THE
WASHING MACHINE
MANUAL

Graham Dixon

DIY Plumbing ☐ **Maintenance** ☐ **Repair**

First edition published 1988
Reprinted 1988, 1989, 1990, 1991
Revised Second Edition published 1992
Reprinted 1993 (twice)
Reprinted 1994
Revised third edition published 1999
Reprinted 2000 (with minor amendments)
Reprinted 2001
Reprinted 2002
Reprinted 2003
Reprinted 2005
Revised fourth edition published 2006

Published by: Haynes Publishing, Sparkford,
Yeovil, Somerset BA22 7JJ, UK

British Library Cataloguing in Publication Data
A catalogue record for this book is available
from the British Library.

ISBN 1 84425 348 7

Printed in the USA.

Contents

Contents

Contents

Acknowledgements

The author would like to extend his thanks and gratitude to the following people and organisations for their help in the compilation of certain sections.

Crabtree Electrical Industries
Oracstar Ltd
Proctor & Gamble plc
UK Whitegoods
Chrysalis Youth and Community Centre – Appliance Recycling Castleford
Very special thanks to Graham Mitchell and Ann Crabtree
Chris Rapson for various new artwork additions

The author would like to point out that any references to manufacturer's names or model numbers etc., used throughout this manual are for identification and reference purposes only. Whilst every precaution has been taken to ensure that all information is factual in every detail, the author cannot accept any liability for any errors or omissions or for any damage or injury caused by using this manual.

Introduction

Today's modern automatic washing machines are the highly refined offspring of their predecessors. Many of the refinements have been made to aid production and to cut production costs for the manufacturer, although it is fair to say that improvements to washing and spin speeds have also been incorporated. The automatic washing machine has changed little in its basic operation over the years, apart from the obvious cosmetic changes and additions of faster spin speeds and increased wash variations. These changes have not significantly increased the overall cost of automatic machines in real terms, they are actually cheaper now than twenty five years ago. With the use of electronics to control motor speeds and the high demand for machines, mass production techniques and a competitive market have kept costs relatively low.

The main drawback has been the cost of repairs and servicing your appliance once the guarantee has expired. Many people have opted for the five year cover offered by manufacturers only to find that in some cases the defective part only is covered and not the wear and tear, and in particular, not the labour charge for fitting the replacement part. This often results in a small repair, e.g. replacement of a belt, still costing around £90. The breakdown of which is the cost of the belt, approximately £10, is waived, but the call-out and repair charge of £80 or more, plus VAT, is levied.

This book looks in detail at front loading automatic washing machines and is designed to help you to understand the function and operation of the internal components of your machine with the view to assist you in finding the fault and the knowledge to repair it. It has been written for those who possess little or no practical knowledge of washing machines or their faults. Seasoned DIY car mechanics will find the book useful as many of the problems found with the washing machine are similar to those on cars, e.g. worn or noisy bearings, faulty hoses, suspension, etc. The information will also be useful for those wishing to gain employment in the service industry. Those already in the service industry will find much of the information of help when they are studying for their servicing NVQ.

Flowcharts, diagrams and step-by-step photographic sequences are used to create a logical pattern to fault finding. This enables the reader to follow a sequence of events in theory (using the flowcharts) in practise (using the photographic sequences) and in detail using the diagrams.

Approached in a logical step-by-step manner, not as a haphazard guess, most if not all faults are within the capabilities of the DIY person. The book is best read cover to cover to gain the gist of flowchart use and to familiarise yourself with procedures and the best ways to locate and rectify faults that may occur. You can then use the book as a quick reference guide before and during repairs. It is impossible to deal specifically with any particular machine as models vary considerably with each manufacturer having their own style of pumps, hoses, bearing sizes, etc. but the concept of an automatic washing machine differs very little between manufacturers. This will become apparent after reading through the book.

Having read the book, you will become more aware of safety around the home owing to a better understanding of your electrical items and their limitations. Regular checks for faults which can be rectified prior to failure or accident greatly increase the safety of your appliances. You will also gain more efficient use of your items through understanding their correct operation.

The machines in the photo sequences have been selected as a cross section of some of the most popular ones found in homes today. Both old and new machines are used in the sequences to highlight actual fault areas and faults to look out for. All names and model numbers are used for customer reference purposes only. At all times, before working on a machine, make sure that it is isolated from both the electrical supply, i.e. switch off socket and remove plug, and from the water supply by turning off the feed taps. This ensures your safety and that of the machine.

We hope you will use this manual to assist you in the Do It Yourself repair of your machine. With most repairs you will find it speedier than calling a repair company, and at the same time save the added burden of call-out and labour charges that repair companies must charge to cover overheads and operating costs. With this in mind, we hope that your faults are few and far between, but remember . . . prevention is better than cure, and regular checks and servicing of your machine can prevent many bigger problems arising in the future.

Chapter 1
Emergency procedures

With such symptoms as leaking, flooding, unusual noises, blowing fuses, etc. it is best to carry out the following procedure. It is essential that the machine is NOT allowed to continue its programme until the fault has been located and rectified.

Firstly – do not panic

Isolate the machine from the mains supply. That is, turn the machine off, switch off at the wall socket, and remove the plug from the socket.

Turn off the Hot and Cold taps that the fill hoses of the machine connect to. This is done because, even with the power turned off, if a valve is at fault, it may be jammed in the open position. The machine will still fill, as turning the power or the machine off will make no difference to this type of fault.

At this point, the power and water should be disconnected. Even now, if there is still water in the machine, it could still be leaking. Any water remaining in the machine can be extracted by syphoning e.g. lifting the outlet hose from its usual position, and lowering it to the level of water in the machine. This will allow the water to drain (unless of course, there is a blockage in the outlet hose!). The easiest method is if the outlet hose will reach to an outside door, where all that is needed is a little movement and the water should drain. Alternatively, the water can be caught in a low bowl using the same technique to drain the water. **Note:** *It is essential that you allow the water remaining in the appliance to cool sufficiently before draining it this way.* To stop the water lift the pipe above the height of the machine. Repeat this process until the machine is empty.

Do not open the door to remove the clothes until all of the previous steps have been carried out, and a few minutes have elapsed to allow the clothes in the machine to cool. In cases where the machine was on a very hot wash, wait about half an hour. When all of these steps have been carried out, and the clothes have been removed from the drum, it is then possible to calmly sit down and start to work out what the problem may be, and form the plan of attack in a logical and concise manner.

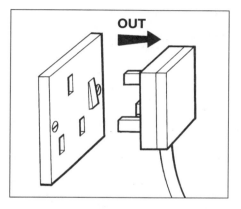

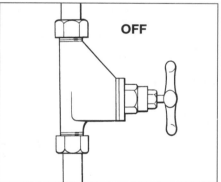

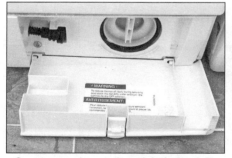

On some makes and models (especially those with internal anti-syphon chambers – see page 22) a small drain hose is located behind the filter cover
Note: *Ensure that the water remaining in the appliance has cooled sufficiently before use.*

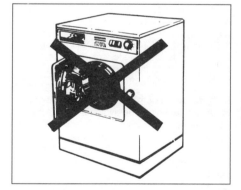

Opening the end cap allows the trapped water to drain into a low bowl/container
Note: *Ensure that the water remaining in the appliance has cooled sufficiently before use.*

Chapter 2
A general safety guide

Electricity at all voltages is to be respected. Those who do not observe the basic rules of electricity are not only a danger to themselves but to those around them. Electrical accidents should be regarded as avoidable. Most are due to plain carelessness and the failure to follow basic rules of electricity even when they are already known.

There are in the region of sixteen million homes in Britain supplied with electricity, each home having on average twenty five electrical appliances. With such a volume of items, it may be a surprise to find that fatalities due to electrical accidents are less than eighty per year. Although this is a small percentage figure in terms of population and only represents 1 per cent of the 8,000 deaths resulting from accidents in the home, the figure is still too high.

The three most common causes of shock or fires from electrical appliances are:

1 Faulty wiring of the appliances, i.e. frayed or damaged flex or cable, incorrect fuse, poor socket, poor/damaged plug, incorrectly wired plug, etc.
2 Misuse of the appliance. The combination of water and electricity greatly increases the possibility of injury.
3 Continuing to use an electrical appliance knowing it to be unsafe, for example with a cracked casing, faulty plug, damaged cable, faulty on/off switch, etc.

By being aware of the need for safety, several of the above faults can be avoided. Others can be eliminated by regular inspection and immediate correction of faults, failure or wear. As for misuse, this may be due to a purely foolhardy approach or genuine ignorance of danger. This can be overcome by understanding and, above all, acting upon the guidelines in this book. If at anytime you feel you lack the ability to do a particular job yourself, then it is best not to try. You can still carry out the diagnosis of the

problem thus ensuring that any work carried out by a repair company is correct. This alone can sometimes save much time and expense.

DOS

● Thoroughly read all the information in this book prior to putting it into practice.
● Isolate any appliance before repair or inspection commences.
● Correctly fit the mains plug (see *Plugs and sockets*), ensuring the connections are in the correct position, tight, and the cord clamp fitted on the outer insulation of the cable.
● Check that the socket used is in good condition and has a sound earth path (see *Basics – electrical*).
● Take time to consider the problem at hand and allow enough time to complete the job without rushing.
● Follow a methodical approach to the stripdown of the item and make notes. This helps greatly with reassembly.
● Double-check everything.
● Ask or seek help if in doubt.
● Ensure that only the correct rated fuse is used. It is dangerous to exceed the required rating. Even if the appliance appears to work normally, little or no protection will be afforded should a fault occur.

DON'TS

● Do not work on any machine that is still plugged in even if the socket switch is OFF. Always isolate fully – PLUG OUT.
● Do not in ANY circumstances repair damaged flex or cables with insulation tape.
● Do not sacrifice safety by affecting a temporary repair.

General

C onsider your own safety and that of other people.
A ct in a way that prevents incidents from becoming accidents.
U se your common sense and think before acting.
T idy workplaces make safer workplaces.
I dentify hazards.
O bserve the rule of Safety First.
N ever underestimate the dangers.

S witch off! Always withdraw plug and disconnect from mains.
A ppliances vary – make sure you have a suitable replacement part.
F or screws use a screwdriver, for nuts a spanner, for knurled nuts use pliers.
E xamine and clean all connections before fitting new parts.
T ighten all screws and nuts firmly.
Y our safety depends on these simple rules.
F uses: Up to 250 watts 1A; 750 watts 3A; 750 to 3000 watts 13A.
I nsulation is for your protection. Don't interfere.
R enew worn or damaged appliance flex.
S ecure flex clamps and all protective covers.
T est physically and electrically on completion.

Plug wiring
Plug wiring must be connected according to the following code to ensure safety. The colours are as follows:

Live – Brown (or Red), symbol 'L'

Neutral – Blue (or Black), symbol 'N'

Earth – Green/Yellow (or Green), symbol 'E'

The colours in brackets are those used until the current international standards were introduced. They may still be found on some equipment. Plug terminals are identified either by colour (old or new) or by the letter symbols shown.

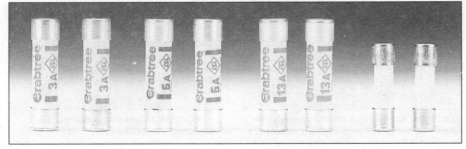

Ensure that only the correct rated fuse is used. It is dangerous to exceed the required rating. Even if the appliance appears to work normally, little or no protection will be afforded should a fault occur

Chapter 3
Plugs and sockets

Problems with electrical appliances may not always be the result of a failure of the item itself but with the electrical supply to it via the socket. A three-pin socket must have a Live supply, a Neutral return and a sound Earth path. When a plug from an appliance is inserted in the socket, a firm contact must be made at all three points. If the live or neutral pins of the plug or connection point within the socket fail to make adequate contact or are free to move, localised heating will occur within the socket. Appliances used from spur outlets must be connected correctly and securely. The spur outlet must also have a double pole isolation switch and great care must be exercised to ensure the outlet is switched OFF prior to disconnecting or working on the appliance. It is good policy and strongly recommended to isolate the spur outlet by both its switch and by removing the relevant fuse (or switching OFF the MCB) supplying that circuit at the consumer unit. Furthermore, confirm the spur has no power by using a non-contact voltage-sensing device like the one shown. DO NOT simply rely on the fact that the appliance connected to the spur outlet does not work, power could still be present. Ensure you check before proceeding.

Problem spotting

Tell-tale signs of this type of fault often show themselves as:
1 Burn marks around one or both entry points on the socket.
2 Plug hot to the touch after use of appliance in that socket.
3 Pungent smell from socket when appliance is in use.
4 Pitting and burn marks on and around the pins of the plug.
5 Radio interference to nearby equipment caused by internal arcing within the socket creating spurious radio emissions. These may pass along the ring main to hi-fi units, etc.
6 Intermittent or slow operation of the appliance being used.
7 Failure of the fuse in the plug. In this instance, this is not caused by a fault within the appliance but by heat being transferred through the live pin and into the fuse which fails by over-heating.

All these conditions are more likely with appliances such as washing machines, heaters and kettles, etc. which draw a high current when in use.

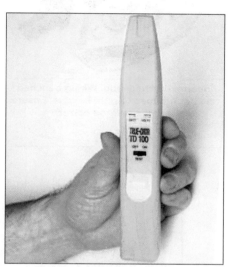

Non-contact voltage testers are used to check if a spur or outlet is isolated. This particular type of tester has a self-test facility to maximise safety and emits both audible and visual indication if voltage is detected. The use of neon test screwdrivers should be avoided at all costs

Why does it happen?

The reasons for such problems are various and may be caused by one or a combination of any of those listed below:
1 Repeated use of the socket, opening up the contact points within the socket. In other words general wear and tear.
2 Poor quality socket or plug.
3 Loose pins on plug.
4 The use of a double adapter. This can cause a poor connection purely by the weight of cables and plugs pulling the adapter partially out of the wall socket. Worse still is allowing a number of high-current-draw appliances to be run through one socket thus causing overloading. Examples might be a fan heater and kettle or washing machine and tumble dryer. Whenever possible, avoid the use of adapters by provision of an adequate number of sockets and do not exceed 3 kW load on any single socket.
5 Use of a multi-point extension lead when the total load on the trailing socket can easily exceed the 3 kW load of the single socket supply.
Note: *It is unwise to use a washing machine or similar items via an extension lead. Make provision for a convenient 13A supply socket to accommodate the original length of the appliance cable.*

Socket highlighting overheating. Both plug and socket will require replacing

This adapter was overloaded by connecting a washing machine and a tumble dryer to it and often using them at the same time. This effectively draws 26 amps through the single 13-amp connection. The weight on the adapter also created a poor connection within the socket. The result was severe overheating and the potential for a fire. DO NOT use adapters for major appliances and check all electrical fittings (plugs and sockets) regularly. When damage of this nature is found ensure that both the plug and socket are renewed

Note: *The corrosion on the earth pin of this plug also indicates that it was exposed to moisture. In this instance it was plugged into the double socket behind the kitchen work top with the right-hand socket used to power the kettle. Unfortunately, the kettle spout was often left pointing towards the protruding adapter resulting in condensation forming on and within it – quite simply a disaster waiting to happen. It was spotted during an unrelated repair visit from a knowledgeable service engineer.*

Rectification

First, DO NOT use the socket until the problem has been rectified. If the socket is found to be showing any of the previously described faults, it must be renewed

Internal view of severe burn out caused by poor connection to terminal. A new plug is required and the cable cut back to sound wire or renewed

Incorrectly fitted plug. Wiring bunched and not trimmed to right lengths. Ensure all plugs are fitted correctly

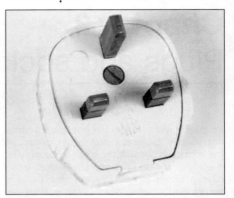

Typical resilient plugs which can stand up to rugged use without cracking

High quality three-pin plug ideal for home appliances

Always look for the ASTA/BS sign when purchasing electrical fittings

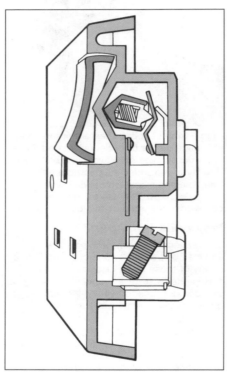

Internal view of 13A socket

The earth

All of the faults mentioned previously relate to the 'live' supply and neutral return on the socket, the plug or both. There is, of course, a third pin. Although it takes no active part in the operation of the appliance, it is, however, the most important connection of all. The function of the earth system is explained in 'Basics – Electrical'. Products that have three core cable must have the yellow and green earth wire securely connected to the earth pin of the plug or pin marked E.

The earth path of an appliance can be checked easily using a simple test meter (see Electrical circuit testing). Remember, a path of low resistance is required from all items within the product that are linked into the earth path via the yellow and green cable.

Note: The earth path of an appliance from its exposed metal parts to the earth pin of the plug should be a maximum of 1 ohm (BS3456).

Checking the socket will require the use of an earth loop test meter which needs to be operated correctly. As these meters are expensive and problems could be encountered with distribution boards fitted with an RCD, it is advisable to have these tests done by a qualified electrical contractor. A simple plug-in tester like the one shown can be found in most good electrical shops and DIY outlets. This is most useful for checking the socket for reverse polarity. In other words, it will show if a socket has been incorrectly wired. An incorrectly wired socket can still work and outwardly give no sign of any problem. This type of fault is dangerous and not uncommon. The plug-in tester also indicates if an earth path is present. However, the quality of the earth in the socket is not shown. That is to say, it may have a very high resistance but would still allow the neon of the tester to light. If the earth resistance is high, remember this may result in a failure to

completely. If it is a single socket it may be wise to have a double socket fitted as a replacement. Numerous DIY books describe the renewal of sockets, so I won't duplicate the instructions here. Suffice to say that caution should be exercised when tackling socket renewal. When buying a replacement socket, make sure it is a good quality one as there are many of dubious quality to be found. Price is a good indicator of quality in this field.

It is advisable to renew all plugs that have been used in the faulty socket because damage may have been caused. It is possible, of course, that a faulty plug damaged the socket. To continue using the old plugs could result in premature failure of your new unit.

As with sockets, plugs can be found in many styles and qualities. While some of the poorer quality plugs may prove to be reliable on low current consumption items like lamps, TV and radios, they may not be so good for washing machines and heaters, etc. Although British Standards do apply to these items, quality does vary considerably. When buying plugs and sockets, go to outlets that can give advice and that carry a good selection. This will allow you to compare quality and build of the products. Look for the ASTA mark which proves that the design and manufacture has been approved by the Association of Short Circuit Testing Authorities. Replacement fuses should also carry this mark.

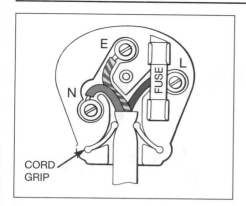

CORD
GRIP

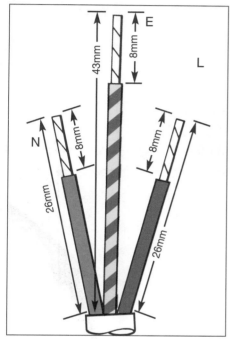

blow the fuse which may cause overheating at the high resistance point or allow a flow of electricity through anything or anyone else that can give a better route to earth.

There is however, a plug-in tester that in effect combines the abilities of the expensive contractor's earth loop test equipment with the simplicity of use of the basic plug-in tester. This type of unit retails at around £50 and when used automatically provides a whole range of checks as well as an earth loop test. Although they are often quoted as being able to test RCD-protected circuits without tripping you must always ensure that you have access to reset the RCD prior to testing should tripping occur. To prevent an RCD tripping the device uses a very low test current which is below 30mA. However, if the circuit/property being tested or an appliance connected to it already has a slight earth fault (below the RCD's 30mA limit) when the test unit is used it is possible for the RCD to trip due to something called cumulative effect. This simply means that an existing earth fault of say 20mA would not cause a 30mA RCD to trip.

Simple plug in socket tester

However, when the plug-in tester applies say another 15mA during its test, then the circuit has a cumulative total of 35mA (original 20 + 15 for the test) and this will result in tripping the RCD protective device. Even the most expensive of 'non-tripping' earth loop test equipment can be affected by cumulative effect. It can also result in what appears to be nuisance tripping of a protective RCD when two appliances are used at the same time (i.e. washing machine and dishwasher etc.) but each will function without tripping if used individually.

Plug fitting

The fitting of a plug is often believed to be a straightforward task that needs little or no explanation. On the contrary, this is an area where many problems are to be found and dangers encountered if the fitting is not done correctly. Do not neglect this most important item.

The following text and photo sequences deal specifically with modern 13A flat-pin plugs. If your property has round-pin plugs and sockets, the indication is that the house wiring may be old and it would be wise to have it checked thoroughly by an expert.

When wiring a plug, it is good practice to leave the earth wire (yellow/green) longer than is necessary merely for connection to the earth terminal to be accomplished. The extra length is taken up in a slight loop shape within the plug. Doing this means that, should the appliance flex be pulled hard accidentally and the plug's cable grip fail to hold, the live and

Make sure a moulded plug removed from an appliance cannot be inadvertently plugged in. Remove the fuse and bend the pins

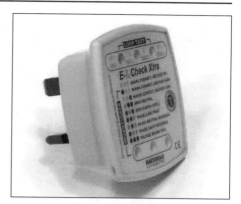

Plug in earth loop tester

neutral wires will detach from the terminal first, leaving the earth loop intact to provide continued safety cover. The photo of the pillar type plug shows how the extra little bit of earth wire is contained inside the plug.

Moulded plugs

Some appliances may be supplied with one-piece moulded 13A plugs fitted to the mains cable. If for any reason this type of plug has to be removed (e.g. to allow the cable to be slotted through a hole in a work surface, or due to damage), because of its moulded construction, it is not possible to take it off in the normal way. The plug has to be cut off with suitable wire cutters and a new plug fitted correctly as shown.

Warning: *Any moulded plug removed in this way must be disposed of immediately. It is wise to remove the fuse and to bend the pins of the plug as soon as it is removed to make sure that it cannot be inadvertently plugged into a socket. Do not leave it lying about or dispose of it where children can find it and plug it in.*

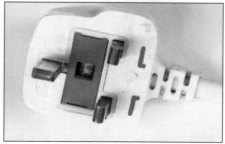

Typical moulded plug

Dos and Don'ts

● DO ensure the cable insulation is removed carefully. Use of correct wire strippers is recommended.

● DO make sure that connections are the right way around.

● DO ensure that wires are trimmed to suit plug fixing point and no bunching is present. See poorly fitted plugs illustrations.

● DO make sure that all connections are tight and no strands of wire are left protruding from terminals. To prevent this, twist the strands together as shown, prior to fitting.

● DO make sure that the cord grip is fitted correctly around the outer insulation only.

● DO ensure correct rating of fuse is used to suit appliance.

● DO ensure the plug top/cover fits tightly and securely with no cracks or damage present.

● DO NOT damage the inner core of wires when removing the outer or inner insulation. If you do, cut back and start again.

● DO NOT fit tinned ends of cables into plugs. Some manufacturers tin (dip in solder) the end of the exposed inner conductors. The tinned/soldered end, if fitted to the plug, will work loose and cause problems associated with loose connections. Although tight when fitted, constant pressure over a long period will compress the soft solder resulting in a loose joint. A second problem associated with tinned conductors is the excessive length of exposed inner wire which the manufacturer usually provides. This can protrude below the cord clamp bunch within the plug to allow the cord clamp to grip the outer insulation only. Both of these practices are dangerous and must be avoided. Always cut cable lengths to suit the plug. If this poor method of fitting is found on an appliance it must be corrected immediately.

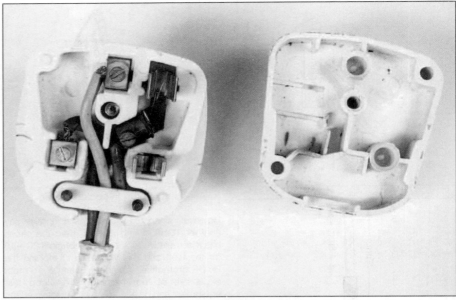

Wiring not cut to correct length. As a result the cord grip is fixed across inner wires, not outer sheath

● DO NOT allow strands of wire to protrude from any fixing points.

● DO NOT fit incorrect fuse ratings. Always match fuses to appliances and observe the manufacturer's instructions.

● DO NOT re-use overheated or damaged plugs.

● DO NOT by-pass the internal fuse.

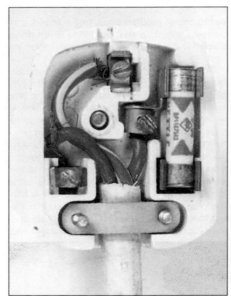

Conductor wire protruding from plug pins

Note: *All of the above photographs are used to illustrate the lack of attention to safety to this small but vital component. Always fit plugs correctly and safely. To give further assistance, a step-by-step photo guide for the two types is given.*

Wiring a plug – pillar type

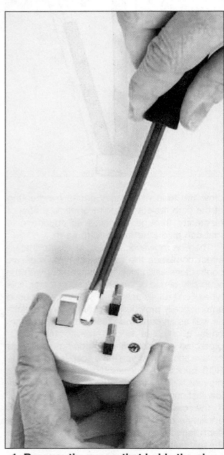

1 Remove the screw that holds the plug top-cover in position, taking care not to lose it

Wiring incorrectly bunched into plug to allow cord grip to hold outer sheath

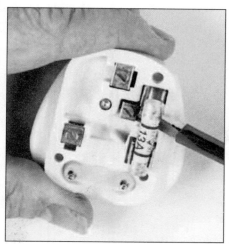

2 Ease the fuse from position (if using a screwdriver, take care not to damage the fuse)

5 Offer the wiring to the plug base with the outer sheath in its correct position resting in the cord clamp area. Next, cut the inner cables as per the manufacturer's instructions, if these are not available allowing 13mm (½in) past the fixing point. Don't forget to allow a little extra on the earth cable to form a slight loop

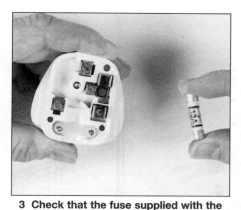

3 Check that the fuse supplied with the plug is of the correct rating for the appliance. Many plugs are supplied with 13A fuse already fitted, but do not be tempted to use it unless it is right. In this instance a 13A fuse was required

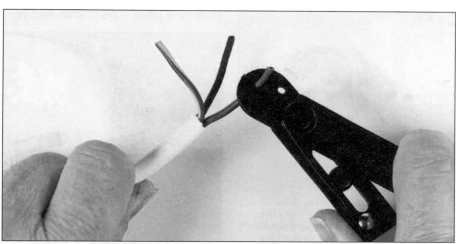

6 Carefully remove 6mm (¼in) of insulation from the end of each wire. This must be done with care to avoid damaging or cutting any strands of the conductor

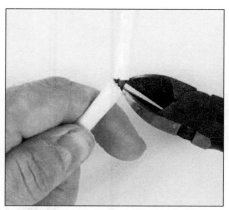

4 Carefully remove the outer cable sheath to expose the inner wires. If damage should occur to the inner wires in the process, cut back and start again

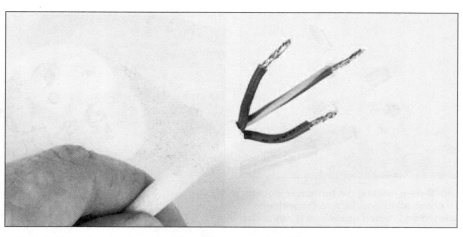

7 Twist the strands of each wire securely together. Make sure there are no loose strands

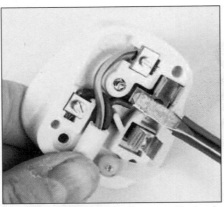

8 Fit each wire into its correct pillar and tighten each screw ensuring that it grips the conductor firmly (with thin wires it will help if they are folded over on themselves first). Make sure the wire fits up to the insulation shoulder and no wires or strands protrude from the pillar

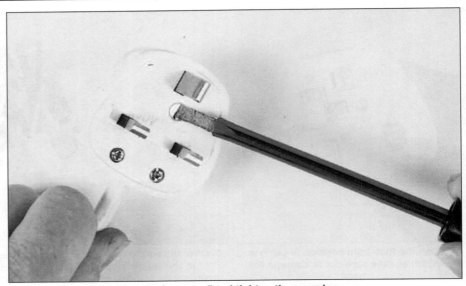

11 With top/cover refitted tighten the securing screw

Wiring a plug – post and nut type

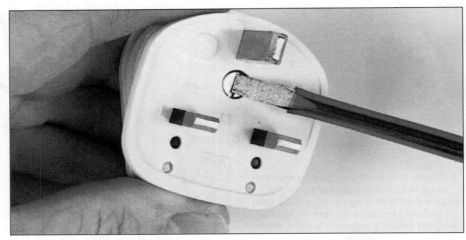

1 Remove the screw that holds plug top/cover in position

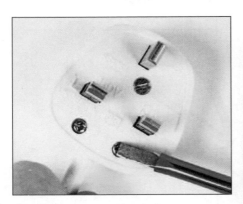

9 Fit the cord clamp over the outer sheath and screw it firmly into position while being careful not to strip the threads of the plastic grip

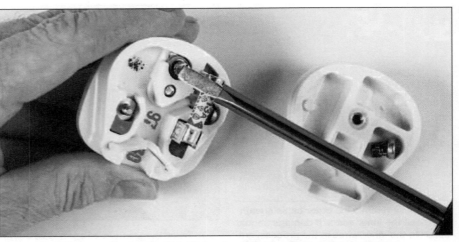

2 Remove the knurled/slotted nuts and place them safely in the top

10 Before refitting the top/cover, double check all fixings. Ensure the wiring is seated and routed neatly and is not under stress or bunched. Fit the correct rated fuse, making sure that it is firmly and securely positioned

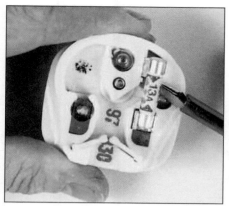

3 With the plug top/cover removed, the fuse can be eased from its position. If using a screwdriver, take care not to damage the fuse

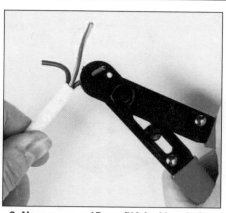

6 Now remove 15mm (⅝in) of insulation from the end of each wire. This must be done with care to avoid damaging or cutting any strands of the conductor

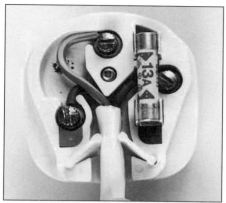

9 Fit each conductor (wire) to its correct terminal. Make sure each is fitted in a clockwise direction, otherwise it will be pushed out as the nut is tightened. Ensure only the conductor is gripped and not the outer insulation

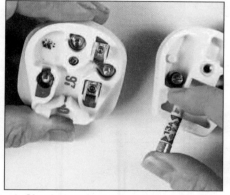

4 Check that the fuse supplied with the plug is of the correct rating for the appliance. Many plugs are supplied with 13A fuse already fitted but do not be tempted to use it unless it is right. In this instance a 13A fuse was required

7 Twist the strands of each wire securely together. Make sure there are no loose strands

10 Securely tighten all three nuts. Ensure that the wire fits up to the insulation shoulder and no wires or strands protrude from the terminal. Before refitting the top/cover, double-check all fixings. Ensure the wiring is seated and routed neatly and is not under stress or bunched. Fit the correct rated fuse, making sure that it is firmly and securely positioned

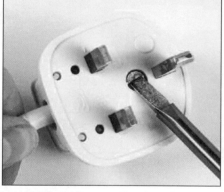

11 With top/cover refitted tighten the securing screw. This type has a captive screw with a shockproof washer to prevent it working loose during use

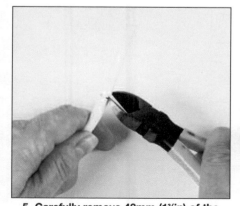

5 Carefully remove 43mm (1¾in) of the cable sheath to expose the inner wires. If damage should occur to the inner wires in the process, cut back and start again. Next, cut the inner cables as per the manufacturer's instructions, in this instance trim the live and neutral wires to 34mm (1⅜in)

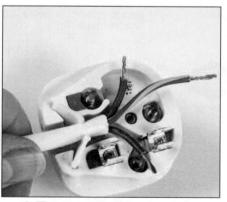

8 The prepared cable can now be inserted into the cord grip ensuring only the outer sheath of the cable is gripped

Plugs and sockets

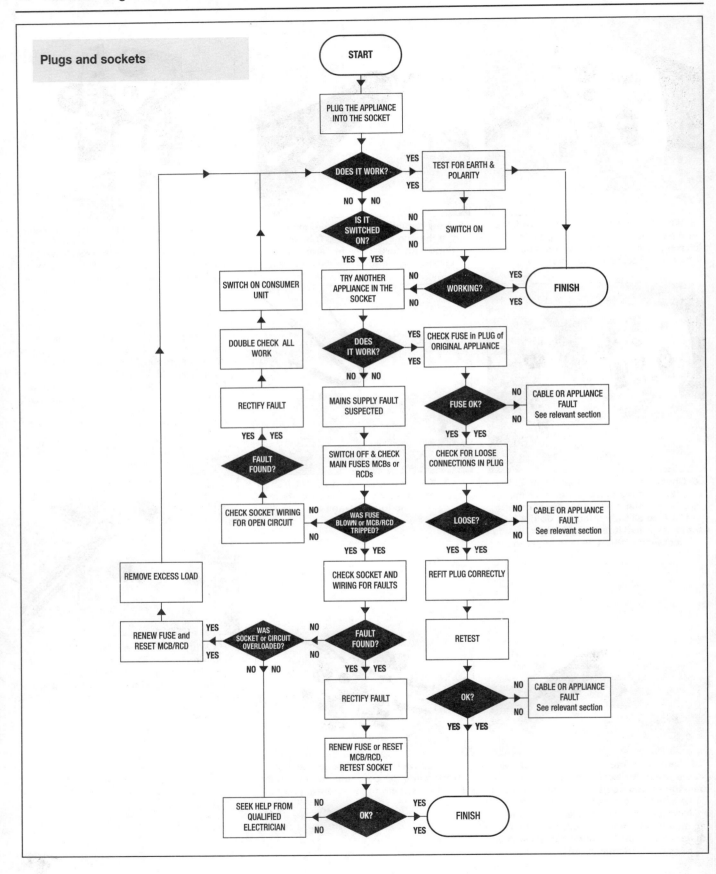

Chapter 4
Basics – electrical

Special note: *Variations may be present in supply systems used in countries other than the UK.*

As detailed in the text in this chapter, various types of earthing systems may be encountered – one of the most popular being the PME system whereby neutral and earth are BONDED (linked) at the supply point to the property. The choice of which supply system (and ultimately which earth system your property has) is a matter for your supply authority. The requirement of a sound earth path however is common to all domestic systems.

For the sake of safety around the home or office, a basic understanding of electricity is essential. Even if you don't intend to carry out any repairs or servicing of your appliances yourself, a sound understanding of household electrical supply will prove invaluable in the long run. Ignorance is no protection against either your or a third party's errors, whether it be on repairs, servicing or the installation of appliances. It is with this in mind that this chapter has been written. It is not an in-depth study of the subject – there are many books that contain more detailed information for those who want to know more about electricity.

In this instance, the aim is to impart a safe knowledge without too much technical data. Some may argue that a little knowledge is a dangerous thing, but I believe that total ignorance is a much greater danger. To be informed is to be enlightened – to be aware of danger helps one to avoid it and to understand how and why certain safety criteria should be adopted.

The top illustration shows a simplified, but typical household supply. The substation has power supplied to it at very high voltage (400,000 volts) in three-phase form. This supply is converted at the substation, via a transformer, down to 230 volt single-phase and is then distributed to our homes. In normal circumstances, current flows from the live supply of the substation's transformer, through the electrical items being used in the house and back via the neutral conductor (cable) to the substation transformer's neutral pole (a closed loop). The neutral terminal of the transformer is in turn connected to the ground (earth – meaning in this case, the general mass of the earth), as shown in the centre illustration. It is usual to use the armoured sheath of the electricity supply authority's cable in order to provide a low impedance continuous link back to the supply transformer's start point. Various types of

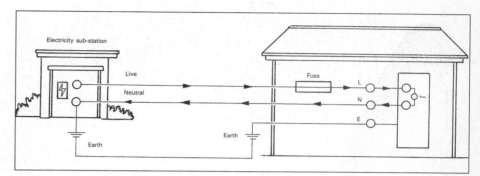

Typical household supply

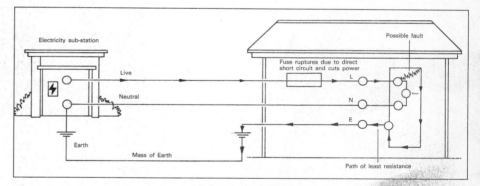

Earth path if fault occurs

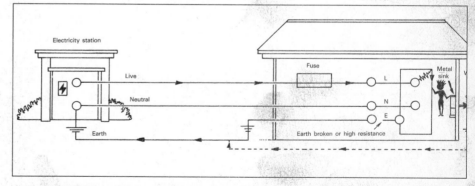

Result of high resistance or break in normal earth path. Fault will find path of least resistance

earthing can be encountered: connection to the armoured sheath of the authority's supply cable; own earth rod; transformer earth rod via general mass of the earth; or the increasingly popular neutral conductor of the authority's supply cable (often called PME – protective multiple earthing or TN-C-S system).

The earth loop path is designed to encourage current to flow, in the event of an earth fault, to enable the protective devices within the consumer unit (fuse, MCB or RCD) to operate in order to isolate the supply to the circuit. Failure to cause the protective device to operate will result in the appliance remaining live with the consequence that any person

Plug-in earth loop tester, details of which can be found in the *Plugs and sockets* chapter

touching the appliance will receive a nasty, possibly fatal, electric shock. Remember, electricity always takes the route of least resistance, therefore a person standing on the ground touching a live appliance can provide a low resistance alternative earth path resulting in a severe shock or worse. For this reason, the resistance of the earth loop path must be low enough to allow sufficient fault current to flow to operate the protective fuse or circuit breaker.

The term used for testing the earthing resistance of the supply outlet is earth loop impedance, which means checking to see if the current flow is impeded and if it is, by how much. This test requires a specialised meter giving resistance figures in ohms, the maximum reading recommended by the IEE (Institution of Electrical Engineers) being 1.1 ohms for a domestic earth path, unless a Type 1 MCB is in circuit in which case a 2 ohm maximum is acceptable.

Note: *A professional earth loop test meter or plug-in earth loop tester (details of which can be found in the* Plugs & Sockets *chapter) provide a clear indication of earth quality by means of a resistance reading or indication.*

What is an earth fault?

An earth fault is defined as the condition where electricity flows to earth when in

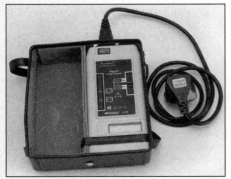

A professional earth loop test meter gives the only true indication of the earth path quality

A versatile test meter incorporating 500 V DC insulation test facility

normal circumstances, it should not do so. There are two recognised ways in which this may happen: direct and indirect.

Direct – when contact is made directly with the current-carrying conductor which is designed to carry that current.

Indirect – touching a part of an appliance, that would not normally carry current but is doing so due to a fault.

What is a consumer unit?

The consumer unit is where the supply into the house is split into separate circuits, i.e. those for lights, sockets, etc. It houses a main isolation switch or combined RCD which is used to isolate (remove power from) all the circuits in the house. Also housed within the unit are various fuse-carriers for cartridge or rewirable fuses or

a Miniature Circuit Breaker (MCB) in place of fuses. Each circuit leading from the consumer unit has its own rating of fuse or MCB and only that fuse rating and no other must be used.

NOTE: *Even when the consumer unit is switched off there is still a live supply to it. Do not remove the covers of the consumer unit or tackle any inspection or repair to this item without seeking further information. Faults other than fuse renewal are best left to skilled electrical engineers. Although assistance may be available from other publications, extreme care should be exercised. As mentioned earlier, it is not the aim of this book to encourage the repair or maintenance of items that are not fully isolated.*

All about fuses

Two versions of fuse are to be found: the cartridge type and the rewirable type. The rewirable type is difficult and fiddly to rewire and the cartridge type, although easier to renew, is often difficult to obtain. Both these systems have drawbacks in being awkward and not very 'user friendly'.

An ordinary fuse is simply a weak link designed to break at a preset rating. If a circuit is overloaded or a short circuit occurs, the resulting overload will cause the fuse to melt and sever the supply. Unless a direct short circuit occurs, however, the overload on the fuse may not be enough to cause the fuse to blow because it has a fair degree of leeway over its rating value. It therefore offers only basic safety and will not afford any personal safety as the time taken to break is usually too long.

To the old familiar imperial ratings for fuses and circuit breakers have now been added

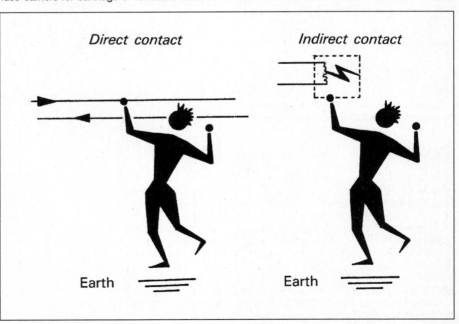

Direct contact

Indirect contact

Earth

Earth

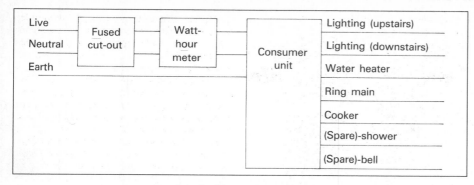

A typical house insulation

the international Renard ratings. A complete changeover will eventually be effected for European standardisation.

Fuse manufacturers are still using the imperial sizes whilst circuit breaker manufacturers have mostly changed to the new ratings. An equivalence chart is shown below:

Current Rating Imp	Renard	Typical Circuit
5	6	Lighting
10	10	
15	16	1mm. htr
20	20	
30	32	Ring main
45	40	Cooker/shower

Typical older-style consumer unit with isolation switch and wired fuses only

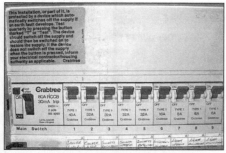

Modern consumer unit with RCD main switch and MCBs on all circuits

Miniature circuit breakers

The miniature circuit breaker (MCB) is now widely used and overcomes all the problems associated with ordinary fuses. The MCB is a small sophisticated unit that affords a much higher degree of protection than an ordinary fuse. It is tamper-proof and the unit involved is easily identified when one has tripped (switch moves to 'OFF' position). Most importantly, MCBs cannot be reset if the fault still exists which

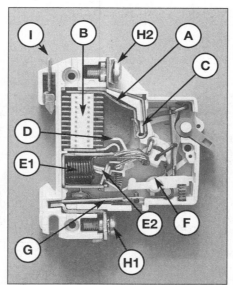

Mechanism of miniature circuit breaker

A   Arc runner
B   Arc chamber
C   Fixed contact
D   Moving contact
E1 Solenoid coil
E2 Moving core
F   Trip bar
G   Thermo-metal
H1 Wiring terminal
H2 Wiring terminal
I   Fixing

eliminates the practice of putting in the wrong fuse wire or cartridge to get things working – a foolish and most dangerous practice. MCBs are available in similar ratings to ordinary fuses and operate in two ways. Referring to the accompanying photograph, current flows into the unit at H1 and along G through coil E1 and on to the moving contact D (shown here open circuit). Contact D in the ON position would be resting on fixed contact C and so current would flow to H2.

Two fault conditions may arise; firstly – short circuit. This type of fault would quickly increase the current flow through the unit. Section E1, being a coil would increase its magnetic field and as a result attract E2 into the coil centre. This action trips the mechanism arm F and causes C–D to open circuit. Conductor A and arc chamber B act to suppress the arc formed on the contact point. This is done by the arc runners drawing the arc across the arc chamber where it is chopped into small arcs which are quickly extinguished. The action of the MCB is much quicker than an ordinary fuse wire. The second type of fault could simply be an overload on the circuit and, although exceeding the safe working load of the circuit, it would not cause the solenoid to trip. In this type of situation, the current flowing through G causes the conductor to heat up. The conductor is made of a tri-metal plate that bends when heated. The bending action of the conductor trips arm F, causing C and D to open circuit as before. This operation again is much better than fuse wire and calibration to higher tolerances is possible.

Note: *These units are factory-calibrated to extremely accurate tolerances and must not be tampered with nor attempts made to readjust them. The internal workings are only shown to help understand their operation. In the event of faults or failures, a new replacement unit must be fitted. No repair or adjustment is possible.*

Unfortunately, neither fuses nor miniature circuit breakers alone can give protection to anyone involved in a DIRECT EARTH situation. Indeed, the same can apply in the case of an INDIRECT EARTH contact. This may sound confusing, but it should be realised that in a 'direct contact' situation a person is literally shorting out Live and Earth, whereas in an 'indirect' contact situation, the Live to Earth path is already there because the equipment itself is connected to earth. The reason the fuse hasn't blown or the circuit breaker tripped is because the fault is not great enough to operate the safety mechanism, yet is great enough to be fatal. For instance, a 10A fuse would never blow with an 8A earth fault on the circuit, yet 8A constitutes a very dangerous level of earth fault current.

Residual current devices

To afford a higher degree of protection, another device has been developed, and is available in various forms.
1 Mounted within the consumer unit to protect all or selected circuits.
2 As individual socket protection.
3 An adapter to be used as portable protection and used where required.

The name given to this device in all its forms is the Residual Current Device (RCD). It may also be called a Residual Current Circuit Breaker (RCCB). In the early days of its introduction, it was known as an Earth Leakage Circuit Breaker (ELCB).

The primary protection is the integrity of the earthing, RCDs, in addition to the earthing, provide a much higher degree of protection depending upon the degree of sensitivity. For personal protection it is recommended that a sensitivity of 30mA is used.

It is generally considered that an earth fault of 1A or more is a fire risk, 50mA or more provides a shock risk which can have varying effects upon the human body depending upon the value of earth fault current and the body resistance of the person and, of course, their state of health. The heartbeat cycle is about 0.75 second. It is therefore necessary to cut off the fault current in less than one cardiac cycle. The Wiring Regulations stipulate that for Indirect Contact protection isolation must occur within 0.4 second.

How does an RCD work?

An RCD protects by constantly monitoring the current flowing in the live and neutral wires supplying a circuit or an individual item of equipment. In normal circumstances the current flowing in the two wires is equal but, when an earth leakage occurs due to a fault or an accident, an imbalance occurs and this is detected by the RCD which automatically cuts off the power in a split second.

To be effective, the RCD must operate very quickly and at a low earth leakage current. Those most frequently recommended are designed to detect earth leakage faults in excess of 30mA (30/1000ths of an amp) and to disconnect the power supply within 200ms (the rated sensitivity); these limits are well inside the safety margin within which electrocution or fire would not be expected to occur.

It should now be apparent that RCDs are designed to sever mains current should your electrical appliance malfunction electrically, or should you cut through the mains cable of your lawnmower for instance. They are simply a fail-safe device and should be used as such. In my opinion, used correctly they are an invaluable asset to your household.

Note: *The use of an RCD must be in addition to normal overload protection, i.e. fuses or MCBs, and not instead of it. All residual current devices have a test button facility. It is essential that this is tested regularly to verify that the device operates. For use with adapters or sockets, or for outside use, test before each operation. If failure occurs (does not trip, or trip appears sluggish or hard to obtain) have the unit tested immediately. This will require an RCD test meter and is best left to a qualified electrician.*

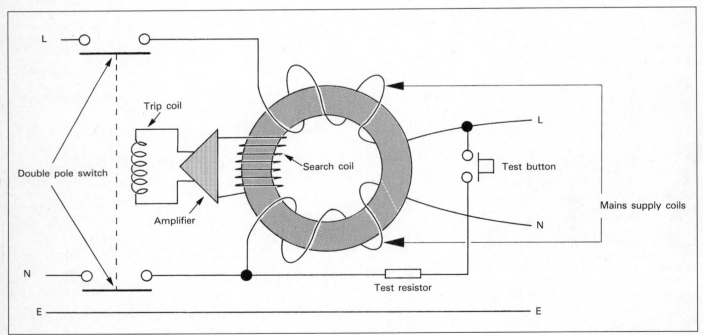

A simplified RCD circuit

Chapter 5
Basics – plumbing

Although the machine may have been working correctly for some time in its present position, incorrect installation of a machine may cause faults several months later. Because of this time span, the faults are not associated with bad plumbing and can cause the DIY engineer to look for other faults, which is very time consuming and annoying. Having said this, it is therefore worth a few minutes examining the existing pipework, and checking the manufacturer's installation details. These details will be found in the manufacturer's booklet that came with the machine. Even if the installation of your machine was left to an 'expert', it is still advisable to read this section, as the chances are that they will not have read the installation details either!

For those of you who cannot find the manufacturer's booklet – what follows is a brief description of plumbing requirements that apply to nearly all automatic dishwashers and washing machines, and the reasons why they should be observed.

Inlet hose

If the machine is to be plumbed in 'Hot and Cold', then isolation taps must be fitted. This enables the water supply to be cut off (isolated) between the normal house supply and that of the washer. **Note:** *The rubber hoses connected to the isolation taps should be positioned so that they don't get trapped when the machine is pushed back, or rub against any rough surfaces during the machine's operation. Both of these conditions can cause the pipe to wear, due to the slight movement of the machine when in use. Ensure also that no loops have been formed in the hot inlet hose. In the beginning this will not cause any trouble, but as the pipe gets older and the hot water takes effect, the pipe will soften and a kink will form. This will then cause a restriction or complete stoppage of water to the machine. This can also happen to the cold inlet hose, although it is very rare, owing to the increased pressure in the cold system.*

The next thing to do is check that there is adequate water pressure to operate the hot and cold valves, (see also *Functional testing*). On hot and cold machines, select a hot-only fill, the machine should fill to working level within four minutes. The same should apply when a rinse cycle has been selected. This gives a rough indication that the water pressure is adequate to open and close the valves. This is because the valves are pressure-operated and a 4p.s.i. minimum is required for their correct operation, (see *Water inlet valves*). The cold pressure is usually governed by the outside mains pressure, but the hot water pressure is governed by the height of the hot water tank or its header tank.

Problems can arise when the tanks are less than eight feet higher than the water valve they are supplying. This is often found in bungalows and some flats. If a slow fill is suspected, check the small filter that can be found inside the hot and cold valves, when the inlet hose is unscrewed. These can be removed and cleaned by simply pulling them out gently with pliers. Care must be taken not to damage the filter or allow any small particles to get past when you remove it. Clean water is normally supplied to the valves, but in many cases old pipework or the limescale deposits from boilers, etc., can collect at these points.

Kinks and loops can also affect the outlet pipe and cause several problems to the wash, rinse and spin programmes.

Some machines may use larger and more specialised inlet hoses – for details of these types of systems, refer to the Chapter: *Water inlet valves*.

Outlet hose

The outlet hose SHOULD fit into a pipe larger than itself, thus giving an 'Air Brake' to eliminate syphoning. The height of the outlet hose is also important if syphoning is to be avoided. Syphoning can occur when the end of the outlet hose is below the level of water in the machine, which would result in the machine emptying at the same time as filling, and if the machine were to be turned off, would continue to empty the water from the machine, down to its syphon level.

Syphoning is a common fault and can give rise to some unexpected faults, such as:

Failing to start to wash (always filling).
Excessive filling time.
Programme failing to advance through rinses.
Washing times longer than normal.

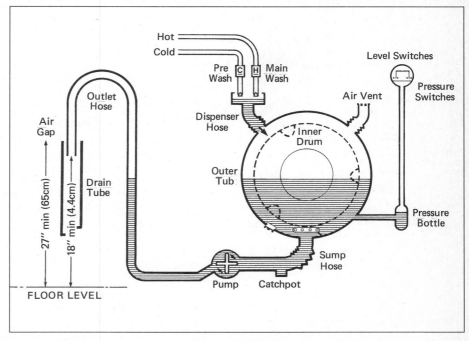

Correct plumbing

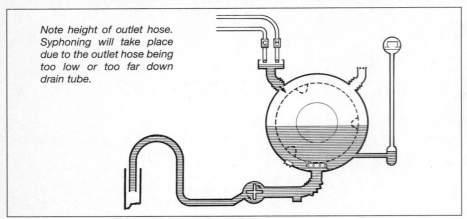

Note height of outlet hose. Syphoning will take place due to the outlet hose being too low or too far down drain tube.

Incorrect plumbing, causing syphoning

ANTI-SYPHON CHAMBER

The diagrams show correct and incorrect plumbing techniques, which will cause and cure any syphoning. This also shows that some of the 'major' faults that appear, can be attributed to something as simple as syphoning and can be cured almost immediately.

All of the above faults can be attributed to syphoning, although this may not be the only cause.

Under-sink drain connections

It is now common practice for the washing machine drain hose to be connected to a combined sink and drain connection or self-bore plumbing-out kit as shown in the following chapter.

Both these types of drainage systems have the drain hose of the appliance fitted onto a small drain connection rather than into a larger free standing pipe as recommended by most appliance manufacturers. Although this does not break any rules or water by-laws the smaller diameter outlet point can become blocked more easily if badly installed or poor fittings are used.

The self-bore plumbing-out kit shown on pages 24 and 25 has an internal non-return valve to prevent waste water from the sink entering the appliance drain hose when the sink is emptied. Although this prevents water from entering the drain hose waste from the sink and/or the washing machine debris can collect at this point resulting in poor draining, or a complete blockage.

The combined sink and appliance waste system does not have a non-return valve thus allowing the back feeding of waste water from the sink into the washing machine. This occurs when the drain hose of the appliance leads directly to the combined drain connection See Diagram 1.

This can lead to a wide range of problems such as:

● Foul odour from washing machine when left unused for a short period of time.
● Poor wash results due to the machine using the dirty sink water for part of the wash fill cycle. **Note:** *Relating to problems above; as it takes a fair amount of water to*

fill the outer tub it is unlikely that water will be visible in the drum if the appliance is used on a fairly regular basis.

● If the appliance is not used for several days but the sink is, it is possible for the back feed water to become visible in the drum and in certain circumstances to reach the door level and flood out when the door is opened to put clothes in. **Note:** *This fault must not be confused with that of a weeping water inlet valve (See Chapter 17) as in this instance the water would be dirty from the sink as opposed to clean water simply dripping in via a faulty inlet valve.*

● Machines that have pressure-operated door interlocks (See Chapter 20) can be activated by the build up of back-fed water to the point that the door becomes locked. This can be rather confusing as when the appliance was last used it worked correctly and the clothes were removed, but several days later, when you need to put a new wash load in the drum you cannot open the door. **Note:** *Only a relatively small amount of water needs to collect in the outer tub to operate the door interlock pressure lock system so it is unlikely that you will see water through the door glass.* Simply

(See Chapter 17)

Some makes and models may have a plastic anti-syphon chamber similar to the one shown here. In addition to preventing syphoning by creating an 'air break' this type of system allows the drain hose to be connected near the top of the appliance which also prevents back feeding of waste water which can occur with some types of plumbing situations

turning the appliance to a drain programme and waiting for the time delay of the interlock should allow the machine to empty the unwanted build up of water and allow the door to open correctly – thus confirming the diagnosis.

It is unlikely that to cure the problem of back feeding you would opt for changing the plumbing system, so the following alternative is often the best option.

To prevent waste water from running down the drain hose and back filling the appliance ensure that a portion of the drain hose is looped as high as possible up the side of the sink as in Diagram 2. This simple yet effective action will prevent water from running all the way down to the appliance. It will not of course prevent sediment building up between the connection point and the outlet hose so regular checking and cleaning is advisable.

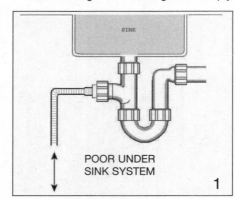

When the drain hose of a washing machine is connected to an under sink waste like this the water can flow both ways allowing waste from the sink to back fill the appliance

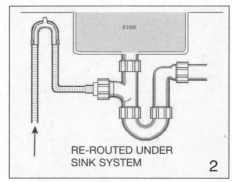

To prevent back flow from the sink ensure that the drain hose is positioned as high as possible in relation to its connection point. This will only allow water to pass out of the appliance and prevent back filling when the sink empties

Chapter 6
Do-it-yourself plumbing

Inlet hose

When a machine is to be fitted in close proximity to an existing sink unit, you can take advantage of the new style 'SELFBORE' taps and outlet systems now available. These simple and effective DIY fittings will save both time and money.

In most cases, the fitting of these taps can be done with only a screwdriver and no soldering is required. You do not even need to drain or turn off the main water system at all.

At this stage, I feel it is better to give you some visual help rather than pages of text. The following pages show you how easy the fitting of such units can be!

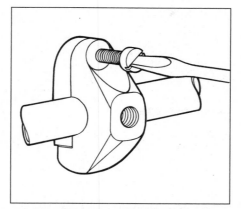

3 Engage screw and tighten until clamp is secure. Do not over tighten

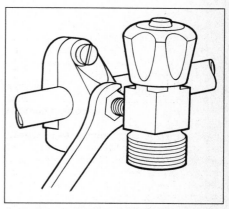

6 Tighten hexagonal nut towards the pipe. This secures tap in position

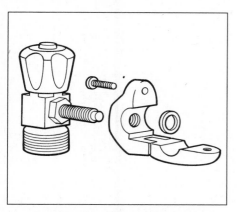

1 First, unscrew tap and open clamp

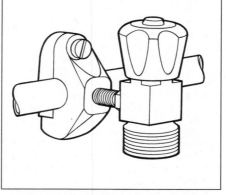

4 Insert tap assembly into clamp. Ensure tap is in 'off' position

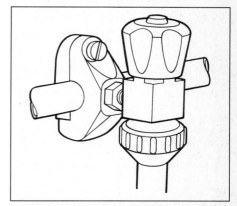

7 The tap is now ready for use. Connect hose to 3/4 BSP thread on tap and turn on

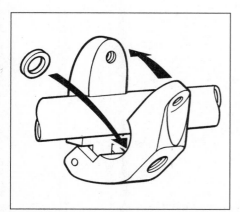

2 Fit clamp around copper pipe in required position. Make sure washer is in position

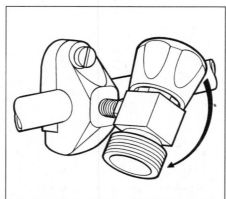

5 Turn clockwise until pipe is penetrated. Set tap to position required

Outlet hose

1 Select the most convenient place in the waste pipe 31mm (1¼in) or 38mm (1½in) dia.

2 Disconnect components. Place saddle halves around waste pipe, removing saddle inserts if pipe is 38mm (1½in) dia. Ensure that 'O' ring is seated in recess. Tighten screws by stages to give an even and maximum pressure on waste pipe.

3 Insert cutting tool and screw home (clockwise) until hole is cut in waste pipe. Repeat to ensure a clean entry.

4 Remove cutter and screw in elbow. Use locking nut (5) to determine final position of elbow and tighten, or screw non-return valve (3) directly into saddle piece.

5 To complete installation, choose correct size hose coupling to suit drain hose and secure hose with hose clip (not included).

It is important to remove regularly lint and other deposits from non-return valve. Simply unscrew retaining collar (4).

This information has kindly been supplied by Oracstar, a leader in the field of Self Plumbing kits, whose wide range of DIY fittings and accessories can be found in most leading DIY stores.

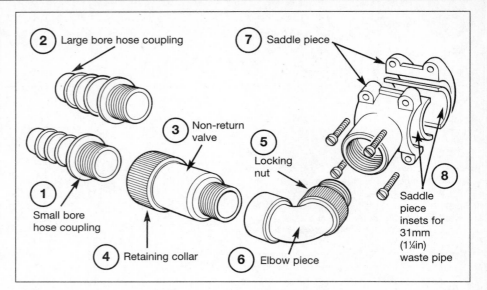

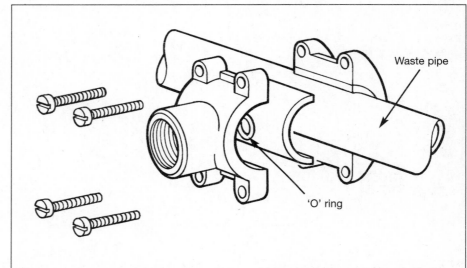

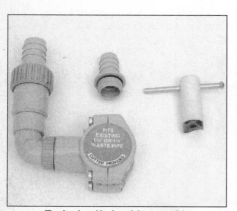

Typical self plumbing out kit

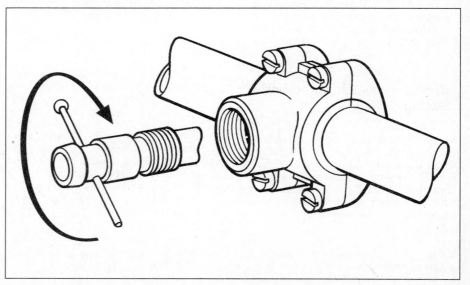

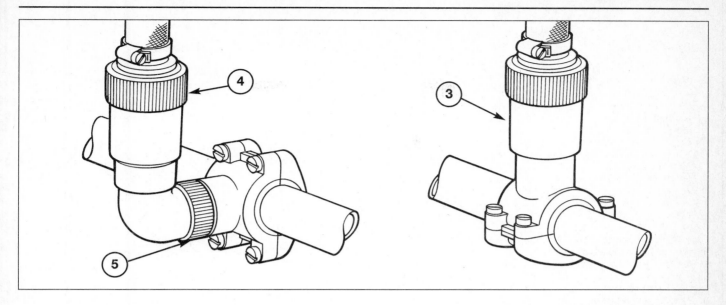

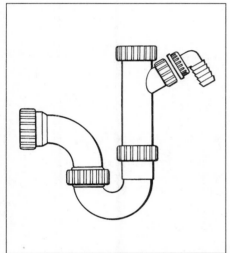

Discharge into a combined sink and washing machine trap. This trap allows water from the sink to drain away as normal but has an extra branch for attaching the washing machine hose

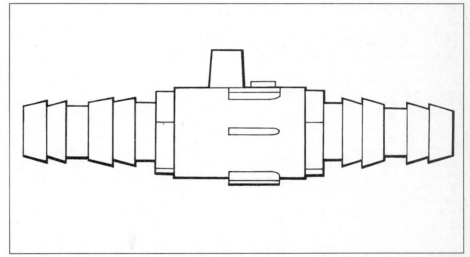

This unit provides an in line air break to prevent syphoning occurring via your appliance drain hose. Full fitting instructions are supplied with every unit

Causes of drain and outlet pipe blockages

As the ingredients in modern cleaning or washing products are specifically designed either to break down into harmless waste, or remain in very minute particles that are not large enough to form deposits of any noticeable size, they cannot actually cause a blockage.

Research has shown that blockages are nearly always caused by something becoming trapped in a drain or waste pipe, which acts as a nucleus around which other matter can form. Broken buttons, pins and poorly finished pipe joints are generally the root cause of a problem. This can slow down the passage of waste into drains so that other soil, such as grease from food or a wash load, particles of dirt and lastly a washing product, will start to build a deposit, which can lead to a blockage.

Caustic soda is normally very effective at clearing any blockages in waste pipes and should be used periodically down a sink waste pipe if this leads to the same drain as any washing appliances. Great care should be taken when using this substance, which is available from pharmacists and hardware stores.

Chapter 7
Tools and equipment

Modern automatic washing machines do not require very specialised tools. Many of the routine repairs such as blocked pumps, renewal of door seals and hoses can normally be completed with a selection of the following tools: crossblade and flatblade screwdrivers, combination pliers, simple multimeter, pliers. Most people who are DIY orientated will own one or more of these items already. A useful addition to this selection would be a self-locking wrench, a socket and/or box spanner set, soft-face hammer and circlip pliers. These would help with the larger jobs, such as motor removal and bearing removal, etc.

Bearing removal/renewal and the like may also require certain things such as bearing pullers. As these can be expensive to buy, it is advisable to hire them from a tool hire specialist for the short period that you require them. Local garages may also be willing to let you hire them for a small deposit.

In addition to the standard fixings some makes and models may have security/anti-tamper screws/bolts which prevent removal by standard tools. There are many different types and sizes in use and to remove them you will require a tool with the correct end style and size. Adapter sets like the one shown which has five different styles in a wide

 Tri-wing

 Allan and Hex Key – with centre pip

 Off-set cross-head

 Slotless

 Torx – with centre pip

A socket set

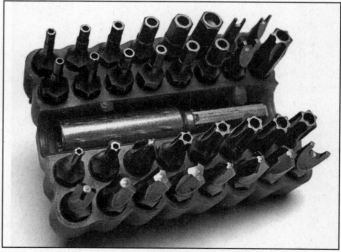

A security/anti-tamper bit set

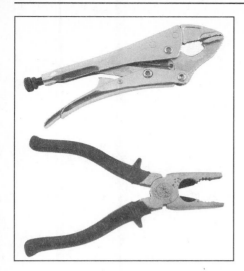

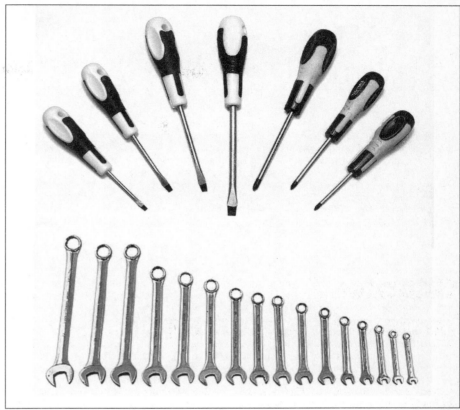

range of sizes are now quite readily available from appliance parts suppliers and good tool shops.

It will not prove difficult to build up a selection of tools capable of tackling the faults that you are likely to encounter on your machine. Most of the large DIY stores will stock the tools that you require, often at a good saving. An excellent safety-related addition to the household tool set would be a plug-in loop earth tester similar to that described and shown in Chapters 3 and 4.

When buying tools check the quality; a cheap spanner or socket set is a waste of money if it bends or snaps after only a short period of use. Having said that there are many tools on the market that are of a reasonable quality and are inexpensive. Try to buy the best that your budget will allow. Remember, the tools that you buy are a long-term investment and should give years of useful service.

As with any investment, it is wise to look after it and tools should be treated the same. Having spent time and money on tools, they should be kept in a clean and serviceable condition. Ensure that they are clean and dry before storage.

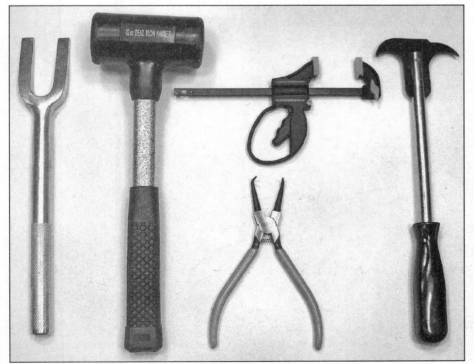

Useful additional tools

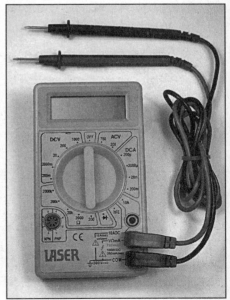

Chapter 8
Locating a fault

Whenever possible the symptoms of the fault should be confirmed by the judicial operation of the machine up to the point of the suspected fault, using the appropriate test sequence, whereupon the machine should be stopped, disconnected from the mains supply and the relevant flowchart followed. For major leaks, blown fuses, etc., this is not practical. In these cases, the fault is known and further confirmation would be of little benefit. This may in fact, result in further damage to the machine or its surroundings.

Being able to assess and locate a fault may at first seem a difficult thing to do, but if a few simple procedures are carried out prior to starting the work, they will help reduce the time spent on the machine. Hopping in a random fashion from one part of the machine to another, hoping that you will come across the fault and subsequently repair it, is hardly the best approach to repair work. This is not the way to tackle any job. Without doubt, the best method of fault finding is to be gained

from your own experience of the machine, the fault with it and its location and rectification based on all the available information. Always remember that a methodical approach to the work in hand, saves time and effort by eliminating unnecessary replacements based on guesswork.

There are, however, a few things that can be done before such testing. These will confirm if it is the machine itself that is at fault or if an external/user fault is the source. Indeed, a large percentage of repair calls are not a fault of the machine at all therefore before jumping to conclusions, pause for a moment. You will not only save time and effort, but money as well.

Remember these points when starting a repair:

1 Allow yourself enough time to complete the task in hand.
2 Do not cut corners at the expense of safety.
3 Try to ensure adequate working space wherever possible.

4 Make notes about the position of the part/s to be removed, the colours and position of wires, bolts, etc.

If you can acquire this practice, it will help you in all repairs that you carry out, not only with your washing machine.

A few simple checks

a) CHECK – that the machine is turned on at the socket.
b) CHECK – that the fuse in the plug is intact and working. This can be checked by replacing the suspected fuse with one out of a working item of the same rating.
3 CHECK – that the taps are in the ON position.
d) CHECK – that the door is closed correctly, and that a wash cycle is selected and the knob or switch has been pulled/pushed to the ON position.
e) CHECK – that the machine is not on a RINSE HOLD position. This on most machines will cause the machine to stand idle until instructed to do otherwise.

If the fault still remains, the next step is to determine its true nature, and subsequent repair.

Making notes and drawings as the work progresses.

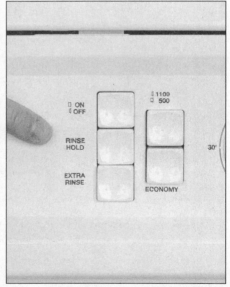

Check that the machine is simply not on the delicate programme rinse-hold position

Chapter 9
General care and attention

For many repairs it is best that the machine is laid on its front face or side. Generally it is best to lay the machine on the side opposite the timer. (The timer is located directly behind the main programme knob.) This is to avoid the tub and drum assembly coming in contact with the timer.

Always ensure that the outer shell of the machine is protected with a suitable cover when attempting to lay the machine down. The machine should be lowered slowly, to avoid excessive movement of the suspension. When lowering the machine, it is a good idea to place a strip of wood under the top edge of the machine, to provide room for the fingers for lifting the machine back into its correct position after the repair.

When laying the machine over, care should be taken to protect oneself from injury. Firstly, ensure that the machine is completely disconnected from the mains supply, and that the inlet and outlet hoses are removed. Secondly, before attempting to lay the machine over, decide if you need any help. These machines are very heavy and a little help may prevent a back injury. Thirdly, before attempting to move the machine, ensure that the floor is dry. A wet floor has no grip, especially if the water is soapy.

The correct rating of fuse must be used as per the manufacturer's instructions. As a general guide, the applications for the three main ratings of fuse are listed in the *General Safety Guide* chapter. Plug wiring must be connected according to the following code to ensure safety. The colours are as follows:
LIVE – BROWN
NEUTRAL – BLUE
EARTH – GREEN/YELLOW

The author would like to point out at this time, that any references to manufacturer's names or model numbers, etc., that are used throughout this manual are for the reader's information, and reference purposes only. Whilst every precaution has been taken to ensure that all information is factual in every detail, the author cannot accept any responsibility for any errors or omissions appertaining to this manual, and shall not be responsible for any damage or injury whilst using this manual.

Blockages in the washing machine

Blockages in the washing machine itself cannot be associated with the use of a particular brand or type of washing detergent.

Although many cite detergents as the cause of the problem, extensive research was undertaken to establish the actual cause of the problem. The results showed conclusively that blockages are not linked to the use of powders or liquids. What was found was that internal blockages are associated with calcium salts and grease residues that have detached from the inside of the machine. In some cases these residues can form a blockage in the narrow tube that leads to the pressure chamber.

A build-up of calcium and grease residue is usually caused by under-dosing the washing detergent (even slightly) over a long period of time, and a problem can arise when a change of detergent, such as from a powder to a liquid, means that the recommended dosage is used. This extra detergent can loosen deposits inside the machine and then it is possible for a blockage to occur.

The recommended dosage of detergent, as stated on the pack, should always be used, and extra detergent should be added if items are heavily soiled or stained.

A maintenance wash should be carried out 2 or 3 times a year (this is often recommended by machine manufacturers in the machine instruction booklet). The procedure involves running the machine through without any clothes in the drum, on the hottest wash possible, with the normal dosage of powder containing a bleaching agent, such as Persil Performance powder, Radion powder or Surf powder. This process will emulsify any grease deposits, which have built up, and the detergent will specifically be working on cleaning the machine rather than cleaning soiled clothes.

Regular inspection points

A regular internal inspection of your machine, may enable you to identify a part that may not be running properly, or find a perished hose before a leak occurs.

It is recommended that the following points are checked regularly.

Inspect	When	Special notes
Pump filter (if fitted)	Weekly	As per manufacturer's manual, often depends on usage.
Valve filters (hot and cold)	6 months	If dirty, pull out with pliers and wash out.
Door seal, door glass	6 months	If seal is tacky to the touch, seal may be in need of renewal soon. Rub any sticky fluff off door glass with non-abrasive pad.
All hoses	6 months	As above. Ensure that all corrugations in all hoses are checked thoroughly.
Pump and sump hose catch pot	6 months	Check for any items that may have collected in or at these points. Remove as necessary.
Suspension	6 months	Check suspension mounts on tub and body of machine. If slide type, see *Suspension* chapter.
Motor brushes (if fitted)	6 months or yearly	Check for wear and /or sticking in slides. If below half normal length, renew.
Belt tension	6 months or yearly	Check and adjust belt tension if necessary. See *Main drive belts* chapter.
Level machine	Yearly, if machine is moved	Check that the machine is standing firmly on the floor, and that it does not rock. Adjust by unscrewing the adjustable feet, or packing under the wheels.
Check plug and connectors	Yearly, prior to every repair	Prior to repair, look for poor connections in the plug and socket. Also look for any cracks or other damage. Renew as necessary.
Taps and washers	Yearly, prior to and after every repair	Check taps for free movement, corrosion and/or leaks.

Chapter 10
Functional testing

Throughout the book, reference is made to functional testing to ensure that the action of the machine is correct and installation is suitable. Use this sequence as a guide to ensuring correct operation after installation, repair or servicing. The purpose is to test where practical, all functions of the machine and plumbing installation in the most efficient manner. The test will suit most types of machines which use mechanical timers/programmers. Some slight modification may be required to suit model variations. Electronically controlled machines, i.e. non-mechanical timers, will have selectable self test programmes similar to this sequence. See *Timers (programme control)* chapter.

A typical installation and functional test

1 With the machine in its correct operating position and levelled correctly, and with all panels fitted, ensure that both hot and cold taps and power supply socket are turned on.
2 Ensure the door is correctly closed and latched.
3 It is not necessary to put a wash load into the machine or detergent in the dispenser for this type of test.
4 Select a hot wash cycle (90–95 degrees). On most machines this will only energise the hot fill valve and therefore test the flow rate/pressure supplied to it. The machine should fill to low level within four minutes if the water pressure is adequate. If the fill time is more than this period, check that the hot supply tap is fully turned on. In most instances little can be done for slow hot filling, (see *Basics – plumbing*) and will in general cause only minor problems such as failing to dispense powders effectively from the drawer. In severe cases either connect to cold supply with a 'Y' joint or alternatively, the powder could quite simply be sprinkled over

the wash load in the drum, (only if the wash is to be started immediately), still allowing the machine to take the hot fill at its reduced rate.

Note: *Some machines can be modified internally. Instruction for this will be given in the accompanying user handbook/installation document supplied with the machine. Follow the instructions given and do not attempt alteration without the detailed instructions of the manufacturer. As with any repair, inspection or maintenance, isolate the machine thoroughly prior to removing any panels.*

5 Check for drum action when machine has filled to low level. Some machines may require the timer to be advanced slightly to avoid a paused heat only cycle before drum rotation takes place. See *Timers (programme control)* chapter (Thermostop). Check for clockwise and counter-clockwise drum action.
6 Check that the door interlock operates and that the door will not open during this cycle.
7 Switch the machine off and move it to the special treatments (fabric conditioner) position. This will select a higher level fill via the cold valve. Some machines will possess a choice of the positions for this – one before the short or delicates spin and one before the normal or fast spin. Remember on delicate cycles the machine will stop full of water after the special treatments cycle and will only move on to the spin when instructed to. Each machine has its own way of impulsing to the spin from this 'hold' position so make yourself aware from your handbook. See also *Machine will not empty* chapter.
7a If you choose the position prior to the normal spin, the machine will fill to its high level using the cold valve and therefore a check of the cold inlet can be made. Wait four minutes maximum for the high level to be reached. As the cold inlet pressure is usually governed by the street mains to the house the pressure is normally well above the minimum required.

8 When the high level is reached check for rotation, again clockwise and counter-clockwise.
9 As the programme of Special Treatments is short, allow the machine to impulse normally to the pump out stage. (If delicate cycle, use the normal advance mechanism.) Check that the machine empties within one minute or thereabouts (verifying that the pump rate and outlet are correct).
10 Allow the machine to impulse on to the spin and through to the 'off' position. Time and spin speeds will differ depending on whether special treatments cycle or whichever spin speed was selected.
11 Check immediately after the 'off' position has been reached to see if entry to the machine is correctly inhibited by the interlock.
12 Time the delay of the interlock minimum one minute up to two minutes (for basic electrical interlocks). Check that after such time the door can be opened correctly. Do not be impatient and force the latch mechanism or handle.

This simple sequence is likely to take 10–15 minutes.

If at any point a fault should occur, the correct action can be implemented.

These simple steps have in effect, confirmed (or otherwise) the operation of both water valves and pressure supplied to them, the pressure system for water level control, hoses and seals, outlet pump and waste, programmer (though not in depth) and spin speed. However, what this relatively simple test has not shown is whether the wash heater works or if the wash thermostat operates correctly. To confirm this, the time taken to heat up to the selected temperature should be noted, also the correct impulse from the thermostat for that particular programme setting. These two items will be tested on the next full wash cycle after the basic functional test proves satisfactory. It is therefore advisable to check both heating and correct temperature advancing on a normal wash cycle.

Chapter 11
Using a flowchart

Flowcharts are used throughout the book, and are designed to help you quickly locate the area or areas of trouble, and to show that a step-by-step approach to even the most difficult of faults is by far the best way to ensure they are found and rectified easily.

The use of flowcharts to those with some experience of home computers will need little explanation. To those of you who will be seeing them for the first time, here is how they work.

How flowcharts work

To the uninitiated, the use of flowcharts may seem a difficult way of fault finding. This is not the case, and will be quite simple if a few small, but important points are remembered. As you will see in the examples, there are only three main types of symbols used. A rectangular box, a diamond and an ellipse. With a little practice, you will become aware how invaluable this method can be in all areas of DIY work. The construction of one's own flowchart before attempting the job in hand will be of help when the time comes to reverse the stripdown procedure, i.e. notes can be made next to the relevant boxes on the flowchart, of what was encountered at that point, i.e. number of screws, positions of wires, etc. Small points – but so vital, and so often forgotten with an unplanned approach.

The rectangular box

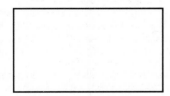

This is a process, i.e. in the box is an instruction. Carry it out and rejoin the flowchart where you left it, travelling in the direction indicated by the arrows.

The diamond

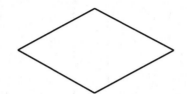

This asks a question, i.e. if the answer to the question in the diamond is yes, then follow the yes line from the diamond. If the answer is no, follow the no line.

The ellipse

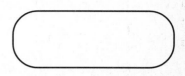

This is a terminator. When this box is encountered, you either start a new chart or finish one. The text in the box will indicate the action.

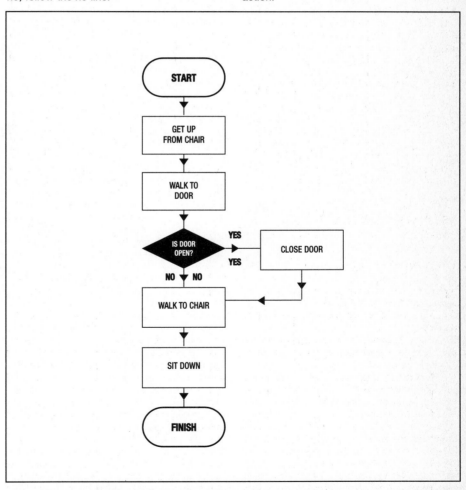

This example flowchart illustrates the steps involved in carrying out the simple task of making sure a door is closed. The arrows indicate the direction to the next step, so as to guide you through the logical sequence

Chapter 12
Determining the fault

Through the manual, flowcharts are used to aid the fault finding process. The location of faults will become much easier as you become more conversant with your machine, i.e., through regular servicing of your machine before faults have arisen.

Selecting the correct flowchart for the job will be made easier if it is remembered that faults fall into three main categories, mechanical, electrical and chemical.

Mechanical faults will normally become apparent by a change in the usual operational noise level of the machine, for instance a faulty suspension may cause a banging or bumping noise. A broken or slipping belt (incorrect tension) may give rise to excessive noise during the spin cycle or little or no drum rotation. This may also indicate a drum or motor bearing fault.

Electrical faults fall into two major categories:

Impulse path faults
A fault is classed as an impulse fault when an internal, pre-determined instruction has failed, e.g. thermostat does not close or open at the required temperature, or the timer fails to move on after a given time sequence. This constitutes an impulse path fault. Simply, this is the failure of the machine to move correctly through its selected programme. An instance of this type of fault is explained below:

The timer supplies power to the heater, but due to a fault in the thermostat circuit, the timer is not supplied with the information that the correct temperature has been reached. Because of this the timer does not move on, but remains on the heat position and exceeds the selected temperature. It should be noted that there is no fault in the timer, just in one of its impulse paths. A similar fault would

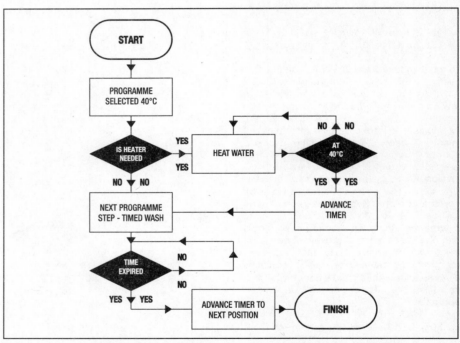

Shown is a simplified flowchart of the operation described

arise even if the thermostat circuit was OK, the thermostat closed at the correct temperature, but the timer failed to move on after the correct time had elapsed. This would be a fault of the timer's internal impulse path via its timing mechanism, and would constitute a component fault, i.e., timer coil, thermostop or complete timer unit. See *Timers (programme control)*.

Component faults
A fault is classed as a component fault when a complete unit has failed. If the pump, heater, motor, etc., should fail, the fault is said to be a component fault.

Chemical faults

These are normally associated with the detergent being used and will create such problems as poor washing, scaling problems, blocking, etc. A comprehensive guide to washing problems and useful hints will be found at the rear of this manual, in the chapter *Common causes of poor washing results*.

Fault finding guide	Chapter title
Machine will not work at all	Basics – electrical Basics – plumbing Locating a fault Door switches (interlocks)
Machine leaks	Emergency procedures Locating a fault Leaks flowchart, fault finding Water level control Pumps Motors Water inlet valves Suspension
Machine will not empty	Emergency procedures Locating a fault Pumps Basics – plumbing Wiring and harness faults
Machine will not fill/take powder	Basics – electrical Basics – plumbing Locating a fault Water inlet valves
Machine does not wash clean	Locating a fault Main drive belts Common causes of poor wash results Basics – plumbing Pumps
Machine is noisy	Noise faults Suspension
Machine washes but no spin	Locating a fault Door switches (interlocks) Pumps
Machine will not turn drum	Main drive belt Motors Door switches (interlocks)
Machine spins on all positions	Locating a fault Motors Timers (programme control)
Machine won't move through programme	Basic plumbing Temperature control (thermostat) Water heater inlet valve Timers (programme control)
Machine sticks through programme	Locating a fault Basics – plumbing Pumps Timers (programme control) Water inlet valve
Machine blows fuses	Emergency procedures General safety guide Basics – electrical Low insulation

The lists following the main fault headings indicate the sequence with which they should be examined.

Chapter 13
Noise faults

Noise can be one of the first signs that something is going wrong with your washing machine. Noise faults are easily ignored, and over a length of time can be accepted as the norm, and because of this it is important that such faults be examined immediately.

As with other faults, noise faults become easier to locate the more conversant that you become with your machine.

Noises and their most common locations

A loud grating or rumbling noise would indicate a main drum bearing fault. See *Bearings* chapter.

A loud, high-pitched noise would indicate a main motor bearing or pump bearing fault. See *Motors and Pumps* chapters.

A noise just before and after spin would indicate wear or water penetration of the suspension mounts. See *Suspension* chapter.

A squeaking noise mainly during the wash cycle would indicate a poorly adjusted drive belt. Instructions on how to adjust the drive belt appear in the *Main drive belts* chapter.

A rather unusual though not uncommon fault can be found on machines with cast aluminium pulleys. If a crack or break develops in one leg/spoke of the pulley, a noise very similar to that of main bearing failure can be heard. Check such pulleys closely for this type of defect and also for tight fit on the shaft of the drum, i.e. it should not be loose. See *Bearings* chapter. This type of fault may be apparent on both wash and spin cycles alike.

Coin damage

Coins and other metal items are easily trapped in the machine, and can cause a great deal of damage. These can become lodged between the inner drum and outer tub, and should be removed before damage to the drum occurs.

Coin damage can be identified by small bumps on the inner drum or a rattling noise when spinning. On old models with enamel drums or tubs, this may be accompanied by small flakes of enamel in the wash load.

Many modern makes and models have glass reinforced/plastic outer tubs, and coins and similar metal objects can knock holes through them or create hairline cracks

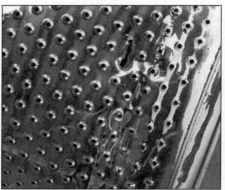

A coin between the inner drum and outer tub turned sideways during the spin and tore the inner drum open. It is possible for coins and other items to enter the space between the drum and the outer tub via the gap that exists between the rotating drum and fixed door seal. This gap varies between makes and models and can be quite large on some appliances

which can result in leaks that can be difficult to trace without taking the whole tub unit apart.

There are also some makes and models that have stainless steel outer tubs, and although they are resistant to corrosion, they can still be easily damaged by foreign objects in a similar way to that described in the following paragraph relating to stainless steel drums.

Unlike early makes, most modern machines have stainless steel drums and it is not uncommon for the drum to be torn open by coin damage. Take care when checking the drum interior and the outer tub unit for this kind of damage as the torn metal edges can be extremely sharp. If there's damage to the inner drum or outer tub unit (or worse still, both) the damaged item(s) will need to be renewed, as a repair is not possible. The design of many stainless steel drums means that they will have raised plastic paddles/lifters fixed to the inner surface of the drum. There are many ways in which these are secured from simple slot and click to screw fixings from the outer surface of the drum. Small pips of plastic found in the wash load may indicate the presence of a coin or similar item trapped between the inner and outer tub which is chipping off protruding pieces of the plastic paddles as the drum rotates (usually on a spin cycle).

Where there is no damage to the drum, it may be possible to avoid a full strip

The coin damage to both inner drum and outer tub on this machine was extensive and was not worth repairing due to the cost of replacement parts. Simply checking pockets before loading the machine could have saved the cost of having to buy a new machine

Typical coin damage to an enamel outer tub. The chips on the enamel coating will quickly lead to corrosion. To slow down the corrosion process, treat the affected areas with an anti-corrosion compound. This is readily available in motorist shops and is generally used for minor car bodywork repairs

When applying the above compound, please ensure that the manufacturer's instructions are followed carefully, and that the compound does not come into contact with rubber hoses or seals, etc. Always use this type of substance in a well ventilated area.

Do not apply anti-corrosion compound to plastic tubs

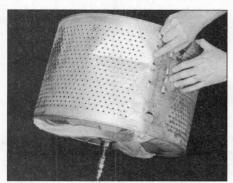

Severe coin damage to a stainless steel drum. This kind of fault can be easily avoided by carefully checking pockets, etc., prior to loading the washer. In this instance the drum had not been torn or holed but dented and it was possible to carefully remove the dent by pressing from within the drum with a gloved hand. However, if there had been any sign of damage to the surface of the drum the only cure would have been to renew the drum assembly

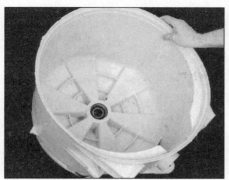

Plastic outer tubs are generally more resistant to coin damage

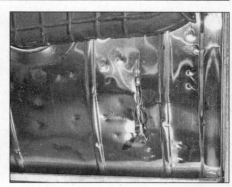

Stainless steel outer tubs can also be badly damaged by coins and other similar items

down/removal by taking out the offending items/coin from the drum/tub gap by removing the heater; see *Heaters* chapter. The item can either be removed via this opening, or manoeuvred into the sump hose, where it can be extracted easily.

Note: *Any large items such as bra wires, keys, etc., can be removed via the heater opening avoiding the sharp 90° into the sump hose. All such problems could of course be avoided by first removing all items from pockets, etc., before washing. This simple action can save a lot of time and money in the long run.*

This plastic outer tub unit has had a hole punched through it by a coin being trapped between the metal inner drum and the plastic outer tub during the spin cycle. This is an obvious fault but cracks in plastic outer tubs are more common and close inspection will be needed to find them

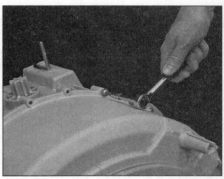

To gain access to the inner drum this tub unit splits in half by removing a series of screws. Further details can be found in the Bearings chapter

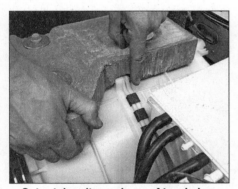

Outer tub units made up of two halves can be found on a wide range of makes and models and many different methods are used to secure the halves together. The two sections of this outer tub unit are held together by large metal clips. Further details can be found in the Bearings chapter

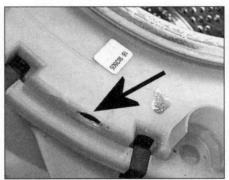

The impact from a coin trapped in the space between the fixed outer tub and the free-to-rotate inner drum knocked a hole clean through the plastic front of this outer tub. A new outer tub front and joint seal were required to correct the problem

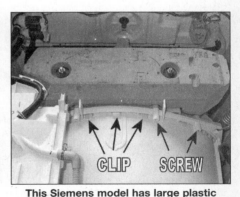

This Siemens model has large plastic clips and self-tapping screws holding both parts of the outer tub together
Note: *The screw heads are facing the rear of the appliance. Although this range of appliances has good front access (facia and front are removable) the outer tub unit needs to be removed from the shell of the appliance to enable the tub to be split (similar to the Beko/ISE bearing sequence shown in the Bearings chapter).*

Chapter 14
Leaks fault finding flowchart

This fault is by far the one that causes the most mess and inconvenience. A small leak/weep over many months can damage carpets, cupboards, floorboards and other parts of the machine whilst the appliance appears to function normally. Above all, the safety factor of a mains powered machine with a water leak should be considered. If a machine has a leak, regardless of how small, it must be checked out and cured. A very small and inexpensive seal may be the cause of the leak that is possibly damaging the main motor. The hoses should have been inspected regularly, as stated in the chapter *General care and attention*.

With the above in mind, the flowchart can be followed. At first it may seem obvious where the leak is coming from, but it would still be wise to follow the flowchart through.

Box 1
The smallest of holes in the door boot (door seal) can be the cause of the biggest leaks. The condition of the seal should also be checked and replaced if any holes are found or if it feels sticky or tacky to the touch. The seal between the door glass and the seal should be a good one, with no scaling or fluff adhering to the door glass. If this is the case, it can be removed easily by rubbing gently with a non-abrasive scouring pad. Details of door seal replacement can be found in the *Door seals* chapter.

Box 2
The clamp band that secures the door seal to the outer tub lip should be checked for tightness. Details of different types of clamp bands can be found in the *Door seals* chapter.

Box 3
The dispenser hose is located at the base of the soap dispenser, and forms the connection with the tub. Again, thorough inspection of this hose is advised, as all of the water that the machine uses passes through this hose, and can therefore lead to some quite large leaks. This hose is usually of a grommet type fitting, and should be checked for tightness, i.e., it should not rotate. A sign of a bad fit is scaling/powder marks running down the outer tub at the fitting point. If the hose feels sticky or tacky to the touch, it should be replaced. **Note:** *If this hose has leaked, the water would have contained detergent. If the water has come into contact with the suspension legs it may cause a loud squeaking/grinding noise just before and after the spin. (This fault is more pronounced on early Hoover Automatics). This is because the suspension works its hardest at this time.*

Please refer to the Suspension chapter.

If your type of washer has a hose connected between the outer tub and the rear of the machine, this is called an air vent tube. This in itself cannot leak as no water passes through it, although it may be used if the machine overfoamed, overfilled or was spun whilst still full of water. The hose is of the grommet fitting type, and should be checked for perishing as before. Most modern machines use the soap dispenser as the air vent as well as the water inlet, thus eliminating an extra grommet fitting hose in manufacture.

Box 4
The sump hose is the flexible hose located at the bottom of the machine. Depending on the make and model of your appliance, this will be in one of two configurations:

a) linking the pump and the outer tub.
b) linking the filter and outer tub, with a separate hose linking the filter and pump, thus creating a trap for any foreign bodies to prevent them reaching the pump.

Again this should be checked for perishing and replaced if found to be tacky or sticky. The grommet fittings should also be checked, as explained in Box 3, and the clips should be checked for tightness as explained in the *Pumps* chapter. If the machine is of

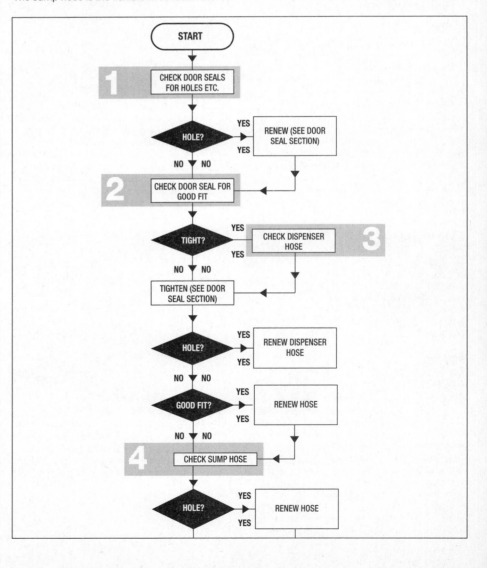

the type with a filter, all hoses to and from the filter housing and the filter seal should be checked for defects. At this point it would be advisable to thoroughly check the pump as detailed in the *Pumps* chapter.

Box 5

The thermostat and heater seal are both generally located on the back half or underside of the outer tub, depending on the make and model of the machine. Many modern makes and models now have the thermostat, heater and pressure vessel located on the front of the outer tub, directly below the door seal. Access to these components is gained by the removal of the front panel of the machine. Details of this are to be found in the *Door seals* chapter.

If the heater seal is found to be leaking, this can sometimes be stopped by tightening the centre nut. This increases the width of the rubber seal by squashing it 'vice like'. If the leak persists at this point, the heater will have to be changed completely, as the seal is not available as a separate item.

Box 6

The connection between the pressure switches and the tub should be checked now, as detailed in the *Water level control* chapter.

Box 7

The hoses and clips on the inlet valves should now be checked in conjunction with *Water inlet valves* chapter. On earlier valves there is a slight chance that the top of the valve can split. This is often shown by a small brown rust patch on the top of the valve.

Box 8

The tub seal and grommets are to be checked now. This means the seal or seals that fit between the separate parts of the main tub assembly. In addition to these seals, small rubber grommets may be found. These will have been fitted to block 'machine holes' that are used in the manufacture of the machine. If these come out or leak, they should be replaced or have sealant applied to them. If the large tub seals leak they should also be renewed. This type of repair is described in the *Bearings* chapter.

Box 9

Any corrosion or flaking of the enamel covering of the outer tub can be treated with a good brand of rust inhibitor, taking care that it does not come into contact with any of the internal rubber hoses, etc., and is used in conjunction with the manufacturer's instructions. Places to note, are where the brackets for the motor and the suspension are welded onto the outer tub. These are stress points where the enamel may crack and flake, and rust will inevitably form. By the time a leak has started at these points, it is too late to save the outer tub, and it must be renewed completely if a lasting repair is to

be made. It is felt that the occurrence of tub renewal on today's modern automatics is very rare. Therefore, the need for a lengthy section in this book would be unnecessary. Also, the cost of such items and all the relevant seals and parts necessary to

complete such a repair would not be cost effective.

If the machine still leaks after these checks, please refer to the *Basics – plumbing* and *Motors* chapters.

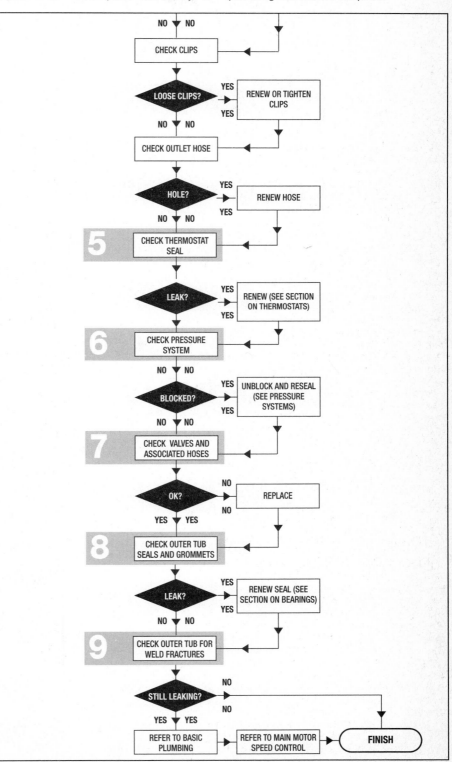

Chapter 15
Machine will not empty flowchart

Of all the faults reported, this must be one of the most common. Often this fault and the 'leak' fault are one of the same. The reason for this being that on many machines there is no 'spin inhibit system'. This is especially true of older machines. If there is no spin inhibit system, it means that if for any reason the machine cannot empty, it will still try to spin. The consequence of this action, is that the increased drum speed pressurises the inner tub, causing leaks from soap dispensers, air vent hoses and door seals. Thus one fault can cause several problems. On most later machines and most of the machines currently produced, the level switch inhibits (stops) the machine before the spin if a level of water is detected. This means that if there is water in the machine the pressure causes the switch to switch to the off position, therefore not allowing the machine to spin. For a more detailed description of the pressure switch, please refer to the *Water level control* chapter.

The 'not emptying' fault can fall into three main categories: blockage, mechanical fault or electrical fault.

Please refer to the following Flowchart

Box 1
Follow the emergency procedure for removing the water already trapped inside the machine.

Box 2
Check the outlet and sump hoses, as well as the outlet filter (if fitted). If a blockage or a kink is found, remove it and refit the pipe(s) and filter.

Box 3
The pump is located at the machine end of the outlet hose, and junction of the sump hose. The small chamber should be checked for blockages. The impeller should

be checked for free rotation, and that it hasn't come adrift from its mounting to the pump motor shaft. If the impeller is found to be adrift from the shaft, this would give rise to no water being pumped, although the motor itself would run. A quick way to check at this stage would be to hold the shaft

whilst trying to turn the impeller. If all is well they should only turn in unison. Remember to turn anti-clockwise, or the impeller on most types will unscrew from the shaft. If a fault or an alternative type pump motor is found at this point, refer to the *Pump* chapter.

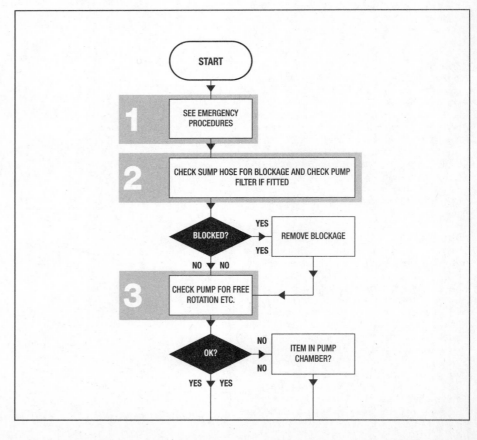

Box 3A

If no blockage is found in the section above, and the bearings are not suspected, the stator continuity of the pump windings must be checked. Please refer to the *Electrical circuit testing* chapter.

Box 4

At this point, the outlet hose should be checked again. An internal blockage such as a coin or button can act as a type of valve, and be very difficult to see. The best method of checking this is to connect the hose of a standard tap, observing the flow of water.

Box 5

The final step is to check the wiring harness connection. Please refer to *Wiring and harness faults*.

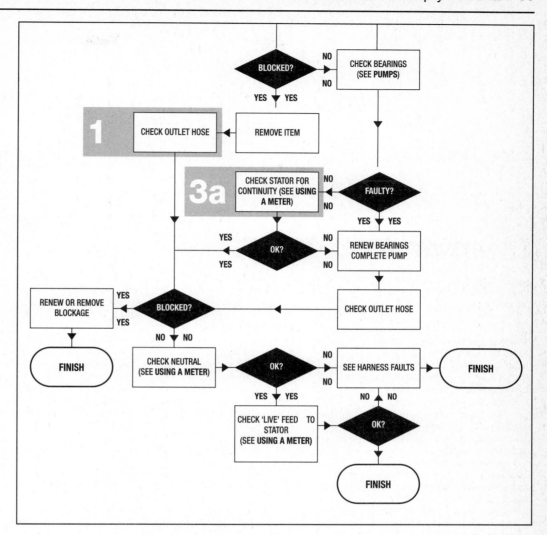

Chapter 16
Door seals

Door seal fitting – helpful hints

Many different types of door seal can be encountered and which type you have depends on the make, model and the age of your machine. The removal and fitting of various door seals is shown in the following photographic sequences. The makes and models shown have been selected for their popularity and to illustrate some of the most common fitting variations as the securing systems and techniques required to remove and refit them are very similar. If your version is not shown you should be able to adapt the information provided to your particular make, model and style of fitting.

The door seal bridges the gap between the outer tub and the shell of the machine. This provides access to the inner drum via the door opening for loading the machine whilst also creating a watertight seal. The seal should be renewed if found to be perished or holed at any point, paying attention to the folds and mouldings of the door seal.

There are essentially three ways that a door seal is secured to the outer tub and all are similar in concept. However, this is an area where manufacturers constantly change the shape of the door seal and the type of securing system. Most of the changes are to assist production with little thought of how this will affect the task of removal and refitting when required, some time later in the machine's life. Although not all the various types of fittings can be shown the most popular and interesting types have been selected for the photographic sequences to illustrate some of the 'tricks' that need to be applied in fitting some of the less obvious securing clamps. If your particular version of fitting is not shown you should be able to adapt the information provided to assist both removal and refitting.

On the outer tub there is a formed lip. When the rubber seal is located on this lip, it is then held in position by a large clamp band, and pressure is exerted by the band to create a watertight seal. There are several versions of clamp bands used in today's machines and several of the most common are described below. The majority of machines will have one or a combination of those listed whereas the others may have a variation of one of those described. Use the list and photographs to help identify the type used in your machine.

1 A simple metal band secured by a bolt, which when tightened reduces the diameter of the band.

2 As (1), but the open ends of the band are secured by a spring.

3 This method is best described as a large rubber band or spring joined together to form an expanding ring. Both types are called garter rings. When fitted correctly, the ring rests in a recess in the door seal, which in turn rests in the recess of the tub lip, therefore creating the watertight seal. Unlike the previous two methods, this band cannot be slackened by the loosening of a bolt or spring, and is best removed by prising the garter ring from its position in the seal recess by using a flat-bladed screwdriver to lift it over the lip. The best way to refit a rubber or spring garter ring is to locate the bottom of the ring in the recess of the fitted door seal slowly working the ring inside the recess in an upward direction with both hands meeting at the top. This can be likened to fitting a tyre onto a bicycle wheel after mending a puncture.

4 A slightly unusual fastening may be encountered where both ends of a wire band are joined by a small metal plate. The ends of the wire band are linked into two holes in the metal plate. The plate has a larger hole/slot in it and if a small screwdriver is inserted into this slot and

This outer tub shows a concrete tub weight in place around the front of it. Variations of this type of configuration can be found in a wide range of makes and models including Beko, Blomberg, Electrolux, Zanussi, Tricity Bendix, AEG and many more. However, some appliances (including many in the ranges listed above) do not have the large concrete weight around the front of the tub, thus allowing greater access to the door seal clamp band
Note: *The tub shown has been removed for the purpose of the photograph – the door seals are fitted with the outer tub remaining inside the machine and with the concrete block left in position.*

forms a tight fit, when turned, a 'cam' action occurs which reduces or increases the overall circumference. Only a small movement is required, approximately a quarter turn between open and closed. When closed correctly, the plate will lock into position. Access to the plate can be gained through the door latch hole after first removing the two interlock fixing screws. This type of fixing is mainly found on machines in the Indesit/Ariston range. The reason for this type of clamp band is that access to a more usual clamp band would be impossible due to a close front fitting circular concrete tub weight which surrounds the door seal tub lip.

Note: *To aid the fitting of a door seal, a little washing-up liquid may be applied to the tub lip or the door seal tub lip moulding. (NOT the front shell lip.) This will allow the rubber to slip more easily into position on the metal or plastic lip of the outer tub.*

The fitting of the door seal to the shell of the machine is similar to the tub lip system in that three major variations are found:

a) The most straightforward seal simply grips the shell lip with no other added support other than the elasticity of the door seal itself (only found on early machines). For safety reasons modern machines now use various methods of secondary fixing to prevent the door seal being easily removed or dislodged from the shell lip. It is essential that such fixings are replaced if they are removed for any reason.

b) This type also uses the shell lip, with the aid of a clamp band. A recess is formed on the outer edge of the seal for a plastic or wire clamp band to be inserted. This ensures a firm grip on the shell lip. As with the inner tub lip, many variations can be found, see photos.

c) The third method involves a plastic flange that is screwed onto the outside of the shell. The screws that hold this flange pass through a recess in the outer front lip of the door seal therefore securing it firmly to the front panel. Variations on both of the later clamps can be found on most modern machines. They are fitted as a safety measure to restrict access to the inner of the machine. It is essential that any such fixing is replaced correctly if it has had to be removed for any reason. Before removing the old door seal a simple examination of the old seal and a note of its correct positioning will aid the subsequent repair and renewal as the new seal will need to fit in exactly the same position. Dome door seals have a definite top and bottom, or pre-shaped sections for door hinges or catches, etc., and will fit no other way.

Note: *It is easier to line up the seal before fitting rather than trying to adjust the seal when the clamp bands have been fitted.* **Note:** *Some machines have one or more of their tub weights*

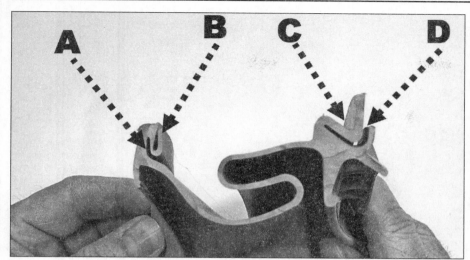

This slice through a typical door seal illustrates the construction of the moulding

A *The recess that fits on to the lip formed around the door opening.*
B *The recess in the door seal into which the outer clamp band fits to secure the seal to the front panel.*
C *The rear shoulder/outer recess around which the rear clamp band sits. The pressure exerted by the retaining clamp around the circumference of the shoulder creates the watertight seal between the outer tub lip and the door seal recess.*
D *The rear door seal recess that fits onto the outer tub lip.*

Removing the front panel of this Siemens washing machine allows excellent access to various components including the rear fixing point of the door seal which is surrounded by a large concrete balance weight
Note: *The seal can be replaced with the weight in place.*

This Siemens machine has a concrete weight encircling the door seal and a spring clamp band is used to secure the door seal to outer tub lip (here being refitted)

mounted on the front section of the outer tub, encircling the door seal and tub clamp fitting, leaving little or no access to the clamp band or tub lip. However, do not remove the front tub weight to aid door seal fitting as it is not necessary for most machines, e.g. Creda, Zanussi, Ariston and Bendix, etc., even though some have front tub weights surrounding the tub clamp bands. The Zanussi and Creda seals can be changed through the door opening in the front panel of the machine, without removing the top at all. (Having said this, removing the top of the machine will provide more light. Remove if necessary).

Door seal deterioration

The material that door seals are made of is a relatively unstable substance, and has a limited life before it starts to perish. This process cannot be prevented, but deterioration can be slowed down by the addition of stabilising ingredients to the mixture before it is moulded.

High-quality washing products themselves do not cause the door seal to deteriorate quickly as they contain chemicals such as silicates to help preserve the material. However, it is possible that lower quality washing products may not have such additives and this may result in quicker than normal deterioration of the door seal as well as other, similar flexible components such as hoses within the appliance. The speed at which deterioration occurs can also be affected by a number of other important factors.

1 Frequency of machine use. The life of a door seal/gasket will obviously vary depending on how often the machine is used. Some people use the machine every day, while others only use their machine occasionally.
2 High temperature programmes. Most chemical reactions tend to happen faster at higher temperatures, so the life of a rubber gasket would be shorter on a machine where the 'boil wash' programme is used regularly.
3 Type of wash load. Certain types of soiling can affect deterioration of the door seal. Oils, fats, and heavy grease soiling on clothes can be deposited on the gasket during the wash process and increase the rate of deterioration.
4 The presence of copper in the wash water. Copper may be present in the water supply through the installation of new pipes and some occupations involve work clothes coming into contact with metal compounds.

Preventative measures

To prolong the life of the flexible door seal/porthole gasket:
1 Always use the recommended dosage of washing product; taking into account the size of the wash load, the amount of soiling on articles, and water hardness.
2 If soiling is particularly heavy use the pre-wash facility, and increase the dosage of detergent, dividing it between the pre- and main wash.
3 Always wipe the door seal/gasket dry after the machine has been used, and leave the door open to allow a free circulation of air.
Warning: It is possible for small children to climb into washing machines and injure

themselves – ensure measures are taken to avoid this. **Note:** *Large-door machines may include a child safety latch that can be set to prevent the door being closed when not in use. Check to see if your machine has this feature and use it as recommended in the instruction booklet.*

The following photographic sequences show the removal and refitting of various types of door seals.

Typical door seal (early Hoover)

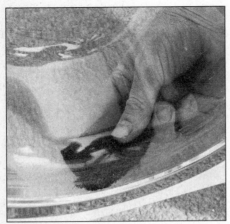

1 Check door glass inner for scale deposit ridge and clean with non-abrasive pad

4 Free complete door seal from front lip and allow seal to rest on inner side front panel

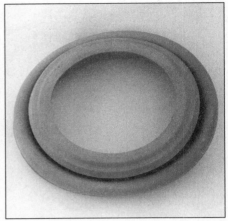

7 New door seal of type to be fitted to the machine shown

2 Grasp the door seal firmly and pull downwards to free from shell lip. Some machines may have a clamp band on front lip. Remove this first

5 With top removed, free the top support springs or tie, and lean outer tub unit back as far as possible

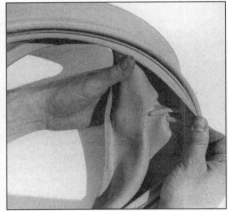

8 View showing inner lip moulding and ridge, the ridge is fitted at the 9 o'clock position when viewed from the front of the machine

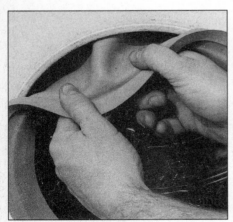

3 When freed from lip, continue pulling in a downward direction

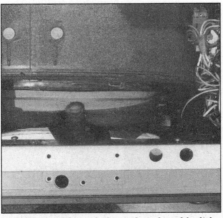

6 With position of clamp band and bolt in view proceed to remove band. Free seal from the clip as shown above

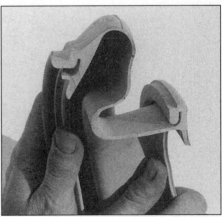

9 Cutaway view of a typical door seal to show intricate moulding and positioning of tub and shell lips of the seal

Early Bendix door seal

1 Remove the plastic flange around the door seal front

4 Picture showing the orientation of the band inside the machine. Must be refitted in the same position

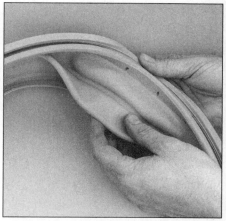

7 New door seal checked prior to fitting and smeared with a little washing up liquid to help slide it into position. (Inner lip only)

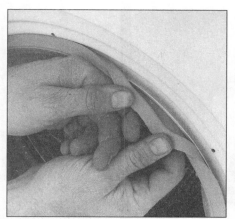

2 Remove the door seal from the front lip

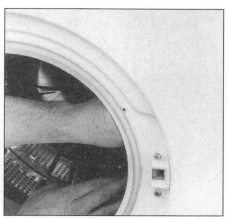

5 Slack off tub clamp band bolt and remove old door seal

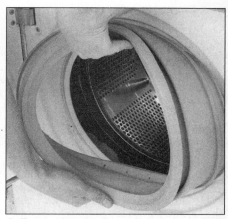

8 Ensure that the three drain holes on the door seal are fitted at the bottom of the tub lip

3 Showing the position of the clamp band with the top of the machine removed

6 View showing the tub lip and weight block gap. (Clean off any scale and/or deposit on the tub lip before fitting the new seal)

BEKO – ISE door seal

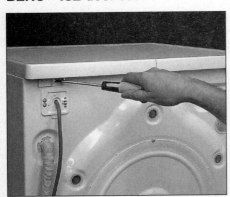

1 With the appliance fullly isolated (switched off, plug removed from supply socket and taps turned off) remove the lid securing screws

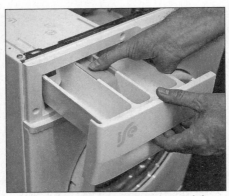

2 Press the dispenser drawer retaining latch and remove the drawer

3 Remove the recessed facia securing screw(s)
Note: *Screw fixings in this area of an appliance are generally stainless steel, so keep them separate to ensure they are replaced correctly.*

4 Clearly mark all electrical connections prior to removal. On this make of appliance they are 'keyed' but were marked anyway as a precaution (a wise working practice to adopt)

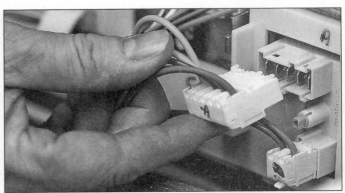

5 Ease the connections free – pull only on the connector NOT the wiring and avoid waggling the connector as this can result in damage to the PCB and IDC wiring connections as used here

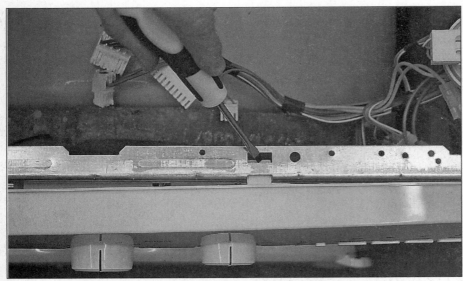

6 Carefully release the plastic latches holding the facia in place
Note: *Do not exert undue force – some plastic latches can be released by finger pressure only.*

7 With all fixings released the facia and control circuitry can be removed
Note: *DO NOT touch the connections or circuit board as the electronics on the PCB can be easily damaged by static discharge.*

8 Note the position of the hidden spring fixing and use a small flat-bladed screwdriver to ease the clamp band free from its recess

9 Grasp the door seal firmly and pull downwards to free it from the shell lip

10 Remove the two screws holding the door interlock in place
Note: *Some makes may use bolts and recessed nuts that are not captive – use your free hand behind the interlock to capture them.*

11 Flip the filter cover down and remove the single securing screws

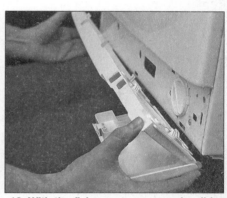

12 With the fixing screw removed – slide the whole of the bottom kick plate slightly to the right to release the plastic 'L' shaped pegs from their slots on the metal shell

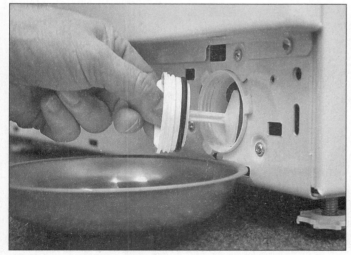

13 Using a suitable low dish to catch any residual water, remove the filter

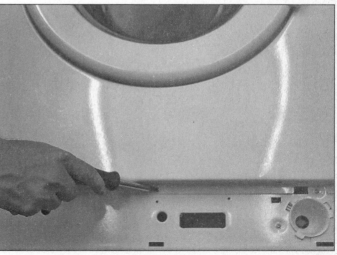

14 Remove the metal front panel fixing screws exposed when the plastic kick plate cover was removed

15 Hold the front panel firmly and press downwards to relase the metal front panel

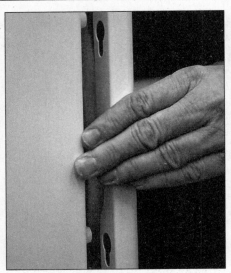

16 This clearly shows the post and captive slot fixing this particular make employs to hold the detachable metal front panel in place

17 Next remove the screws securing the large circular tub weight in place – the fixings used in this instance were large Torx-headed self-tapping screws which simply expand the plastic securing studs to secure the weight

18 When all the fixings are removed invert the door seal into the tub and carefully slide the weight forwards and free from the machine
Note: *The weight is very heavy yet once free of its mounting it can easily be damaged by careless handling – handle with care.*

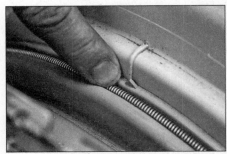

19 This make/model has a clear alignment indicator on both seal and tub. If it had not, a pen would have been used to mark the correct position of the seal prior to removal

20 This door seal is secured to the outer tub by a spring clamp band so a small flat-bladed screwdriver was used to ease the clamp band free from its recess

21 With the clamp band removed, ease the door seal free from the hub lip while carefully noting which part of the seal fitted onto it

22 Prior to fitting, lubricate the tub lip with a little fabric conditioner
Note: *If a door seal has only a small seal recess and tub lip it is best not to apply lubrication of this type as it may cause the seal to slip out of position during fitting.*

23 Orientate the door seal to match alignment of the indicator points or marks made prior to removal of the old seal

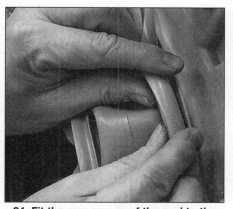

24 Fit the rear groove of the seal to the tub lip. This is often easier if thumbs and forefingers are used then flick the seal into position as opposed to applying too much force, which can be counter productive

25 When the door seal and tub lip are correctly fitted into position, carefully invert the seal into the drum as this will make fitting the spring clamp band easier. If the seal dislodges at this point it means that it was not correctly fitted to the tub lip

26 As the joint of the spring clamp band is the weakest point fit it to the seal recess first as this allows stretching to occur without stressing the joint

27 Stretching the spring into position can require a fair amount of effort. If you find yourself needing a third or fourth hand then the use of simple adjustable clamps or spring grips will be of great assistance

28 Reassembly of the tub weight, front pane, wiring connections, kick strip, etc., are a reversal of the removal procedure. Finally, fit the front recess of the door seal to the shell lip in a similar manner to that used for the inner tub lip. However, in this instance work towards the spring joint as this allows the movement required to allow the wire band to expand. Ensure that the position of the spring matches that of the original. If need be use clamps to aid fitting as in step 27

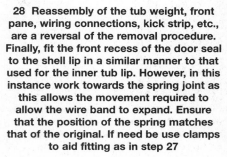

Hotpoint door seal (early models)

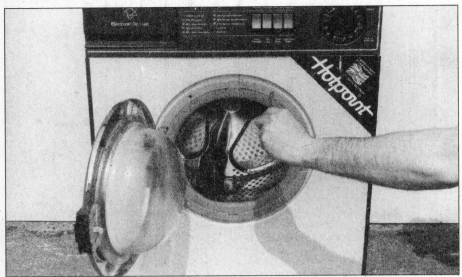

1 Remove outer plastic surround screws, and top and bottom section

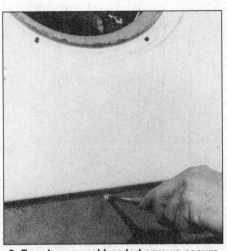

6 Four hexagonal headed screws secure the front panel under the bottom edge. (On later machines, three Philips-headed screws will be found)

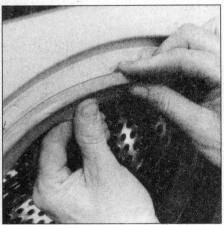

2 Pull seal to release from shell lip, hinge and catch

4 Pull out the soap dispenser drawer completely and remove the front facia fixing screws

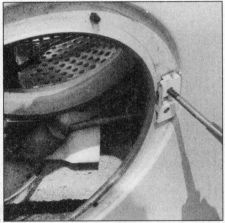

7 Remove door switch assembly and pressure switch bracket

3 Unscrew the timer knob centre and remove the timer knob. Also remove the two front facia fixing screws found behind the timer knob. Note: *Some knobs are secured by a single screw positioned within the machine behind the knob and accessed through a slot beneath the lid.*

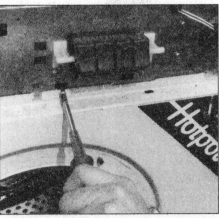

5 With front facia removed, remove the screws securing the front panel of the machine

8 With front panel removed, the clamp band can easily be removed

9 Note the position of hinge and catch mouldings. The door seal can then be pulled free from the tub lip

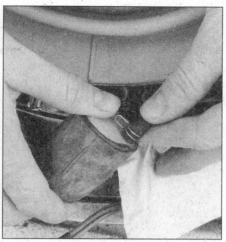

12 With the new door seal in this position it is wise to check that all of the leads, hoses and pressure vessel are correct before refitting the front panel

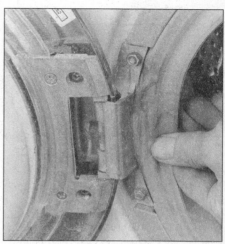

15 Lubricate the hinge and catch points with a little washing up liquid, and ease into position

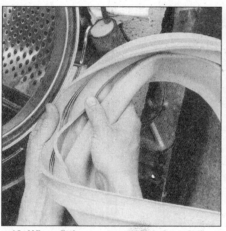

10 When fitting a new seal to the tub lip, the tub gap can be adjusted slightly. (Note: *the inner lip of the door seal is ribbed.*)

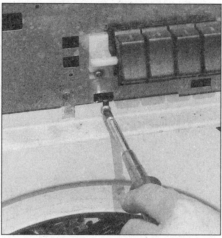

13 Refit front panel, door catch and all front panel fixings

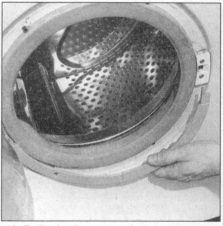

16 Refit plastic surround and ensure that the ends locate correctly. The machine is now ready for the functional test

11 When the new seal is fitted in this position, check that the inner drum rotates without fouling the door seal inner. Adjust if necessary to obtain the smallest gap possible before refitting

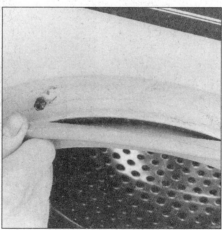

14 With front panel secured, fit the door seal to the front panel lip

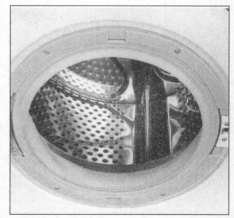

17 When fitted, the new seal should not have undue kinks or twists. It is essential that this is correctly fitted

Typical Hotpoint door seal (later models)

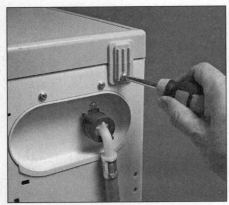

1 With the appliance fully isolated (switched off, plug removed from supply socket and taps turned off) remove the lid securing screws

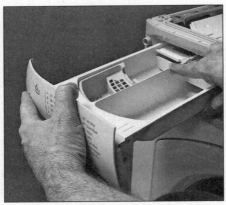

2 Remove the dispenser drawer by pressing the centre retaining latch and pulling the draw forwards

3 Remove the recessed facia screws
Note: *Screw fixings in this area of an appliance are generally stainless steel so keep them separate to ensure they are replaced correctly.*

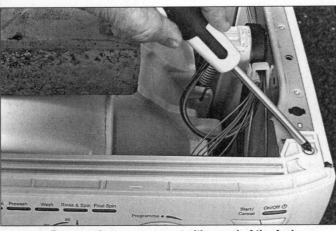

4 Remove the top screws at either end of the facia

5 Carefully release the plastic lathes holding the facia in place
Note: *Do not exert undue force – most plastic latches of this nature can be released by finger pressure.*

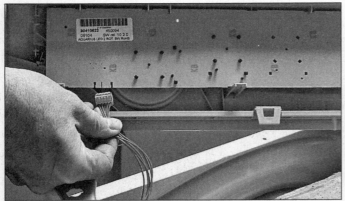

6 Note the correct position of the harness connector and ease it free – grip only on the connector NOT the wiring and avoid waggling the connector as this can result in damage to the PCB and IDC wiring connections. Remove the facia assembly and place it face up to avoid scratching the surface.
Note: *DO NOT touch the connections or circuit board as the electronics on the PCB can be easily damaged by static discharge.*

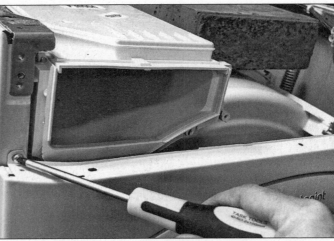

7 Remove the top screws securing the metal front panel exposed after taking the facia off

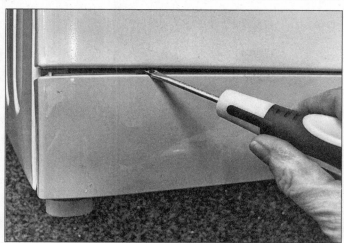

8 Locate the latch access points between the plastic cover plate and the bottom edge of the front pane. Carefully despress them using a small flat-bladed screwdriver

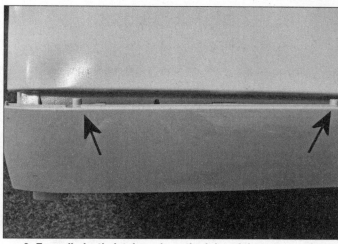

9 Free all plastic latches along the joint of the two panels (shown are the left and centre latches)

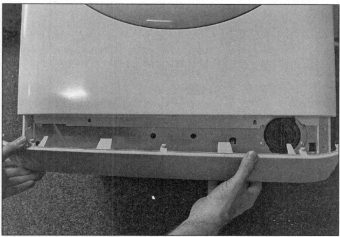

10 When all latches are free tilt the panel forwards and lift it free from the appliance

11 Remove the front metal panel securing screws exposed when the lower plastic panel was removed

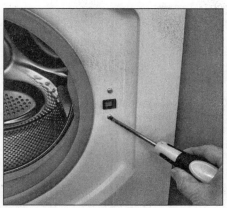

12 Remove the two screws holding the door interlock in place
Note: *Some makes may use bolts and recessed nuts that are not captive – use your free hand behind the interlock to capture them.*

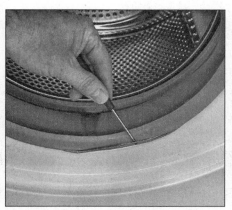

13 Use a small flat-bladed screwdriver to carefully remove the door seal front spring clamp fixing

14 After making a note of the correct position and orientation of the seal, grasp it firmly and pull downwards to free it from the shell lip

15 Hold the front metal panel firmly at either side and lift to release it from its securing posts

Note: This shows the post and captive slot fixing this make employs to hold detachable metal front panels in place.

16 Removing the front panel exposes the inner tub and the door seals rear clamp fixing. In this instance a 'zipper' type clamp was used

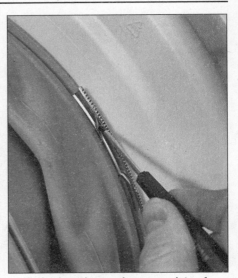

17 A 'zipper' type clamp consists of a pre-shaped wire and serrated metal plate. The wire ends simply engage the serrations. To release the clamp insert a small flat-bladed screwdriver between the wire and metal plate

Note: Both ends will need to be released in this way but only one freed completely.

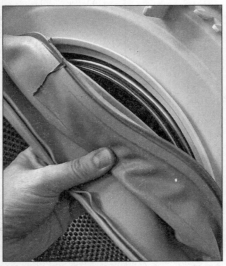

18 With the clamp removed the rear lip of the door seal can be eased from the outer tub lip

Note: Take note which part of the seal fits onto the outer tub lip as this will greatly aid the fitting of the new seal.

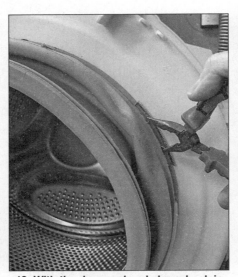

19 With the door seal and clamp back in place the clamp can be tightened using a large pair of long-nose pliers. These should be inserted into the two wire loops of the clamp and squeezed firmly together

Note: Ensure that the position of the clamp matches that of the original.

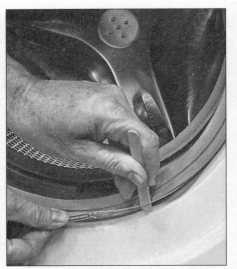

20 Stretching the spring of the clamp band into position can require a fair amount of effort. Avoid the use of metal tools that may slip and damage the front of the appliance. if your hands are not strong enough or the spring simply too strong, a good tip is to use a 'lolly' stick to ease the spring into position.
If you find yourself needing a third hand then consider using clamps or spring grips to hold the clamp in position as you move around it – refer to the previous door seal renewal sequence for further details

Note: Ensure that the postion of the clamp matches that of the original.

Spring clamp band door seal (Zanussi, late Bendix, Electrolux, etc.)

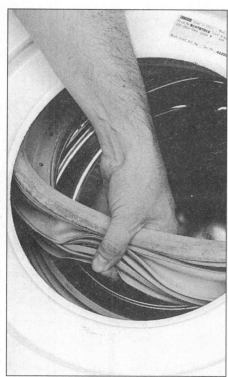

1 To remove a spring type inner clamp band you will need access to both the inner and outer edges of the inner tub lip, so do not place the front of the seal in the drum. Press firmly on the inside of the seal at the bottom and using your fingers or a flat bladed screwdriver ease the seal free from the tub lip (this may require a degree of force). Place your forefinger through the gap created and meet up with your thumb on the outside of the seal. Ensure you have both the seal and spring encircled and simply pull the seal and spring free

2 When fitting the new seal ensure it is correctly orientated and placed within the tub and shell gap

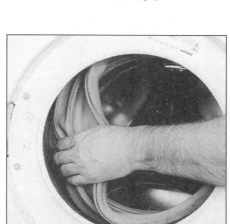

4 Press firmly around the perimeter to check that the seal is correctly positioned and seated on to the tub lip

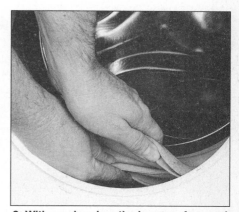

3 With one hand on the inner surface and the other on the outer, use your fingers to correctly locate the seal recess to the tub lip starting at the bottom. Work around the tub lip until fitted

5 When satisfied that the seal is located on the lip, invert the front section into the drum. This will allow better access for fitting the spring clamp band

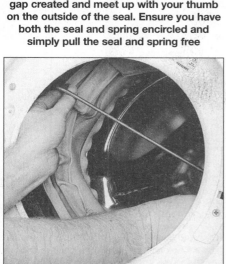

6 Place the spring in the bottom of its recess and with both hands work upwards allowing the spring to slip into the securing recess like fitting a bicycle tyre

7 Refit the front of the door seal to the shell lip

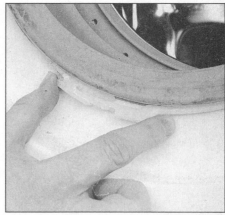

8 Ensure the front clamp band is refitted

Chapter 17
Water inlet valves

In this section we deal with several of the most common reported faults: not taking powder, not filling at all, not filling in certain parts of the programme. Please refer to the flowchart found later in this chapter.

Many configurations of water valve can be found from single hot or cold to much larger units consisting of three or more individually operated valves grouped together to control the flow to several outlets from one inlet. All inlet point threads are the same size ¾ BSP, but outlet hose connections from the valve may differ. A wide variety of fixing brackets are also used, outlet angles can be in-line (classed as 180 degree valves) or angled downwards (classed as 90 degree valves). Operation of the electro-mechanical action follows and covers the general operation of all such valves.

A solenoid coil of some 3 to 5000 ohms (3 to 5k ohms) resistance when energised (i.e. supplied with power), creates a strong

A 90° double inlet valve

magnetic field at its centre. This field attracts up into the coil a soft iron rod or plunger, and will hold it in that position as long as power is supplied to the coil. When power is

Triple valve: Generally cold supply, found in some automatic washers and dishwashers

removed (de-energised) from the coil, a spring at the top of the plunger recess returns it to its resting position.

A double inlet valve with block connector fittings

A single (red) hot valve with terminal connections

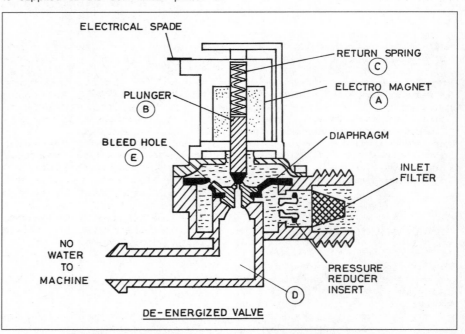

ELECTRICAL SPADE

RETURN SPRING
C

ELECTRO MAGNET
A

PLUNGER
B

DIAPHRAGM

BLEED HOLE
E

INLET FILTER

NO WATER TO MACHINE

PRESSURE REDUCER INSERT

D

DE-ENERGIZED VALVE

The de-energised valve (at rest – no power supplied).
With no power supplied to the solenoid coil (A) the soft iron core (B) is pressed firmly onto the centre hole of the flexible diaphragm by spring (C). As chamber (D) is only at atmospheric pressure and the water is at least 4 lbs p.s.i. (somewhat higher), pressure is exerted on the top of the diaphragm*, effectively closing it tight. The greater the water pressure the greater the closing effect of the valve, therefore no water will flow

*The pressure on top of the diaphragm is via a small bleed hole marked (E). It is essential that this very small hole is not obstructed. Though very small, it is a major factor in the correct operation of these types of pressure operated valves

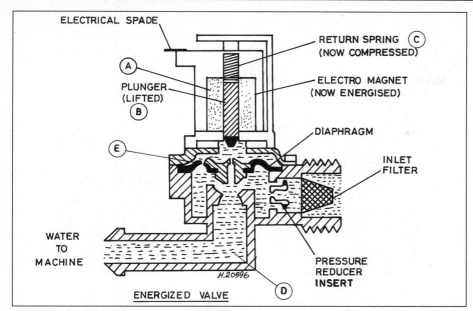

ELECTRICAL SPADE

RETURN SPRING (C) (NOW COMPRESSED)

PLUNGER (LIFTED) (A) (B)

ELECTRO MAGNET (NOW ENERGISED)

DIAPHRAGM

(E)

INLET FILTER

WATER TO MACHINE

PRESSURE REDUCER INSERT

H.20596

(D)

ENERGIZED VALVE

The energised valve (power supplied to it). When power is supplied to the solenoid coil, the resulting magnetic attraction of the coil overcomes the power of the spring (C) and pulls the plunger up into the coil centre. This allows an imbalance of pressure to occur by exposing the centre hole of the diaphragm. The imbalance lifts the flexible diaphragm and allows water to flow into chamber (D), thus water flow is achieved. It is easier for the water to lift the diaphragm than to balance the pressure by flowing through the very small bleed hole. Any enlargement or blockage of this vital bleed hole will render the valve inoperative

How does it work?

Shown here in detail are the two states of the water valve.
Main benefits of such valves
1 The higher the pressure supplied to it the tighter the valve will close.
2 Cost is relatively low.
3 Very reliable.
4 Simple to change if faulty.

Typical faults to watch for

1 As with ordinary house taps, the valve seat may wear and allow a small trickle of water to pass even when de-energised. This will cause the machine to fill when not in use if the taps are left turned on over a long period of time and the machine will overfill, resulting in a possible flood.
2 The valve, when de-energised will fail to allow the plunger to return to its normal resting/closed position. This problem will cause severe overfill and flooding.

Note: *Turning off the machine will not stop the overfilling in such cases. Complete isolation of both power and water supply is required and, as with step 1, complete renewal will be necessary.*

3 The valve fails to allow water to flow due to open circuit in coil winding. See *Electrical circuit testing* chapter.
4 The valve fails to allow water to flow due to a blocked filter on its inlet. Carefully remove and clean. Do not allow any particle, no matter how small, to escape past the filter as it could block the bleed hole.

Water valves come in many sizes and an assortment of shapes – single valves, double valves and triple valves or a combination of all three. On the double and triple valves, each solenoid operates one outlet from a common inlet. Unfortunately, a fault on one coil or one outlet will generally mean a complete renewal of the whole valve assembly, as individual spare parts are not available.

Verify the suspected fault

In this theoretical instance, the machine was loaded and a programme selected but it failed to fill. Moving the timer/control to a pump out position confirmed that power was being supplied and that the door interlock was working. See *Door Switches (interlocks)* chapter.

Box 1

Reselect wash programme to confirm that the machine was originally set and turned on correctly.

Box 2

With the machine correctly set, this confirms that, although the machine has electrical feed, no water is entering to begin the filling/washing action.

Box 3

This may seem too obvious to mention, but many an engineer has been called out to find the taps were in the OFF position. This normally brings the comment that the taps are 'never turned off', and in this case it must have been some other devious member of the family or innocent plumber that has done the dirty deed! This comment brings in the cardinal rule that all automatic washing machines and dishwashers should be turned OFF at their isolation taps when the machine is not in use. This may seem a quite pointless task, but the objective is simple. If an inlet pipe should split, or an inlet valve fails to close correctly, a quite disastrous flood could occur. However, if the taps were turned OFF between each use of the machine this could not happen.

Box 4

This section is to help identify which water supply is at fault, hot or cold. Normally whites-only washes fill at the start of a programme with hot water only, so selecting this programme will verify (or not) if the hot supply is at fault. Rinses use only cold water so selecting a rinse fill sequence will verify (or not) if the cold supply is at fault. See the chapter on *Functional testing* to assist in this task.

Box 5

By unscrewing the hose from the valve, this can be easily checked by turning the tap to which it is connected, on and off, ensuring that the free end of the hose is held in a suitable container. Failure of water flow could be due to a faulty tap or tap shaft or an internal fault of the supply hose. Some makers of machines supply rubber inlet hose seals which have a metal or gauze filter moulded into them. It is recommended in the manufacturer's instruction booklet, that the two washers supplied with the filters are fitted at the isolation tap end of the supply hose as a first line filter for the valves. Check if such filter washers were used during the original installation by unscrewing the supply hose from the isolation tap. Clean or renew as required.

Box 6

Checking of the water valve inlet filter can be carried out while the hose is removed for Step 4. Take care not to allow any particles to escape past the fine mesh filter and into the valve. Carefully clean the filter of all scale and debris, etc., and replace. **Note:** *The filter can be removed by gently gripping the centre with pliers and pulling it free of the main valve body.*

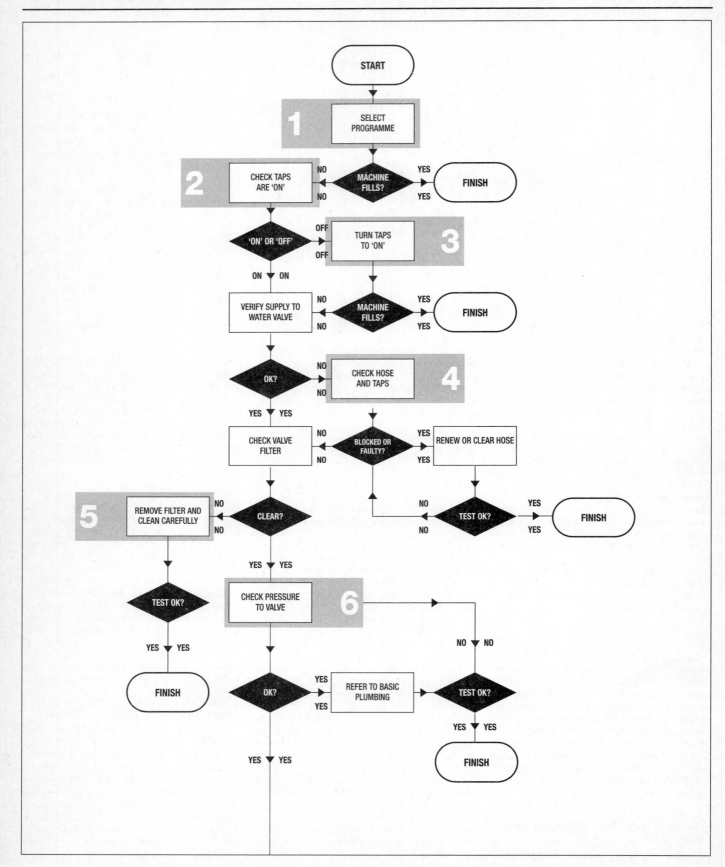

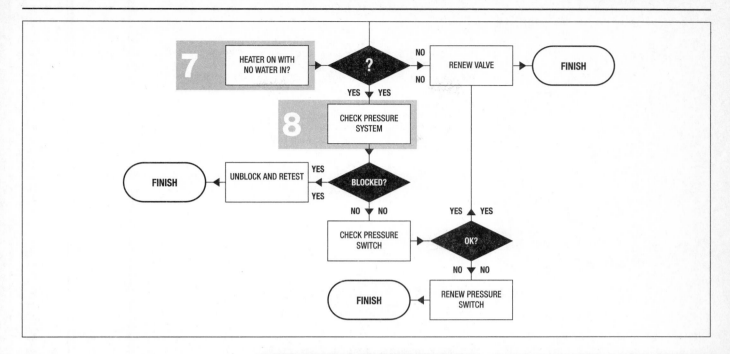

Box 7

Ensure that the water supply to the valve is adequate to operate the valve. See: *Basics – plumbing* chapter.

Box 8 & 9

If the heater is found to be switched ON when there is no water in the machine, a pressure system fault is indicated and should be checked. Details of this process will be found in the *Water level control* chapter (pressure system section). If the heater is OFF when there is no water in the machine, the valve would appear to be suspect. The valve is easily changed by removing the fixing screws and detaching the internal hose/s from the valve. Making a note of the wiring and those connections that are on the valve, remove them and replace with a new valve assembly by simply reconnecting the hoses and wires in a reverse sequence.

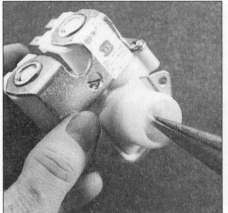

If the valve filter requires cleaning, carefully remove it as shown, ensuring that no debris slips past

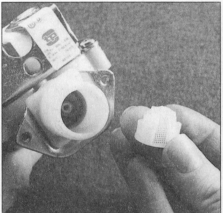

Once removed, the filter can be thoroughly cleaned and inspected for damage. Note: *This can be done with the valve in situ. It was removed in this instance for photographic purposes only.*

Anti-flood inlet hoses

Most automatic washing machines are supplied with standard hot and cold inlet hoses normally 1.5m in length with ¾ BSP threaded connections, to help with awkward plumbing situations 2.5m hoses are available. However, alternative flood protection hoses are to be found on some models. A description of the two most popular types is as follows.

Water block inlet hose pressure activated

The water block hose is a mechanical protection system primarily to reduce the chance of flooding should a fill hose split or leak. The water block hose consists of several layers making a hose within a hose configuration. Only the inner hose carries the water from the valve to the appliance. If the inner hose should perish or leak, the pressure will be trapped within the next layer and used to close a mechanical valve situated at the inlet end of the hose. Most hoses have a means of indicating that the safety valve has been activated, for obvious reasons, once tripped this device cannot be reset. If required, this type of hose can be used to replace ordinary fill hoses to increase the level of protection.

Note: *On most machines this type of hose can be fitted in place of a standard inlet hose.*

Water block inlet hose electrical/mechanical

This system consists of a special one-piece inlet hose and inlet valve combination often referred to as an 'Aquastop' hose. It can be activated in two ways, either electrically or mechanically via pressure (similar to the water block hose). On some versions safety is further improved by the use of a water inlet valve with a two-solenoid configuration i.e. two valves in series. The valve(s) and solenoid(s) are housed in a large protective container at the water entry point of the fill hose with the valve screwing directly on to the isolation tap connection. The power supply for the water valve solenoid(s) and the hose from the valve outlet to the appliance run through a bulky corrugated plastic cover. The reason for this configuration is to alleviate the constant pressure carried by conventional flexible inlet hoses where the inlet valve is situated at the machine end. The fill hose consists of several layers with the inner hose carrying the water from the inlet valve to the appliance. Should the inner hose leak, the pressure will be contained within the next layer and used to close a mechanical inlet valve. For obvious reasons once tripped this device cannot be reset.

Note: *In essence the 'Aquastop' system alleviates the potential for leakage problems that may not be covered by the appliance's internal overfill protection system. However, the hose is bulky and the large end connection can be difficult to connect unless the correct plumbing requirements are in place. Additionally, simple valve failure will result in a complete new 'AquaStop' hose being fitted which can be expensive. These points should be weighed against the incidence/failure rate of conventional inlet hoses, which are often and unwisely left under pressure (ideally the isolation tap(s) should be turned OFF after each wash cycle).*

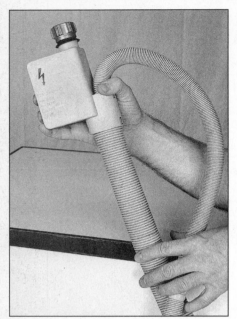

Typical water block (Aquastop) inlet hose

This particular version of Aqua-stop hose is a full-sealed system with no access to the water inlet valve housed within the white plastic block

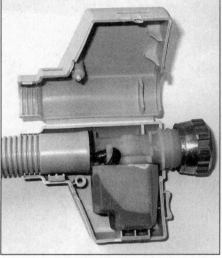

The internal view of a Siemens Aqua-stop hose showing the sealed inlet valve within the clipped together unit
Note: *This internal view is shown for information purposes only as faults with this type of system will require a complete new hose assembly.*

The base of this washing machine houses a float-operated flood protection system. When a leak occurs the water collects at the base of the appliance and lifts the polystyrene float which in turn operates a switch mounted above it. This will shut of the water inlet valves(s) and power the drain pump to evacuate the remaining water from the tub
Note: *When carrying out any servicing or repair, prevent accidental operation of the flood protection system by ensuring that any spillage of water within the appliance is thoroughly mopped up.*

Models with flood protection systems usually clearly indicate they have this useful feature

A water inlet valve combined with a flow sensing system, details of which appear in the following chapter, Water level control

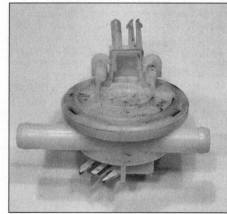

An independent flow-sensing system, details of which appear in the following chapter, Water level control

Chapter 18
Water level control

Modern front-loading automatic washing machines have several fill levels each of which corresponds to the type of wash cycle selected, e.g. high-level fill for delicate programmes and lower level for the more robust wash programmes. There may also be the facility for an intermediate level option if a half load selection is available to the programme. Some machines such as the Jets System models use small volumes of water for the wash cycle which is constantly sprayed over the clothes during the wash cycle by means of an additional pump. Depending on the make and model the circulation pump may be fitted to a reservoir situated beneath the outer tub or in line with heater and sump hose. To dilute the detergent during rinsing, normal levels of water are used. Irrespective of which type of machine you have, the way in which the amount of water taken in during a wash programme will ultimately be governed by either a 'Pressure system' or a 'Flow control system', and on some makes and models you may find a combination of both.

What is a pressure system?

The pressure system governs the level of water in the machine.

Where is it located?
The pressure switch has no standard fixture location, but is usually to be found at the top of the machine. It can be identified as the large circular switch that has several wires and a plastic tube attached to it leading to a pressure vessel. Several variations of pressure vessel are available. It may be an integral part of the plastic filter housing located behind the front face of the machine's shell, alternatively it may be an independent unit located to the rear of the machine near the tub. There are also pressure hoses that function in the same way as the rigid pressure vessel. These hoses will either be grommet fitted to the lower part of the outer tub, or directly moulded to the sump hose. Machines that have moulded plastic outer tubs normally have provision for a rigid pressure vessel to be mounted on the lower section. Although the position and style of the switch and pressure vessels vary, the basic way in which they operate does not.

How does it work?
The pressure switch does not actually come into contact with water, but uses air pressure

A typical pressure switch

trapped within the pressure vessel or pressure hose. When water enters the tub and the level rises, it traps a given amount of air in the pressure vessel. As the water in the tub rises, this increases the pressure of the trapped air within the pressure vessel. This pressure is then transferred to a pressure sensitive switch via a small-bore flexible tube.

The pressure switch is a large circular device that houses a thin rubber diaphragm, which is expanded by the corresponding pressure exerted on it. The diaphragm rests alongside a bank of up to three switches, each of which is set to operate at a different level of pressure. The switch is totally isolated from the water ensuring maximum safety.

This large plastic moulding houses the filter, heater, thermostats and pressure vessel. It also has connections for the outlet pump and a second pump for circulating water during the wash and rinse cycles. It is located beneath the tub unit and is a part of a 'Jet Wash System'. Check this type of system for scaling and blockages, especially in hard water areas. Several manufacturers now use water circulation systems similar to this one.

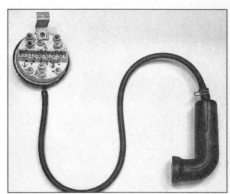
A typical pressure system

Possible faults in the pressure system

To create the highest pressure in the chamber of the pressure vessel, the vessel must be positioned as low as possible in the machine. Unfortunately, any sediment that forms in the machine collects at this point and can therefore easily block the entrance. Similarly, because of its very small internal diameter, the pressure tube can also block. The pressure that this device creates is very small, and can easily be blocked by a very small obstruction, such as a lump of detergent or sediment deposits or the growth of algae.

The seals and hoses of the system are also of great importance. These should be checked for air leaks and blockages. Any puncture or blockage would create a loss of pressure, resulting in the incorrect operation of the switches, i.e., if the air pressure in the pressure vessel were to leak out, the vessel would fill with water, indicating that the machine was in fact empty. The water valves would then be re-energised, thus trying to fill an already full machine, the results would be obvious.

The above example assumed that the air was prevented from actuating the pressure switch. If a blockage occurred whilst the switch was pressurised, the machine would work as normal until the machine emptied. The next time a programme was started the pressure switch would already be pressurised. Therefore the machine would not take any water, but proceed to turn the heater on. Although most heaters are now fitted with a TOC (Thermal Overload Cut-out – see *Jargon*), this may not act until some damage has been done to the clothes inside the drum or worse.

Points to note

a) The pressure system should be checked at yearly or half-yearly intervals, depending on the water hardness in your area.

b) Any hoses or tubes that have been disturbed must be resealed and any clips tightened.

c) Blowing down the accessible end of the pressure tube may seem an easy solution to remove a blockage, but this may only be a temporary cure. Also, water may enter the pressure vessel before you can push the end of the tube back onto the pressure switch. This will render the pressure system inaccurate, if not useless.

d) The use of a quality low lather detergent specifically formulated for use in automatic machines is essential. Failure to use the correct detergent will result in foam entering the pressure system and rendering it, at best, inaccurate.

A pressure switch should only be suspected when the system has been thoroughly cleaned, checked, sealed and retested.

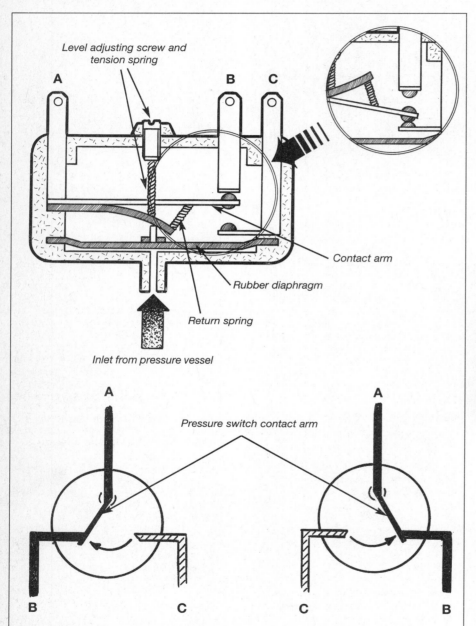

These diagrams illustrate the theoretical operation of a single level pressure switch: A being the live supply. Point B is the empty position of the pressure switch, and in this position power supplied to A via the programme timer would be allowed to flow to the fill valve via B. When the preset level of water is reached, the diaphragm of the pressure switch pushes the contact arm across to contact C. Power to the fill valve is therefore stopped and transferred to connection C which in turn could supply the main motor and heater

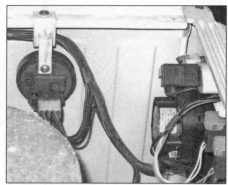

Photograph showing the position of the pressure switch in a typical automatic. The positions may vary with makes, but all will be found as high in the machine as possible

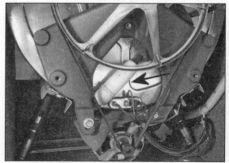

A rear-mounted pressure vessel

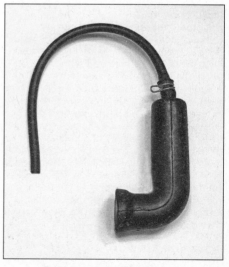

Rubber pressure tubing etc

A combined pressure vessel and sump hose

This Whirlpool model has the pressure switch mounted at the front of the appliance

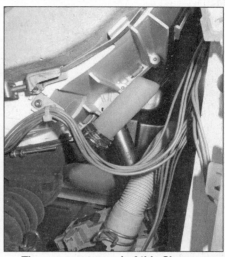

The pressure vessel of this Siemens machine (centre of picture) is connected to a branch of the large sump hose and is secured to the side of the plastic outer tub. Access is via the removable front panel and facia on this model range

Checking a mechanical pressure switch

Blowing into the switch via the pressure tube, the audible 'clicks' of the switches should be heard. This should also happen when the pressure is released. If your machine uses a single level of water, one click will be heard. Two levels of water will produce two clicks. If your machine has an economy button, a third faint click will also be heard. **Note:** *Do not blow too hard as this may damage the switch. Remember, the pressure they operate on is very low.*

Many machines have an overfill level detection system which will activate the outlet pump should any excess water enter the machine for any reason. Several systems use the third or fourth switch of the existing pressure switch bank, operated only by the increased pressure caused by the overfill.

Unfortunately, systems that use the same pressure vessel for both normal and abnormal water level detection may fail to detect overfilling if it is caused by a blocked pressure vessel or hose fault that allows the pressure to escape.

Systems using a separate pressure vessel and a separate pressure switch for detecting overfilling are much less prone to failure of this nature. Nevertheless, they still require cleaning and checking frequently.

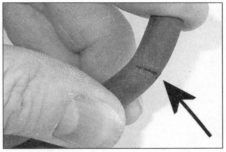

Checking the pressure tube for chafing and small porous cracks. Renew if suspect

Any loose connections on the pressure system will allow the pressure to drop. This will cause overfilling. Ensure a good seal

An internal view of a pressure switch, showing the diaphragm and switches. This pressure switch was faulty due to a small hole appearing in the internal diaphragm. Operation would appear correct, although the pressure would decrease during the wash, and the machine would overfill. If the first functional test was rushed, this type of fault could be overlooked. The switch in the picture was stripped down to confirm the fault only. These switches require replacement when faulty, as they cannot be repaired

Pressure switches may also have the electrical connections in an 'in-line' configuration as in this example. The operation of the switching action remains the same but allows for block rather than single wire connections

Main faults within a mechanical pressure switch

a) When the diaphragm becomes 'holed' or porous, the switch can be operated and clicks heard, but will click back again without being depressurised.

b) The contact points inside the switch may 'weld' themselves together. This will alter the number of clicks heard, as one or more may be inoperative. Movement of the switch can free the points, although this will not be a lasting repair, as the switch will fail again.

Economy Switch
(½ Load Button)

Triple Level Switch

A

B   C   E D

The figure above illustrates the way a 3 level switch is used in conjunction with an economy switch, to give an alternative level as an economy feature

Any of the above faults require the fitting of a new switch. The make, model and serial number of the machine should be stated when ordering, as pressure switches are internally pre-set for specific machines, although the external appearance is similar. Fitting is a simple direct exchange between the old and new.

The diagram illustrates the operation of a double level pressure switch. Fig. 1 shows the machine filling with water. If B and E are taken as hot and cold valves respectively, it can be seen that the machine is filling with both of

the valves. In Fig. 2 the lowest level of water is reached. The pressure breaks the connection with the hot valve (B), and remakes it with the heater switch (C). The cold valve (E) continues filling. Fig. 3 shows the highest level, with the cold fill stopping, switching in the motor (D).

A similar procedure should be followed for all types of pressure vessel and care should be taken to reseal all hose connections that are removed. Remember to wash clear all loose particles, etc., as even the smallest of blockages in this system will cause trouble.

Electronic pressure switches

An alternative to the mechanical pressure switch which has internally operated switches is the electronic pressure switch. The name is somewhat misleading as the item does not contain any switches and really should be referred to as an analogue pressure detector.

How do they work?

Electronic pressure detectors use the same types of pressure vessels, chambers, hoses etc. as the mechanical pressure switches described previously and as such are affected by the same problems of blockages, air leaks etc. However, they operate in a totally different way, having only three connection wires but are capable of accurately detecting even small changes in the pressure within the sealed pressure system. These features result in a wider range of water level control (more levels available) while at the same time being extremely accurate. Unlike the mechanical pressure switch, an electronic pressure detector cannot operate on its own as the signal it produces in relation to the pressure it is detecting needs to be fed to an electronic circuit. It is the electronic circuit (often part of the programme control PCB) that carries out the control (switching) functions.

Although smaller in appearance, the construction, shape and outward appearance of an electronic pressure detector is very similar to the mechanical pressure switch, but

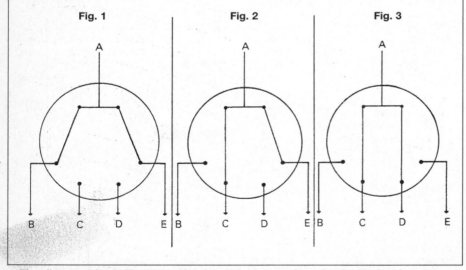

The diagram above illustrates the theoretical operation of a double level pressure switch. Fig. 1 shows the machine filling with water. If B and E are taken as hot and cold valves respectively, it can be seen that the machine is filling with both hot and cold water. In Fig. 2 the lowest level of water is reached. The pressure breaks the connection with the hot valve (B), and remakes it with the heater switch (C). The cold valve (E) continues filling. Fig. 3 shows the highest level, with the cold fill stopping, switching in the motor (D)

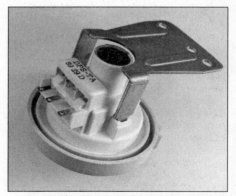

Electronic (Analogue) level detector

internally they are very different. As with the mechanical pressure switch, air pressure in the sealed system distends a rubber diaphragm within the detector and the distension of the diaphragm is proportional to the pressure being applied to it.

The diaphragm is connected to a ferrite core which is free to move within a coil of wire that surrounds it. In addition to the coil and ferrite core there is small circuit board within the unit called an oscillator that feeds the wire coil with a set frequency. The position of the ferrite core within the coil directly affects the frequency due to a phenomenon called inductance and it is this change in frequency that is detected and used by the main circuit board (PCB) as the control signal for the programme routine.

The unit requires three wires – two being used to provide the low-voltage power supply for the small internal PCB and the third is for transferring the frequency information to the main control PCB.

Note: *Electronic level detectors are operated by low voltages of 5 volts or less and may be damaged by test meters that use a higher voltage during testing. Little can be gained from using a test meter on this type of item and may even result in damaging the unit by inadvertently applying too high a voltage during testing.*

As this type of level detector is generally only found on electronically controlled machines, fault identification is best left to reading the error code that the machine will display when a fault occurs. For further information on fault codes see Chapter 26 and prior to suspecting the electronic detector or main control PCB ensure you have thoroughly inspected and cleaned the whole of the pressure system.

Flow sensing water level control

Flow sensing is the ability to measure the quantity of clean water entering the machine rather than reacting to the level of water collecting in the tub. In reality, machines that utilise flow sensing normally combine this primary level control with water level pressure detection as a back up.

The way in which flow sensing works is very similar to the way fuel is metered into your vehicle's fuel tank at a petrol station or a water meter measures the amount of water you use in your home.

However, the system employed in washing machines is essentially much smaller and more compact and can be an integral part of the water inlet valve or be an independent unit situated between the inlet valve and entry to the detergent dispenser/tub.

When the water inlet valve is energised (opened) to fill the machine to the required level, depending on the type of system employed, the water passes through or past a small turbine within the valve causing it to rotate. The number of rotations made during the fill period is proportional to the volume of water entering the machine. A small permanent magnet is embedded into the turbine and an externally mounted, normally open reed switch closes each time the permanent magnet passes by it.

The opening and closing of the reed switch in relation to the magnet's rotation create a series of pulses which are detected by a microprocessor housed on the main programme control PCB.

To fill to the required level for the selected programme the microprocessor simply counts the revolutions (pulses) from the switch. When the required number of revolutions for the selected programme has been attained the control circuit will switch off the inlet valve and continues with the programme sequence.

Metering the clean water intake in this way eliminates many of the problems associated with the pressure operated systems that simply measure the volume of (dirty) water within the outer tub unit.

However, even when measuring the clean water inlet into the appliance problems can still occur and most if not all flow control system will have pressure-operated back-up systems. The primary being:

1 No flow through the valve due to no water supply (tap not turned on), blocked inlet hose or inlet valve filter will prevent rotation of the turbine resulting in no pulses being generated. This will be detected by the microprocessor the programme will be cancelled and an error code or alarm will be displayed.
2 Low pressure or a partially blocked inlet filter may result in water entering the appliance, but not turning the turbine (a pressure of at least 0.2 bar is required for correct operation). This will be detected by the microprocessor, the programme will be cancelled and an error code or alarm will be displayed.
3 Jamming of the inlet valve in the open position will result in the processor continuing to receive pulses even when the required number have been attained and the valve electrically turned off by the control unit. In this instance, the microprocessor will cancel the programme and will power the drain pump to prevent a flood occurring. An error code and alarm will also be displayed.
4 Should the microprocessor develop a fault which results in leaving the inlet valve open i.e. fails to respond correctly to the above problems (2) or (3) the excess water entering the tub will be detected by the pressure-operated back-up level control system. This will normally result in cancellation of the programme and the pressure switch directly powering the drain pump to prevent a flood occurring. An error code and alarm will also be displayed.

An independent flow sensing system

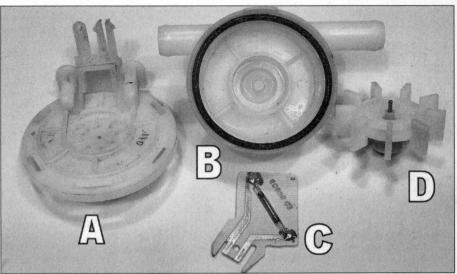

An internal component view of an independent flow sensing system
A – top cover; B – flow chamber; C – small PCB with reed switch; D – turbine

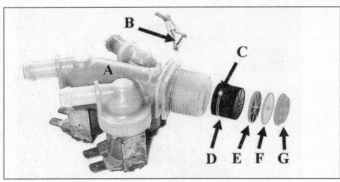

This diagram illustrates the action of the independent flow-sensor unit. When the water inlet valve is energised water enters the flow chamber on the left and exits on the right. As it passes through the chamber the turbine with a permanent magnet mounted in the base is turned by the water flow. The reed switch mounted externally beneath the flow chamber is activated by the magnet's rotation

Flow sensing water inlet valves are essentially normal inlet valves with the addition of the following components fitted within the valve's entry point
A *Valve unit which may be single, double or triple as in this instance;* **B** *Reed switch mounted within the valve's plastic fixing bracket (removed to show detail);* **C** *Small permanent magnet clipped to the inner turbine;* **D** *Turbine body (free to rotate within the inlet);* **E** *Turbine support;* **F** *Flow regulator (to maintain a flow rate of around 8 litres per minute to the turbine);* **G** *Inlet filter. Although small in size the components function the same as described for the larger version*

Pressure switch cleaning

This pressure vessel shows clear signs of sediment build-up

A single screw and 'O' ring hold the pressure vessel in place
Note: *Some models may have a plastic latch/catch in place of a screw fitting.*

With the fixing removed the pressure vessel can be eased free from the outer tub connection point

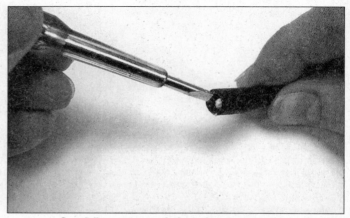

Carefully remove and clean the pressure tube

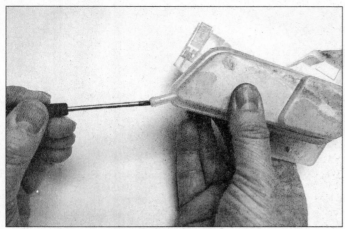

Ensure the pressure tube connection point is also free from sediment

The entry point of the pressure vessel was severely blocked

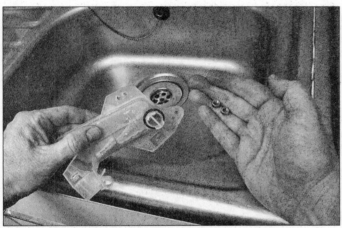

The interior was cleaned by filling the chamber with a little water and inserting two small nuts. The open ends were then sealed and the units shaken vigorously for a few seconds. Several cleaning sequences may be required, depending on the severity of the build-up within the unit

During the cleaning process the pressure vessel was flushed with clean water until all traces of sediment were removed

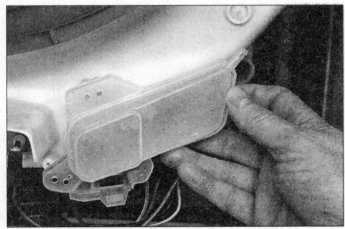

When thoroughly cleaned the 'O' ring was moistened to help it slide back into position

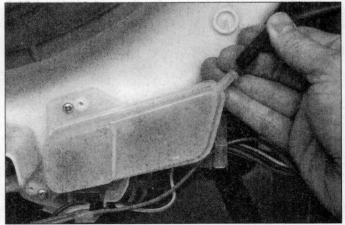

The pressure tube was then securely replaced
Note: *Although not required in this instance clips and sealant may be required on some makes and models.*

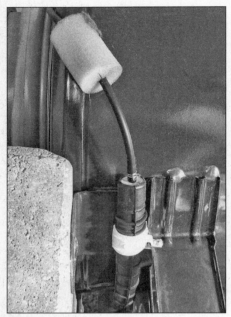

Pressure hose fitting on the underside of the outer tub. The grommet fitting to the tub can leak, so ensure that the good seal is maintained should the hose be removed for cleaning

This Zanussi range appliance has two pressure switches – the smaller of which works in series with the wash heater

A solid pressure vessel with two chambers

Opaque pressure vessels like this one will need to be removed for checking if they are becoming blocked
Note: *How often checking needs to be made depends on the hardness of water and the quality of detergent being used.*

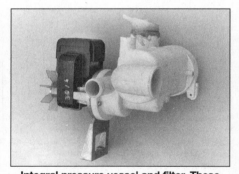

Integral pressure vessel and filter. These units are difficult to clean thoroughly so care is required. Also ensure a good seal on the pressure tube when refitting

This picture shows a pressure vessel which is much longer than usual. Most vessels are much smaller. This type can be found in early Candy machines (pressure vessel arrowed)

Typical small-pressure switches that are used on many makes and models. The left-hand pressure switch has block connections and the right-hand one has individual terminal connections

Typical double level switch is more common

Typical triple level pressure switch

Variable pressure switch as fitted to early Hotpoint top loader machines. The centre button changes the pressure required to operate the diaphragm. This is linked (mechanically) to the wash load select buttons on the control panel

Some pressure switches may have their tube connections on the rear plate. This is only a variation on the fixing type, and does not impair the operation of the switch

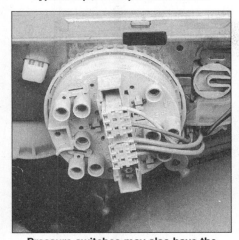

Pressure switches may also have the electrical connections in an 'in-line' configuration as in this example. The operation of the switching action remains the same but allows for block rather than single wire connections

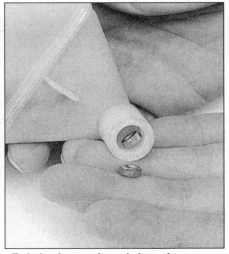

To help clean awkward shaped pressure vessels pop one or two small nuts into the inlet, add a little water, cover the inlet and shake the vessel

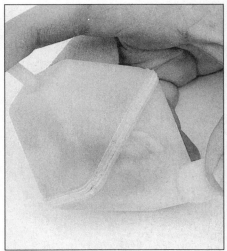

Rinse and repeat this process until the water runs clean. Ensure you use nuts that will fit easily into the vessel and ensure they are removed before refitting to the machine

68

Chapter 19
Pumps

Most washing machines have just one pump, which is used to drain the water from the machine when required. However, some makes and models may have a second pump to circulate the water and detergent mixture during the wash cycle. The most popular of these circulation systems is the Zanussi 'Jet System', although similar systems are used by other manufacturers. The function of a circulation system is essentially very simple. The following information relates mainly to drain pumps but is equally applicable to circulation pumps. Both types of pump can be found in shaded pole or permanent magnet versions. **Note:** *For details of the motors used to power the pump, see* Motors *chapter.*

Leaks

Leaks from the pump may not be apparent, but the resulting pool of water usually is. So here are a few points to look out for.

Firstly, check all clips on the hoses to and from the pump and tighten if they are loose.

Shaded pole pumps

If the leak remains and the pump uses a shaded pole drive motor the shaft seal should be checked. This is the seal that forms a watertight barrier on the rotating shaft of the motor directly between the impeller, and the front motor

bearing. The seal can be broken by a collection of fluff/lint forming between the seal and the impeller itself, thus distorting the rubber seal. To check if this is happening, remove the pump chamber, by removing its securing clips or screws, and whilst securing the rotor of the pump motor, turn the impeller clockwise to undo it from the shaft, i.e., impeller and rotor are usually left-hand threaded. Having done this, remove any objects adhering to the shaft and refit, ensuring the pump chamber seal is in position. If the seal still leaks this will be due to it being worn or softened. On most machines, this means the complete renewal of the pump. (Not so costly as you may think, as many genuine and proprietary pumps of good quality are now available at very low cost.)

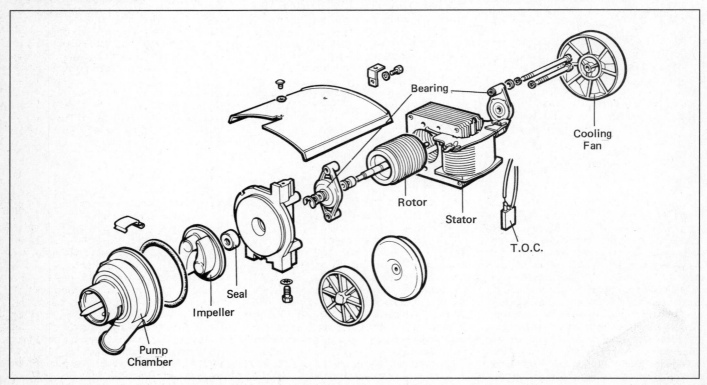

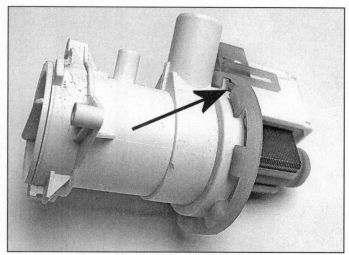

The front chamber of this drain pump is a simple twist fit, often referred to as a bayonet lock. This pump chamber is removed by pressing a plastic latching clip (arrowed) and twisting the two sections apart

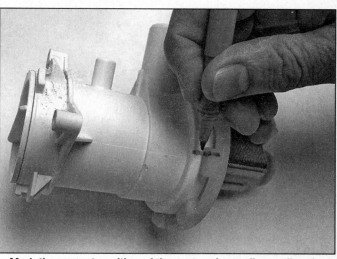

Mark the correct position of the parts prior to dismantling the pump

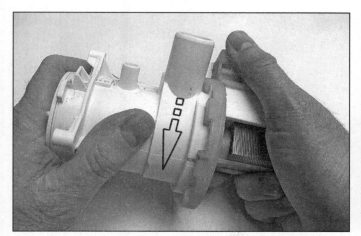

After depressing the latching clip remove the pump chamber by firmly holding the motor while at the same time depressing or lifting the small plastic locking tag and twisting the chamber to remove it

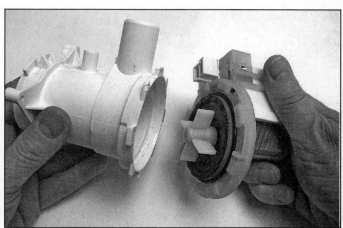

A large 'O' ring creates the water-tight seal between the pump body and filter housing. To prevent the 'O' ring from moving out of position during refitting, wet it with water (DO NOT use any other lubricant) to help slide it into the correct position as the two parts are twisted back into position

This may seem drastic for such a small seal, but the fact is that water, containing detergent would have been entering the front pump bearing long before the leak was bad enough to see. This means it will probably be damaged itself and next in line to cause trouble.

Other leaks can be attributable to the pump, due for example to impeller damage, that is to say blades of impeller broken off or badly worn away by a solid object lodged in the pump at sometime e.g. small coin or tight bearings causing slow running of motor.

Both of the above will result in poor water discharge i.e. slow draining. This in turn may cause the machine to spin whilst some water still remains, thus causing other hoses, etc., on the machine to leak or the machine to fill to too high a level, as some machines have a timed rinse fill action. On other machines, slow drainage may mean that the machine fails to spin at all. This is due to the pressure switch detecting the presence of water in the machine, (that the slow pump failed to discharge in its allotted time), therefore not allowing a spin to take place and either missing out the spin completely or stopping the wash cycle at the spin positions.

Checking the impeller and bearings can be done at the same time as checking the seal.

Permanent magnet pumps

The construction of the permanent magnet drive motor helps alleviate the problem of shaft seal leaks and bearing failure which are common to shaded pole versions. However, water ingress into the sealed rotor chamber can cause the rotor to pop out of its chamber. This occurs when the water that has entered the sealed rotor chamber heats up and expands forcing the rotor out of position. This fault is often accompanied by a chattering noise when the pump is energised and tries to run. The pump may work but inefficiently.

The large entry point of this outer tub-to-drain pump hose houses an 'eco-ball' valve. To avoid problems, ensure it is free to move within the recess and remove any grease, accumulation of detergent or sediment prior to refitting

A combined permanent magnet drain pump and filter unit

A smaller combined permanent magnet drain pump unit

Eco-ball valves

A feature of many modern machines is the inclusion of a large valve within the hose that connects the outer tub to the pump or filter housing. The popular name for this type of system is an eco-ball valve. The function of the device is simple yet effective and when working correctly dramatically reduces detergent loss, which gives rise to its name.

The correct operation relies on the drain hose being installed and fixed properly. Water remaining within the drain hose when the drain pump is turned off after the emptying phase will lift the eco ball against the outer tub exit point. This means that when the machine fills for the next wash cycle all the water and detergent go straight into the tub. On earlier machines (non-eco models) it is possible to wash up to 70% of the detergent straight into an empty filter, pump chamber sump hose and drain hose, resulting in a great deal of wastage. The eco-ball system also ensures that only the water in the tub unit is heated and not the water resting in the sump hose, filter, pump chamber and drain hose, which effectively reduces the amount of electricity required for the wash cycle. To avoid problems and to maintain the efficiency of the system ensure that the appliance is installed correctly (as per manufacturer's instructions) and that the ball is free to move within the recess. Remove any accumulation of grease, detergent or sediment on a regular basis.

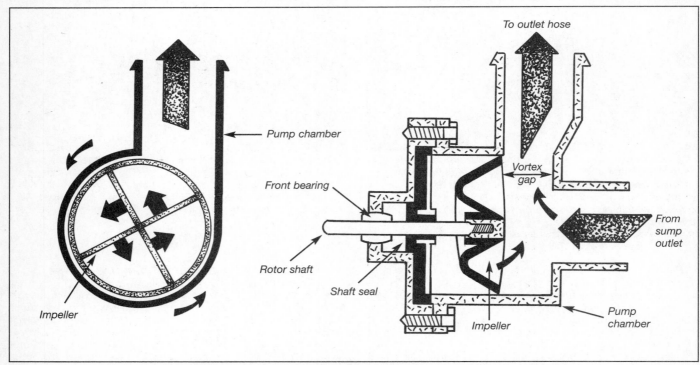

Vortex style pump. Dynamic force exerted on the water in the direction of output.
Above is a simple illustration of the outlet pump chamber and impeller. Water from the sump enters from the front. The rotation of the impeller lifts the water in the direction of the narrower outlet hose.
There are two types of impeller; one is simply a paddle type and more prone to blockages; the second is like the one illustrated and called a vortex pump. This type of impeller is more of a flat etched disc that allows a gap between itself and the pump chamber. This gap lets particles pass through easier than the bladed impeller version. The vortex impeller applies lift to the water as shown in the smaller version, the action is similar to the rotating vortex created when a bath empties

Water retained in the sump and drain hose system from the previous wash cycle lifts (floats) the ball to block the entry point. When the appliance fills for the new wash this simple action effectively prevents the detergent from being washed into the sump hose

Note: *For this type of system to work effectively the appliance must be plumbed with the drain hose positioned at a height no lower than 600mm (2ft). If lower, there will not be enough back pressure to hold the ball in the correct position.*

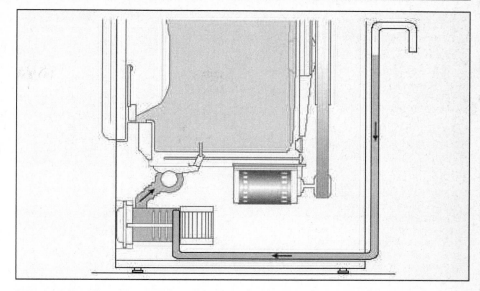

When the tub is filled to its working level the ball will still be held in the closed position by the weight of water in the sump and drain hose system – thus retaining the detergent

Note: *The drain hose must be above 600mm (2ft) somewhere along its length for this to occur.*

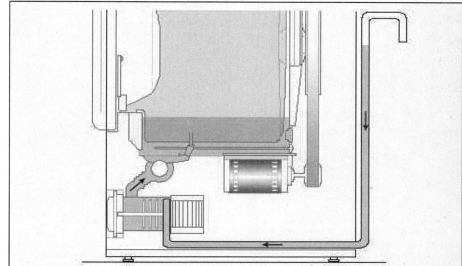

When the pump operates during the emptying phases a pressure differential is created between the water in the tub and drain system that pushes the ball into the sump hose recess allowing water to flow out of the appliance

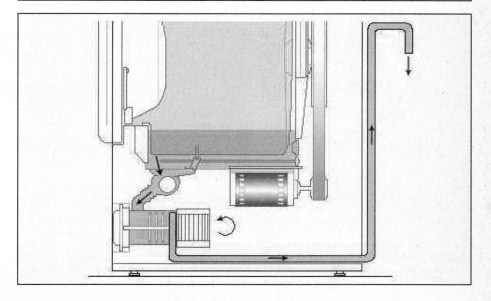

Typical pump replacement

Note: *As with all service work or repair to your machine ensure that it is fully isolated before commencing (switched off, remove plug from the supply socket and taps turned off).*

The make, type and shape of pump will differ between manufacturers and individual models in their range. However, the location of the drain (and a Jet System recirculation pump if fitted) will always be at the lowest point within the appliance.

The way in which they are secured in place also differs with three main variations possible:
1 *Simple self-tapping screw or bolt*
2 *Twist fit to larger filter housing*
3 *Plastic latch and 'O' ring*

Make a note of all connections and position of the pump prior to removing the wiring and hose connections. The first two types of fitting are relatively simple to remove and replace and it was felt that a photographic sequence would not be required.

However, with the third method of fixing the pump is held in place by plastic latches and an 'O' ring and requires a little explanation of how best to remove it.

In the sequence below the pump was failing to operate correctly and needed to be removed to check the chamber for blockages, problems with the impeller or the PM motor.

This style of pump fixing is very common throughout the Zanussi range of appliances and other brands that are part of the same group of companies. This includes the Italian made versions with such brand names as AEG, Electrolux, Bendix, Tricity Bendix and many more. It can be seen in the photographs that similar plastic catches are used to secure other components to the plastic base of the appliance.

In this instance the pump was found to have a worn shaft seal that had allowed water to penetrate the sealed chamber of the permanent magnet motor. A complete new pump unit was required as no individual parts are available. The new pump was refitted by lining it up with the plastic moulding and sliding it forwards until the plastic catches click into their locking positions.

Note: *In most modern machines, the pump has to be changed as a complete unit for even the smallest of problems. This is no excuse for turning a blind eye to leak faults. Such behaviour is false economy.*

This pump is held in place by plastic retaining clips and an 'O' ring and is a very popular configuration. To remove it you need to press in both of these retaining clips

While pressing the two retaining clips together with one hand (or grips) insert a flat-bladed screwdriver between the pump chamber and connection point to create leverage between the two components

When the clips are released correctly the pump unit will then slide out of position
Note: *When refitting or renewing the pump ensure that the 'O' ring is placed on the pump body (male section) and a little water applied to help it slide back into position without distorting the 'O' ring seal. Do not use detergent or similar lubricant as this may lead to poor sealing between the two components.*

Chapter 20
Door switches (interlocks)

General safety

Although failure of an interlock or door latching system, which allows the door of the machine to be opened mid-cycle, is thankfully not too common, such failures can, and do, occur. It is strongly recommended that the correct locking action of the door mechanism and interlock are carefully checked on a regular basis throughout the life of the product. In addition, young children should be discouraged from playing with or near working machines. Impatient adults should not attempt to open the door of their machine until the interlock mechanism has had time to correctly de-latch. Unless this is in the course of carefully testing the integrity of the latch and interlock under a controlled situation, i.e. exercising great care and not in the presence of children.

What is an interlock?

The name interlock is given to an electrical switch/mechanism behind or near the main door latching device of a washing machine door and is designed to give a time delay of up to two minutes, before the door can be opened. The delay time differs between the makes and models of different machines.

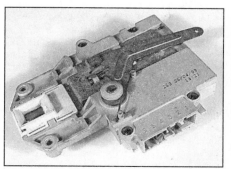
This interlock has an arm linked to a push button on the front facia which, when pressed, releases the door latch

What are the different types?

A machine with a push/pull timer knob action, may also have a manual interlock thus giving double protection. The manual interlock system is quite straightforward, bolting or unbolting the door with the push/pull action of the timer knob, via a latching mechanism. The mechanical interlock acts in much the same way as the electrical version in preventing entry via the door if the machine is turned on except that there is no time delay. Such mechanical interlocks are always in addition to electrical interlocks which incorporate a delay to entry.

An internal illustration of the heater and switch arrangement

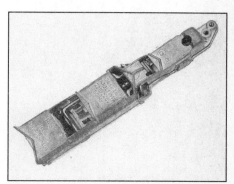
This large metal bodied interlock houses a solenoid operated door interlock and switch

A popular block connector interlock

A block connector interlock popular with Ariston and Indesit

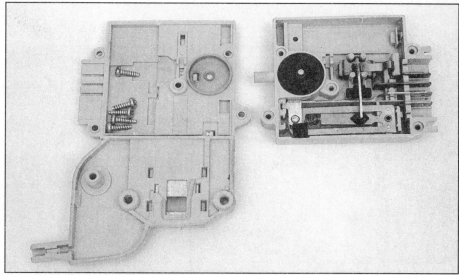
This large rectangular bi-metallic interlock (shown disassembled) also has a small pressure activating locking system

A more recent version of interlock also incorporates a pressure switch type of system, that will not allow the door to open if there is any water remaining in the machine. This again is a mechanical operation and will work even when the machine is unplugged. The door can only be opened when the water has been drained out. This must be remembered in the case of a pump failure or blockage. The system is easily recognisable by the pressure tube leading to the door interlock. Such systems may use a separate pressure vessel or a 'T' junction arrangement from the water level pressure switch tube. Whichever system is used, faults similar to those described in the *Water level control* chapter will be encountered e.g., blockages, air leaks, etc.

Shown is only a small selection of interlocks

to highlight the many variations that can be encountered. Interlocks cannot only change between machine manufacturers but the models themselves may have different variants, i.e., machines with identical external appearance may have different variants of the interlock fitted.

The outer design and fitting of the interlock may change, but the function and operation differs very little between variants.

One type of interlock may be common to more than one manufacturer. It is therefore essential to obtain the correct model and serial numbers of both the machine and interlock when locating a spare part.

Mechanical pecker locks

As the name implies this is a mechanical interlock although it can be found combined with any of the other electrical versions detailed in this chapter. The essence of this type of system is to physically detect movement in one of three key areas: the drum, belt or motor shaft. Only when movement in the area being checked has ceased can the door be opened. The area checked for movement will differ between makes and models, however the principle of operation is similar whichever area is used. A device called a pecker unit is used to detect movement of the belt, motor or drum. The pecker unit is linked to the door interlock mechanism by a bowden cable (similar to a bicycle brake cable). The pecker unit consists of a spring-loaded arm and 'the pecker' mounted on a larger pivot arm. The principle of operation is as follows. The pivot arm and pecker are positioned close to, but not touching, the item to be checked for movement (belt drum or motor shaft). When

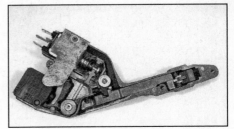
The interlock shown uses a solenoid operated locking mechanism

the user attempts to open the door the bowden cable is tensioned. This transfers movement to the pecker unit and pushes the peck into contact with the motor shaft, belt or drum pulley. If the area being checked (pecked) is moving (in either direction) the pecker will be deflected and the unit will absorb the slack in the bowden cable. However, if the check area is stationary the pecker is pushed directly onto the check area and no deflection occurs. When no deflection occurs the bowden cable remains taut and allows the interlock mechanism to unlatch the door. Correct alignment and adjustment are crucial to the correct operation of the system. Cable adjustment can be made but settings and tolerances differ between manufacturers and models. The main problem areas are: wear often caused by impatient users trying to open the door of the machine while it is still in motion after the spin, damage to the pecker unit often caused by out of balance spinning and incorrect adjustment/position of components.

Coil operated interlocks

This type of interlock uses a solenoid coil to lock the latching mechanism. When energised the solenoid coil magnetically attracts a soft iron core to its centre (similar to the action of a water valve) to lock the latching mechanism. In addition to locking the mechanism the movement of the core slowly expels air from a small chamber. When de-energised the return of the soft iron core to its rest position is damped (slowed down) as air slowly re-enters the air chamber through a very small hole. The damping action of the air chamber creates both a smooth locking action and the required delay at the end of the cycle. The interlock also houses a mechanical switch, which is actuated by the door latch pecker. This type of interlock may be combined with other systems. Due to its simplicity this type of interlock is fairly reliable. However, one common problem is that of excessive noise. This normally takes the form of a buzzing noise, which is magnified by the metal shell of the appliance. Pressing the door or holding the door handle (if fitted) often reduces the noise level. The noise originates in the interlock and is magnified by the shell of the appliance in a similar way an alarm clock

A mechanical pecker system mounted on the main wash motor

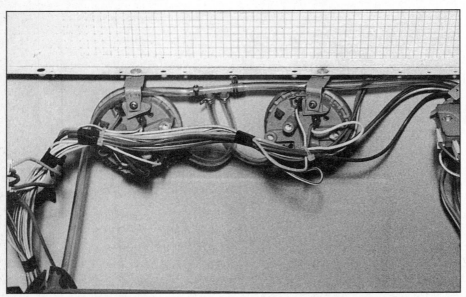
Shown is a machine with twin pressure switches and a pressure operated door interlock. The 'T' junction can be seen between the two circular pressure switches. The tube to the top right-hand side leads down to the door interlock (not shown)

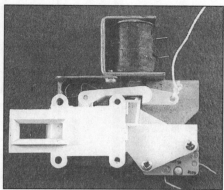

An early electro-mechanical interlock. The cord which can be found on many such interlocks is to allow manual operation should there be an electrical supply failure or fault within the appliance

An early Siemens interlock

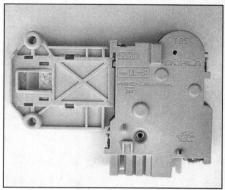

An instantaneous door-type interlock as used by Zanussi and other branded models from the Electrolux group

can be made louder if placed on an empty metal tin. The noise is caused by excessive lateral movement of the soft iron core, which oscillates in the alternating magnetic field produced by the coil. The noise does not affect the operation of the interlock but can be very annoying to those in the vicinity of the machine. To remedy the problem a new interlock will be required, unfortunately even new interlocks have been known to exhibit this problem. **Note:** *There are two reasons why the noise can be alleviated by pressing on the door or holding the door catch/handle. Simply pressing on the door or shell of the appliance damps the vibrations of the metal shell. Holding the door handle or catch partially operates the latch slide within the interlock; the slide is pushed onto the core, which in turn prevents it from vibrating.*

Computer-controlled interlocks

Computer controlled machines (as opposed to mechanically controlled) may have similar electro-mechanical interlocks to those described in the previous paragraphs. Alternatively, depending on make and model, they could be completely different both in the way the door is opened and the way that access is restricted via the door until the programme has finished and the machine is completely empty of water. A breakdown of basic operation is as follows though it does not typify any specific make as manufacturers will incorporate subtle differences to create individuality of product.

Door opening is by means of a push button action that actuates a simple electrical switch which then makes contact and supplies power to a solenoid-operated catch mounted within the machine in place of the door interlock. With power supplied to the solenoid in this way the door latch is released and the door opens. To avoid continuous supply to the solenoid, a microswitch is incorporated within the unit to open circuit the solenoid coil as soon as the door latch pecker is released. The opening operation of the door depends on:

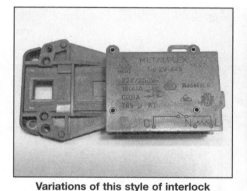

Variations of this style of interlock produced by Metalflex can be found in a wide range of makes and models
Note: *This face of this particular interlock has the internal wiring configuration embossed upon it. Apart from the terminal lettering the diagram (and function) is identical to that shown in diagrams A and B on the following page.*

1 Power being supplied to the machine and the machine being turned on.
2 No programme is currently operating.
3 No motor action or drum rotation is taking place.
4 Any water in the machine is below the lowest detectable level of the pressure switch, i.e. all switches in rest position. See *Water level control* chapter.
5 Door open button is released.

The requirements of steps 2–5 are monitored continuously by the microprocessor within the electronically controlled timer. With condition 1, a power supply is necessary for the door solenoid to operate. However, in power failure or fault situations many machines have means of de-latching the door mechanism manually; *reference should be made to the appliance handbook for further information.* Before carrying out mechanical actuation of the latch, ensure the machine is unplugged (isolated) and that the water level is below the door level, see *Emergency procedures* chapter.

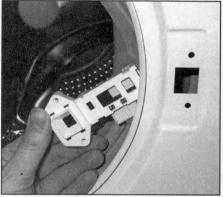

A Siemens door interlock being accessed via the door seal

Several machines use an LED (light emitting diode) or display to indicate when door opening can be activated.

The use of a microprocessor within such machines allows for greater interaction and sensing to be carried out. Due to the larger memory size of the chips used, more variable programming is possible. The way in which the programme is written enables it to react to variations within the circuit of the machine which in turn gives rise to a greater number of criteria being monitored to ensure compliance with safety, etc. The microprocessor board also includes a clock chip which can help in controlling programme times accurately. The timing function can also be used to time a delay to the door open switch if required by the manufacturer of the machine.

How does a basic electrical interlock work?

Because manufacturers prefer to have their own version of interlock, it is impossible to illustrate all of the different types. Because of this, the Klixon (3DB) type of switch is used to illustrate the internal workings and theory.

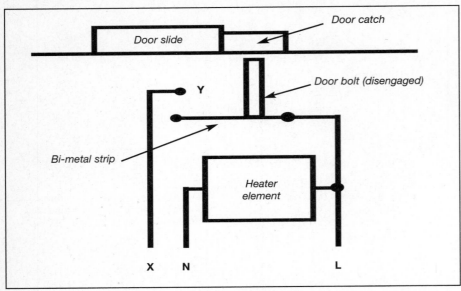

Diagram A

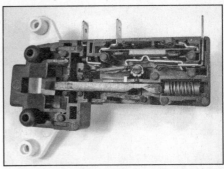

In this internal view of a door interlock the small resistive heater (light rectangle) can be seen attached directly to the bi-metallic strip, which operates the switch and plastic latch mechanism

Note: *The cover of this item was removed for photographic purposes only. Door interlocks are a non-serviceable safety component and when a fault is found or suspected they should be renewed.*

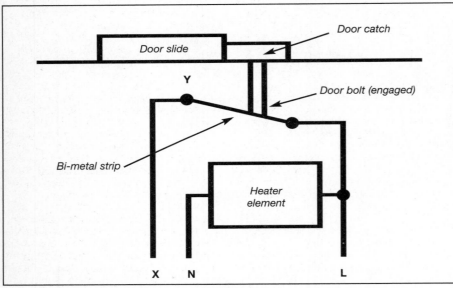

Diagram B

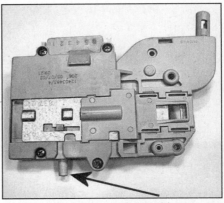

This door interlock along with many others not only has electrical connections (top), but also has a tube connection point (arrowed). The tube comes from a pressure vessel and operates an internal pressure locking device in addition to the electrical locking system. The pressure lock prevents the door from being opened if a detectable level of water remains within the machine

A popular interlock manufactured by Rold – a variation of which can be found on a wide range of makes and models

Diagram A shows the state of the interlock before power at L. It can be seen that the door bolt is disengaged and the bi-metal strip is in its 'rest' position. Because of this, there is no connection at point Y, therefore no power is transmitted to X.

Diagram B shows the state of the interlock when power is applied to point L. The heater is activated, therefore heating the bi-metal strip. This then bends, engaging the door bolt and making the connection at Y, allowing power to flow to X. When the power is disconnected, the heater is allowed to cool and the bi-metal strip then bends back to its rest position. This action can take up to two minutes, thus creating the delay. The delay time (cooling of heater and bi-metal) will vary according to the ambient temperature, style of interlock and position of the appliance. Some makes and variations of interlocks use a small oil-filled piston arrangement in place of the bi-metal strip. When heated, the oil expands and the resulting piston movement is used to actuate the interlock. As with the bi-metal system described, cooling allows the piston to retract and de-latch the interlock.

Note: *The heater referred to in this part of the manual is not the large heater in the drum, but is of minute proportions and is only used to heat the bi-metal strip.*

Modern machines tend to link the interlock to all of the other functions of the machines, so if the interlock should fail, power to the rest of the machine would be severed and the machine would then be totally inoperable. With older machines, interlock failure would only result in no motor action throughout a normal programme.

A two tag interlock (1DB) is called a straight through interlock as, although locking occurs switching does not. (Many early Candy machines use a smaller version of this type of interlock mounted on the switch panel directly behind the door opening button. When the interlock is actuated operation of the door opening button is prevented.)

Note: *The delay time is needed for the continued spinning of the drum after the motor has turned off, and is now a legal requirement. For this reason they must not be bypassed, as the results to small children or impatient adults will be disastrous.*

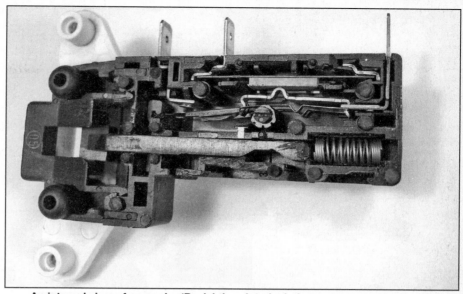

An internal view of a popular 'Basic' door interlock that operates as detailed in diagrams A and B. Although the principle of operation and construction is relatively simple, some manufacturers of appliances charge a disproportionately high price for such door interlocks

Instantaneous door interlocks

This type of door interlock derives its name from the fact that as soon as the major components within the appliance have stopped the user can open the door immediately (i.e. no time delay).

How does it work?

This type of door interlock is a combination of two electromechanical systems operating in one unit. One is operated by a bi-metallic strip and the other by a cam which is moved one step at a time by an electromagnet.

In a similar manner to the interlock described earlier, turning the appliance on supplies power to the small bi-metallic heater, however, latching of the door will not occur until the programme start button is pressed. Pressing the start programme button results in the main programme electronic board sending a 'pulse' (for only a few milliseconds) to the electromagnet. The pulse moves the cam within the interlock into one position which allows the door to be locked, and the

internal switch to close and supply power to the various components.

When the end of the programme is reached and a range of set parameters is met, the programme electronics send two further pulses in quick succession to the electro-magnet. The first pulse and movement of the cam does not release the latch or internal switch but the second pulse and cam movement both unlatches the door slide and opens the internal switch of the interlock.

Before sending the two pulses the main programme electronics check for the following parameters:

1 That the drum is stationary. This is done by ensuring that the motor tacho coil is not sending out any signals (i.e. the motor is not rotating) – see *Motors* chapter.

2 That if water still remains in the machine (for whatever reason) the level is beneath the bottom of the door. This is done by checking the level switch (usually an electronic level detector version – see *Water level control* chapter).

3 Any water remaining in the machine complies with (2) above and is below 40°C. This is done by checking the resistance of the temperature thermistor. See *Temperature control and thermal fuses* chapter.

If the electro magnet coil goes open circuit due to a power cut or the appliance being turned off mid cycle for longer than four minutes the small heater within the interlock will cool and the bi-metallic latch will release the door slide.

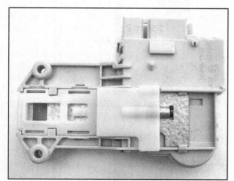

An instantaneous door interlock

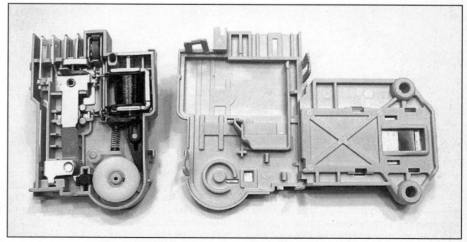

The internal view of an instantaneous door interlock

Chapter 21
Heaters

Metal covered (shrouded) elements are used to heat the wash water and many shapes and sizes can be found. The construction of the sheathed element allows it to be bent and shaped into any one of thousands of configurations to suit any situation. This however, can only be done at manufacture and no modification or bending should be done to old or new elements.

The heating element is housed within a metal tube and surrounded by an insulating material (magnesium oxide) which allows heat to be transferred to the outer sheath, but not the current. When a current is passed through the element its resistance gives rise to heating. Outer sheaths are made from various types of corrosion-resistant metal to suit the particular requirements and conditions.

Where is the heater located?

Most wash water heaters are located in the lower part of the tub in one of the following positions – through the back of the outer tub, through an aperture on the underside of the outer tub or through an aperture through the front of the outer tub, directly below the door seal. An exception to tub mounted wash heaters is the 'remote' heater – so called as it is not located in the outer tub unit at all. Remote heaters are found on models that use

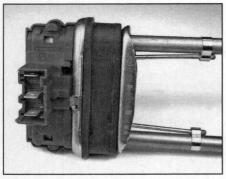

This version of heater has two much shorter metal rods that operate overheat switches housed within the plastic casing. The three terminal connections are closer together to allow for a 'block wiring connection' to be used. Testing and fitting of the element remains the same. However, a point to note is that the 10mm securing nut is recessed within the plastic housing and will require a thin-walled 10mm socket to access it for removal and refitting purposes

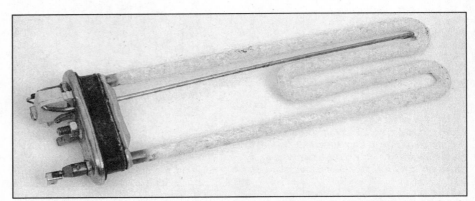

This wash heater has an external safety overheat microswitch actuated by a metal rod that protrudes through the rubber seal and is fixed to the far end of the heater. If the heater comes on with little or no water in the tub the rod will expand beyond its normal size. This expansion pushes the rod forward and in doing so open circuits the switch and turns the heater off. Once pushed through the rubber seal the rod will not self-reset the microswitch even when the heater has cooled down. However, on some versions the switch can be reset by easing the rod back into position
Note: *This must only be done when the original fault has been traced and rectified. If in doubt fit a new heater ensuring it also has overheat protection. There are versions that have a double rod and switch system for increased overheat protection.*

very low volumes of water for the wash cycle (such as 'Jet System' models) which means that the heater would not be sufficiently covered by water during the heating cycle. Remote heaters can be smaller, standard heating elements fitted into a housing beneath the outer tub through which water is circulated during the wash cycle, or a metal tub with an external heater wrapped around it. Depending on the location of the heater in your particular make and model you may need to remove the rear or front panel of the appliance.

Access to a remote heater often requires the machine to be laid on its front, which

This remote heater often referred to as a heat exchanger or through flow heater, has a heating element wrapped around the outside of a metal tube which heats the water as it passes through

allows access both via the back panel and the open base of the machine. Remember to follow the correct procedures of full isolation and protection when gaining access to this or any other parts of an appliance.

Removal and refitting of the heater

After making a note of the connections and removing them, a standard heater can be withdrawn from its position by fully slackening, but not removing the centre nut and tapping it to release the tension and then gently easing the rubber grommet free from its position with a flat-bladed screwdriver.
Note: *Ensure that you are removing the rubber grommet with the heater and not simply sliding the element through the rubber grommet as this will make removal extremely difficult.*

Refitting is a reversal of these instructions, although a little sealant should be applied to both surfaces of the grommet fitting. Care should be taken that the centre nut is not over tightened, as this would cause a distortion of the metal plate. On most automatic washing machines, the inner of the outer tub has a raised flange or cover plate that engages the curved section at the end of the heater. It is important that this is located correctly when refitting the heater. Check that it is located

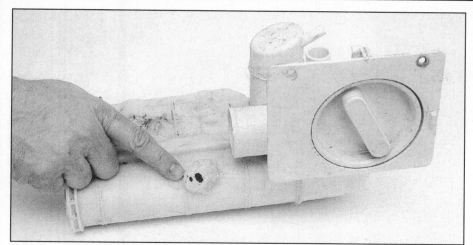

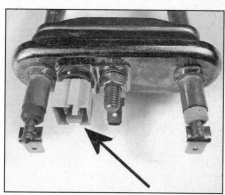

A heater with an integral thermistor

The large bubble on the top of this plastic moulding was caused when the heater came on with little or no water in the system. Blockages within the pressure system led to severe overheating within this combined remote heating, filter and pressure vessel unit

and held correctly by pressing firmly, but carefully downwards on the terminals of the heater while slowly rotating the inner drum. If the heater is not located correctly it will pivot on the grommet mounting and allow the element to come into contact with the drum, resulting in a grating noise and vibration. If such a noise is experienced during this simple test, slacken the heater clamp centre nut, remove the heater completely and relocate it correctly; then try again.

Note: *Do not exert excessive pressure on the terminals of the heater. Try to press down on the exposed outer sheath.*

Machines that have plastic or nylon outer tubs are fitted with overheat protectors (not to be mistaken for heaters that have integral thermistors – see the picture and the following chapter). Overheat protectors are essential and are linked in line with the live feed to the heater. They are fitted for safety reasons, for if a pressure switch or pressure system were to fail, it is possible for the heater to be engaged with no water in the outer tub.

This would be most unwelcome in a machine with a metal tub, although only minor damage would be caused to the clothes. If this type of fault were to happen in a plastic/nylon outer tub, the result would be extremely dangerous.

Note: *Under no circumstances should the overheat protection device be removed or bypassed.*

The overheat protector that is used on early Philips machines was an integral part of the heater and is similar to a capillary thermostat switch. However, on later machines, a simple thermostat is used to open circuit the heater if overheat occurs.

On the later machines the thermostat is connected in the live supply between the door interlock to the pressure switch. If overheating occurs the thermostat goes open circuit and cuts power to all other components apart from the door interlock. Early Hotpoint models used a separate thermal fuse heater protector for boil dry

protection of their plastic outer tub machines and this item along with the late Philips thermostat are available separately.

If such items are found to be faulty, the result would be failure to heat the wash water or failure to move through the programme. If any type of protector is found to be open circuit, it is essential that the cause is identified and rectified prior to renewal. Thoroughly check the pressure system and switch. For more detailed information on thermal fuses and protection devices see the *Temperature control* chapter.

These two heating elements have integral overheat protectors called thermal fuses. The one on the left may appear identical to the normal heater below, however, upon closer inspection it can be seen that the element with the internal thermal fuse has different coloured terminal ends. If the element you are changing has this subtle but important difference ensure the replacement does too. The element on the right clearly has different terminal ends

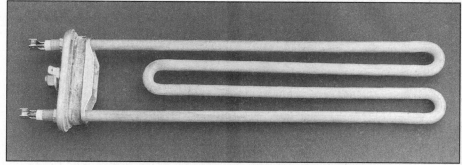

Normal style heater. (Do not fit to plastic tub machines)

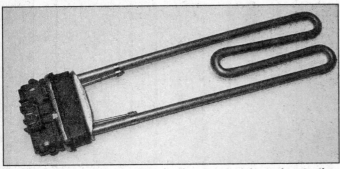

A heater with a block connector and mechanical thermal protection

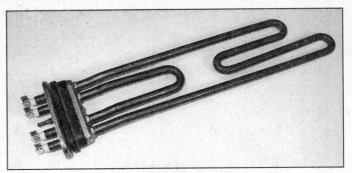

Double element heater

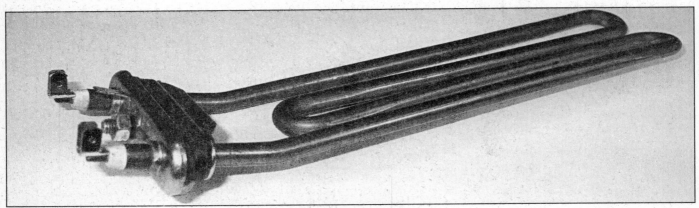

An angled single-element heater

Temperature control

There are several ways in which the temperature is controlled, details of which can be found in the following chapter.

Main faults with heaters

One of the most common faults with all heating elements, is that of open circuit, i.e., no current flows through the heater, therefore no heat is produced. This can simply be due to a broken or loose connection to one of the heater terminals. This then overheats, leaving an obvious discoloration of the connection or terminal, resulting in a break of the circuit at that point. Alternatively, the break in the circuit can occur within the

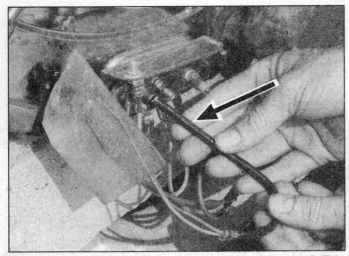

A heater with a removable over-heat thermal fuse (arrowed). This may be found on some early Hotpoint machines with plastic outer tubs. It was superseded by a heater with an integral thermal fuse which is recognisable by having different-coloured terminal insulators

Scaling can lead to element failure. The degree of scaling varies depending on the hardness of the water and the detergent used

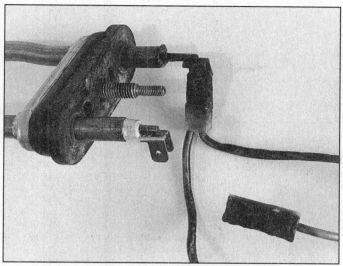

Overheated terminal due to loose connection on live supply

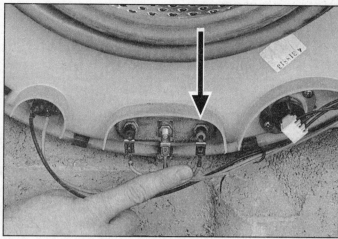

This wash heater has an internal thermal fuse (arrowed terminal). Although a normal heater will fit the aperture, it is essential that any replacement fitted to the machine also has thermal protection

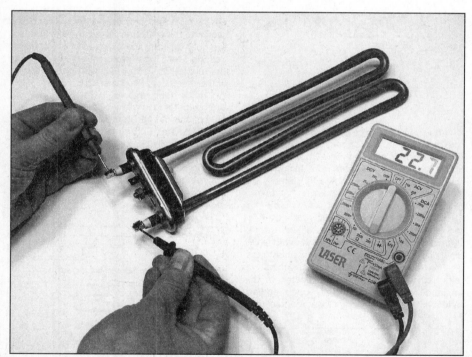

Using a simple multi-meter to check a heating element. With the connections removed the heating element should indicate continuity, i.e. in most instances a resistance of between 20 and 30 Ohms would be found for wattages between 2,000 and 3,000

Note: *The wattage of a heater is often marked on the securing plate (the higher the resistance the lower the wattage. Using Ohm's law to calculate the wattage from its resistance will not result in an exact match to that displayed on the heater. This is due to the resistance when cold being different from its resistance when it is powered).*

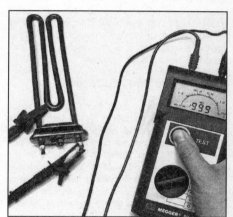

To test a heater conclusively for 'low insulation' (a very common problem) you will require an insulation test meter like the one shown here

A typical through-flow remote heater unit. To the top is an overheat protection thermostat – if this has tripped, check the circulation system for blockage, including scaling of the heater tube

element itself. Heaters can easily be tested for continuity as described in the – *Electrical circuit testing* chapter.

Another fault that can occur is that of low insulation. In this case, please refer to the chapter *Low insulation*. Accompanying the low insulation fault is that of short circuiting of the heater caused by a complete breakdown of insulation of the element. This results in the appliance blowing fuses or earth tripping if an RCD is in circuit.

Should any of the above faults occur, a complete replacement of the component(s) is required.

Chapter 22
Temperature control and thermal fuses

Thermostats

What is a thermostat?

A thermostat (stat) is an automatic device for monitoring temperature. This can be water temperature or the temperature of a component, the thermostat (stat) will either 'make' or 'break' a circuit at a predetermined temperature. Temperature ratings of fixed thermostats are usually marked around the metal perimeter on the back of the stat and are marked NO or NC, i.e. normally open contact (closing and making a circuit at given temperature), or normally closed (opening at given temperature). Some thermostats can and do contain both variants.

Where are they located?

The positioning of each thermostat depends on the task it has to do. Wash temperature thermostats need to be in contact with the wash water, and depending on the make and model, may be located on the back or the underside of the outer tub. Machines designed for front servicing, will often have the thermostat, heater and pressure vessel located on the front of the outer tub, directly below the door seal.

Exceptions to the above are Jet System models where, depending on the make and model of the machine, the thermostat may be located on a reservoir beneath the outer tub on a remote heating element.

Examples of the various positions of thermostats and heating elements can be found throughout the book.

How a fixed thermostat works

Diagram A shows a typical fixed (non variable) thermostat which can have one, two or three settings. Diagram B illustrates how a three position (NO) thermostat works. The power enters the switch at X, but cannot proceed as there is no contact. As the temperature rises and each preset temperature is reached, the bi-metal disc set to that temperature bends, making one of the three possible contacts.

Removing, refitting and testing a standard type thermostat

Note: *Before the repair or removal of any component from the machine, isolate the machine from the main electrical supply by removing the plug from the wall socket.*

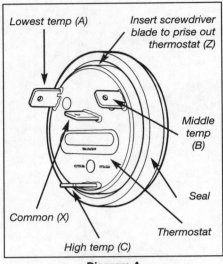

Diagram A

After making a note of the connections on the thermostat, disconnect the wires. Next insert a small screwdriver at point (Z), and ease the thermostat free from its grommet fitting. Do not remove the grommet and thermostat from the fixing point as one unit as the thermostat expands and holds the grommet in place. When refitting, it is advisable to smear a little sealant on the grommet to aid correct fitting and avoid leaks. Refitting is a reversal of the removal process.

The diagram on the right shows an alternative style of fixed thermostat, in this instance 50°C (NO) normally open contact and a 85°C (NC) normally closed contact. The

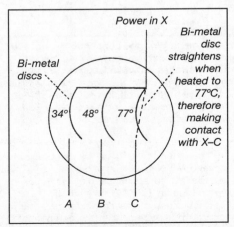

Diagram B

latter is a safety thermostat which operates if overheating should occur within the machine.

The top diagram illustrates the position of the thermostat at rest. Bi-metal discs are mounted directly behind the metal front cover of the stat and are preset to distort at given temperatures (in this instance 50°C and 85°C). They are linked to contact switches by pushrods. Any corresponding distortions of the discs, either make or break the corresponding contacts as shown.

When removed from the machine, the thermostat's operation can be tested by placing the metal cover in contact with a known heat source, e.g. radiator, hot water, etc., which matches or slightly exceeds the required temperature. Allow a little time for the heat to warm the stat and bi-metal discs. Testing for closing or opening of the thermostat can now be carried out as shown in the *Electrical circuit testing* chapter.

Check temperature with a household thermometer and allow a few degrees either way of the marked temperature on the outer rim of the stat, and remember to check if the stat is normally NO or NC. When cool, check that the stat returns to its normal position as indicated on the rim, i.e. NO or NC. **Note:** *NA may be found on some thermostats which are made abroad and is the same as NO which is 'normally open'.*

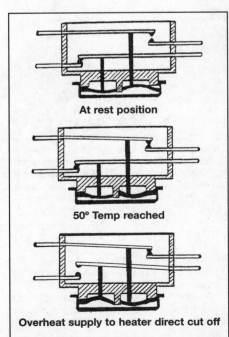

At rest position

50° Temp reached

Overheat supply to heater direct cut off

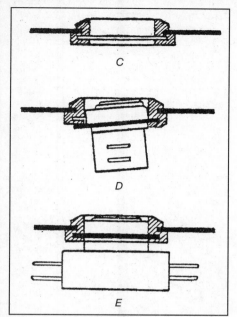

Thermostat fitting

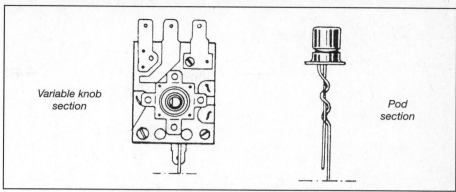

Diagram F – Typical pod type thermostat

Refitting is a reversal of the removal process. See diagrams C, D and E.

Locate one side of the metal lip in the grommet recess (C).

While pressing firmly on the thermostat flick the outer lip of the grommet over the metal lip of the thermostat with the aid of a small, flat-bladed screwdriver. (D). Sealant will help locate and seal the thermostat into position. (E) Ensure that the thermostat is securely located into the grommet and that the outer lip is not trapped at any point.

Thermostats may also be held in position by metal clips or clamps, and again, make sure of a good seal and check that the clips or clamps do not trap or touch any wires or connectors.

The variable thermostat

This is how a variable thermostat works. Diagram F shows a pod-type thermostat. This is found on machines that have a variable wash temperature control. Diagram G is a schematic diagram of the internal workings. This consists of an oil or gel-filled pod which is connected to the switch by a capillary tube. When the oil/gel in the pod is heated it expands within the sealed system and pushes a diaphragm. The diaphragm acts on the switchgear thus 'breaking' one circuit and 'making' the other. When the oil/gel cools it contracts, pulling the switch in the opposite direction. The switch is then in its original position and the process repeats if necessary.

Removing, refitting and testing a pod type thermostat

The pod, which is located at the base of the capillary tube, must be eased from its rubber grommet gently, taking care not to unduly kink or pull on the capillary tube itself.
Note: *When fitting or refitting this form of*

thermostat, the capillary tube must not come into contact with any electrical contacts such as the heater terminals or moving parts such as the main drive belt. When fitted, the tube should be checked along its entire length for any possible contact with these items. Also, a coiled section of at least two large turns should be left at a convenient position to absorb the movement of the tub assembly.

The pod thermostat can be subjected to a known temperature (e.g. radiator, kettle, etc.) ensuring that only the pod itself is immersed in water, and be checked with a small test meter for continuity. This process is shown in the chapter *Electrical circuit testing*.

Note: *Whilst at room temperature, the state of the thermostat should be determined. On pod thermostats, the lowest and highest setting should be selected. During testing, ensure that switch actuates both on rise and fall of temperature, see chapter Electrical circuit testing.*

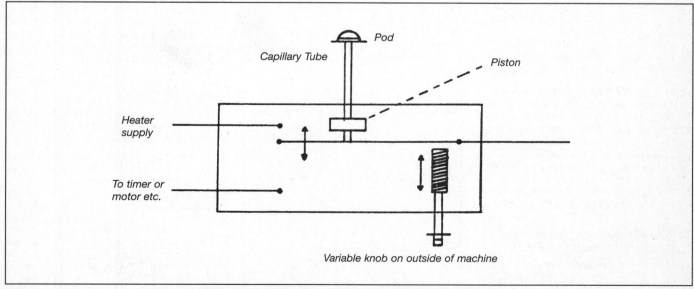

Diagram G – Internal workings of a pod type thermostat

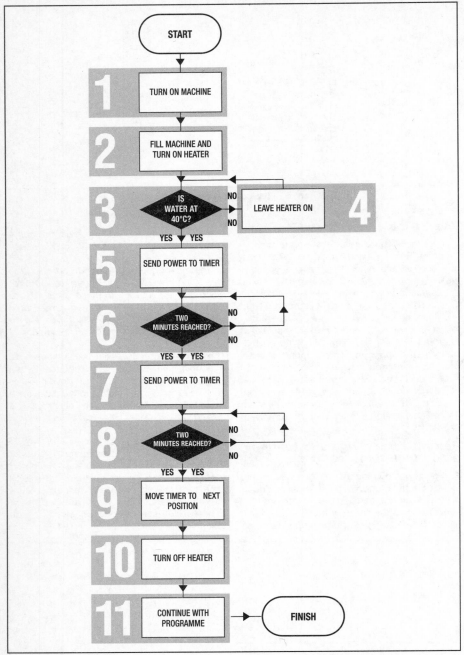

Thermostat operation flowchart

Using the following flowchart, trace the sequence of events:

1 The machine is turned on.

2 The timer impulses, fills the machine with cold water and turns the heater on.

3-4 The thermostat 'waits' until the heater has heated the water to 40°C.

5-6 When the thermostat closes (i.e., the water has reached 40°C, the timer washes for two minutes. The timer starts the washing action for two minutes. (At this point the heater is still engaged).

7-8 The above operation is repeated, again with the heater engaged. When the two minute wash has ended, the water will be 45°C due to the extra four minute heating.

9-11 The timer then moves to the next position, which disengages the heater and would then be ready for the programme to continue as required.

12 For the purpose of this flowchart, the wash will end here, as we are only concerned with the operation of the thermostat at this time.

Note: *This is only used as an example to illustrate the use of the thermostat, and does not actually represent the way in which a wash is formed. For further information regarding the timer, see the chapter* Timers (programme control).

This way of using preset thermostats can give a greater variation in wash temperatures. A combination of preset and variable thermostats is common to give protection to the cooler washes, i.e., should the variable thermostat be accidentally left at 90°C and a delicate wash be selected, the preset stat would override the variable stat, therefore giving some protection to the wash.

The following thermostats show a small selection of those used by manufacturers of washing machines. All types are used directly or indirectly to control wash temperatures. This means that they 'turn off' the heater as soon as a pre-selected temperature has been reached, to allow the timer to advance or a timed heat cycle to commence.

Thermistors

What is a thermistor?

A thermistor is a solid state device used in place of a fixed or variable thermostat. The thermistor's particular properties allow them to be used as infinitely variable temperature sensors that have no moving parts. They are also incapable of going out of calibration i.e. giving incorrect temperature resistance values, but occasionally they can and do go 'open circuit', or connections to and from them may short circuit. Both are faults which will inevitably give rise to temperature sensing problems.

Circular 'three' step thermostat with temperature settings marked on outer edge

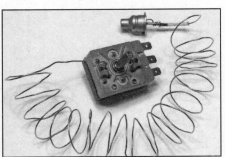

Variable thermostat showing the switches, capillary tube and pod

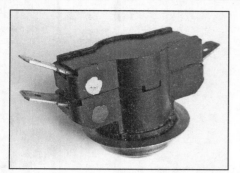

A popular two-step fixed thermostat

An alternative design of two-step fixed thermostat

The rear view of a two-step fixed thermostat

Where is it located?

Like all temperature sensing devices, it must come into direct or indirect contact with the substance (air/water) or the item that needs monitoring. Its location is therefore similar to the other thermostats but methods of fixings will differ.

How does it work?

Unlike other temperature control devices the thermistor cannot work alone. It is an electrical resistor, the resistance of which varies in relation to its temperature. There are two ways in which it varies depending on manufacturer, and the requirements of the finished product. Thermistors can be positive or negative temperature co-efficient. In simple terms, this means a positive co-efficient thermistor's resistance increases as its temperature increases and conversely, a negative coefficient thermistor's resistance decreases as its temperature increases. Thermistors are therefore rated as PTC or NTC respectively. The NTC type of thermistor is the version most often used in temperature sensing circuitry in automatic washing machines; e.g. Hoover, Servis, Hotpoint, etc., a theoretical operation of this is given below. It is essential that only the correct variation of thermistor is used which conforms to the rating requirements of the machine and it's circuitry.

The variation in resistance to temperature change forms part of an electronic circuit, the output of which controls the advancement of the selected wash programme, in either mechanically or electronically controlled machines. On electronically controlled machines, i.e. those without mechanical timers, the resistance of the thermistor is monitored directly by the main programme circuit board or sub module, see *Timers (programme control)*. However, thermistors can be found on machines with mechanical timers/programmers and the way in which they work in this instance is as follows. The resistance of the thermistor forms part of a temperature control circuit. There may be a separate module solely for this purpose or it may form part of the motor control module as in some Hotpoint machines. A theoretical operation of such a system is given below.

Refer to the illustration opposite. In this instance the output voltages at D & C are used to control a triac (an electrical component

within the circuit). The triac in turn switches the thermostop coil on a mechanical timer or impulse to control panel of a computer control machine. See *Timers (programme control)*.

Being an electronic circuit in either mechanical or computer controlled machines, the operating voltage within this portion of circuit will be low (5 volts DC). Therefore, any electrical testing of the thermistor must be with a low voltage test meter as voltages of over 5V will damage the thermistor or module circuitry.

The two resistors Ra and Rb are of the same value. A 5V DC voltage supplied to point A will take one of two routes depending on the resistance opposing it, i.e. A.C.B. or A.D.B. Route A.C.B. has within it four resistors each of which can be switched in and out of the circuit in relation to the programme selected and temperature required for that wash cycle. The diode at point E eliminates reverse supply to the triac. The route A.D.C. contains the thermistor in its second leg D.B. If we assume that the water within the machine is cold, then the thermistor resistance will be high. This will allow a current from D to C thus energising the thermostop or holding the programme on the heat cycle until the predetermined temperature (governed by the switchable resistors) is attained. Releasing of the thermostop or impulse of programme is as follows. As the water temperature increases, the resistance of the thermistor decreases (NTC). At some point the resistance in both sides of the circuit will be equal and then no current will flow between D and C and the triac will switch off. This in turn will release the thermostop on mechanical timers or allow impulse to the next stage of the programme on electronically controlled machines. Variations in temperature are gained by switching in or out the required resistors in the C.B. leg of the circuit, thus

Typical solid state thermistor

A popular two-step fixed thermostat

altering the point at which equilibrium is reached within the circuit. All switches open = all resistors in circuit rc + rd + re + rf would result in high resistance, therefore a cooler wash of say 30ºC is achieved. Quick wash switch closed = resistor rf bypassed, i.e. lower total resistance gives wash of say 40ºC. Switch 1 closed = two resistors in circuit rc & re may relate to 50ºC with option of quick wash switch to further reduce temperature (and time) if required by user. Switch 2 closed = three resistors rc, rd, rf in circuit may relate to 60ºC with option of quick wash switch to further reduce temperature (and time) if required by user. All switches closed = this will leave only rc in circuit at this point, and a high temperature of say 90ºC would be achieved, again with option if required.

Note: *The option to alter the temperature selected by the set programme; i.e. by pressing a quick wash or short wash option button on the control panel, may be bypassed itself by the timer on some programmes. This means that although in the theoretical operation detailed above, each setting could be further affected by the quick wash switch, in reality, this may not be the case as a quick wash may not be suitable for certain types of wash loads.*

Thermistors and temperature controlled filling

In addition to basic temperature control the ability of thermistors to react to any temperature change is used to the full in

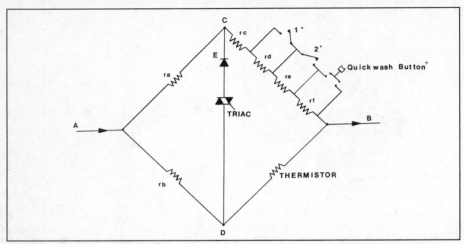

This heating element has an integral thermistor (arrowed)

* = Switches controlled by timer wash selection. (These switches would be electronic not mechanical on computer controlled machines)
+ = Button on facia of machine which is a user selectable option

some computer and hybrid timer controlled models. For instance as the machine fills with water the thermistor's resistance will be proportional to the temperature of the water entering the tub. This known value can be used by the processor to fill the machine (when circumstance permits) with the ideal starting temperature for that particular wash cycle. This is accomplished by energising only the hot valve and allowing the processor to cycle the cold valve as required to achieve the preferred starting temperature. This is very much like what we do when we want to fill a bowl of water to wash with. We dibble our fingers in the water and if it is too hot we turn the cold tap on until we achieve the temperature we want. It may seem a simple task but when this ability is added to a washing machine it can equate to a significant saving in energy.

T.O.C.s

The term T.O.C. is an abbreviation for thermal overload cut-out. In simple terms, if the item the T.O.C. is attached to, or is in proximity with, gets too hot (over a predetermined temperature), the T.O.C. will operate and open circuit the supply. The way in which it works is very similar to the thermostat, both of which use the bi-metal strip system. Thermostats are in fact used on some machines as T.O.C.s to open circuit for instance, the heater if an overheat fault occurs. However, the term T.O.C. generally relates to the smaller devices that are embedded within or on top of motor winding coils of all types.

There are several variations in style and size, each of which being matched to its particular use and position within the appliance or apparatus. It is therefore essential that only the correct style and

temperature rating is used when renewing a T.O.C. Those that are used to protect motors and pumps, etc., are rarely renewable and usually form part of the original winding or moulding. If a T.O.C. has gone open circuit, it will have done so for a particular reason, therefore this safety item must not be bypassed. Always ensure that any replacement component contains a T.O.C. Some pattern spares may miss out this fundamental safety device in order to cut production costs, so take note that such an omission could be unsafe.

Although designs and ratings of T.O.C.s vary, there are two basic types of operation; A. The self-setting T.O.C. This is like a thermostat and resets when a normal working temperature returns which may result in a cycling of the fault, i.e. the safety T.O.C., due to a fault open circuits the heater supply. This would result in the cooling of the heater and the water, in the process the T.O.C. also cools and in doing so returns power back to the heater.

The manual reset T.O.C.
The action of this type of T.O.C. is identical to that described above except for one main difference. Once tripped, it cannot reset itself and has to be reset manually usually by simply pressing a button or rod.

Note: *This must be done with the machine isolated; i.e. unplugged, and only after the cause of the tripping has been eliminated.*

Thermal fuses

Many appliances will contain this type of overheat protection device. It can be found protecting the heater on many makes of machines, especially those with plastic outer tubs. It is essentially a fail-safe device which,

A grommet-fitted thermistor (centre)

To remove a thermistor (or thermostat) from its grommet fixing, carefully insert a small flat-bladed screwdriver and ease it free. Do not attempt to remove the grommet with the thermistor (or thermostat) still in position

when actuated by a predetermined temperature, goes open circuit. It cannot self-set or be manually reset, therefore renewal of the thermal fuse is required once the device has gone open circuit. Renew the thermal fuse only when the fault which caused it to operate has been corrected, e.g. pressure switch system blockage allowing heater to energise without water in the machine.

It is a solid state device and as such contains no moving parts or contacts that may in themselves fail. Thermal fuses alleviate the possibility of fault cycling. Some heating elements may have replaceable thermal fuses like the one shown on the

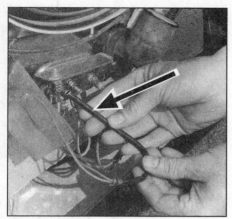

Heater with overheat detector (arrowed). This is found on some machines with plastic outer tubs

right, which are housed in protective sheaths or mouldings and should not be confused with elements with integral thermistors.

Thermal fuses have a wide variety of temperature ratings available to suit the various applications, so great care must be taken when replacing the device to match the original rating/item and if in doubt it is recommended that the manufacturer's part is obtained as a replacement. Do not under any circumstances consider bypassing this removable type of thermal fuse for any reason whatsoever. **Note:** *A photograph and explanation of an alternative mechanical wash heater T.O.C. system based on expansion is shown in the previous chapter on heaters.*

To maximise safety and to prevent a heating element thermal fuse from being bypassed by ignorance (or plain stupidity) heating elements are now produced with integral thermal fuse protection. Once the thermal fuse has operated this design renders the heating element inoperable and eliminates the possibility of the fuse being bypassed for whatever reason. When such a fuse has operated, a new element will be required once the reason for the safety device operating has been identified and corrected.

Not all elements are fitted with integral thermal fuses and it is therefore essential that if the original element had one then the replacement you obtain must also have one too. Do not be tempted to replace a thermally protected element with one that does not have thermal protection. Patterned spares are often available in both versions as there are makes and models that do not require thermal fuse protection. It is up to you to ensure you obtain the correct version and not simply buy on price or availability. If in doubt purchase the genuine component, which should be a direct replacement.

Although at first glance they may look identical closer inspection will often reveal subtle differences which help identify if the element has or does not have integral protection (see photos).

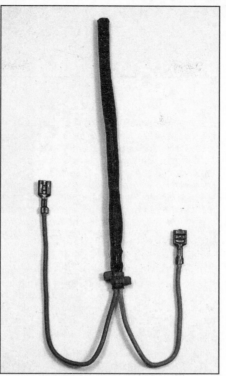

In this instance the thermal fuse is housed within the insulated sheath.

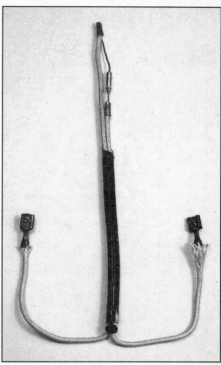

Thermal fuse or micro temp as it is sometimes called. The device will often be housed in an insulated flexible sleeve

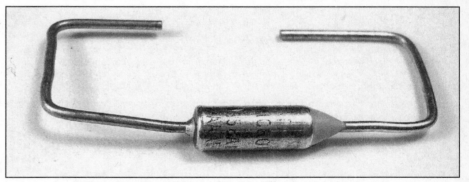

With the sheath removed the thermal fuse can be clearly seen

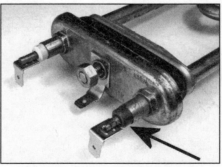

This heating element has an integral thermal fuse (arrowed) and can be identified by the element terminals being slightly different colours when compared with a standard element without thermal fuse protection

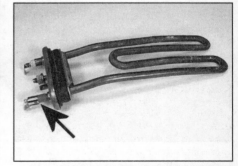

This heating element has an integral thermal fuse (arrowed) and can be identified by the element terminals being slightly different colours when compared with a standard element without thermal fuse protection.

Chapter 23
Suspension

During the normal washing and spin drying operations of front loading machines of all types, a great deal of vibration is produced. The level of vibration increases during the spin sequences, especially if the wash load is out of balance or severely under loaded. If the outer tub unit was fixed rigidly to the shell/outer casing of the machine, damage would be caused to both internal components and to the immediate location of the machine through excessive movement of the free-standing machine.

To avoid the transference of vibration produced during wash and spin cycles, the inner tub unit of front loading washing machines is supported within the shell/outer casing of the machine by vibration absorbing supports, i.e., suspension. Due to the confines of the shell/outer casing of the modern machine, a limited amount of movement is allowed, but any excessive vibration and movement of the tub unit is removed (damped) by the action of the suspension system supporting the unit.

Note: *To prevent damage to components within the machine during transportation/ delivery, some means of packing will be fixed to the machine to stop any movement of the tub unit, i.e., rocking suspension. It is essential that any such packing or transit fixings (as they are commonly known) are removed. There are as many different types of transit packing as there are machines, so read your instruction booklet for a description of how to remove the packing from your new machine. It is advisable to retain the instructions and packing should it become necessary to transport your washing machine again, e.g., moving house. If you do need to refit the transit packing, a good idea is to put a sticker on the door reminding you that the machine must not be used until the packaging has been removed.*

Remember that the suspension is the system that controls all of the movement of the tub unit when it is in use. Without the suspension or when it is damaged, the whole tub unit will move violently when in use. See also *Out of balance protection* later in this chapter.

What different types of suspension are there?

The spring type suspension – simply large strong support springs (used only on early slow spin machines).

Slide and spring damper – supporting the tub from beneath with only small springs or straps at the top for holding the outer tub unit in the mid fore and aft position.

The oil damper and spring suspension – not unlike the system used on motor cars.

The air damper and spring suspension – similar in looks to the oil damper but consist of a chamber and piston arrangement which restricts the escape of air as the two components slide within one another.

The friction damper consists of two arms gripping a metal plate tightly, therefore slowing down the movement of the tub.

What follows are descriptions of each type of system, however a combination of systems may be used on some machines.

The spring only system

The spring only system may also be found. The spring or the mounts can be changed separately if required or replaced as a complete unit.

Slide and damper types

The main faults to check for are those of guide wear, allowing the shaft to jump out of position, and also the top rubbers to soften or wear. This results in a phenomenon called 'twisted tub'. The reason for this is the suspension on one side of the tub is not correctly positioned, therefore allowing one side of the tub to bang on the side of the shell and cause damage. A noise fault can also become apparent at the top of the suspension due to soapy water seeping into the

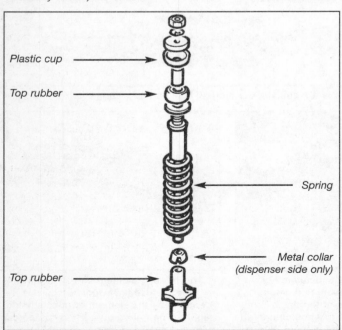

Spring only unit, Hoover type

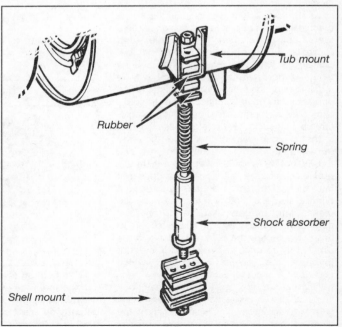

Large damper and mounts

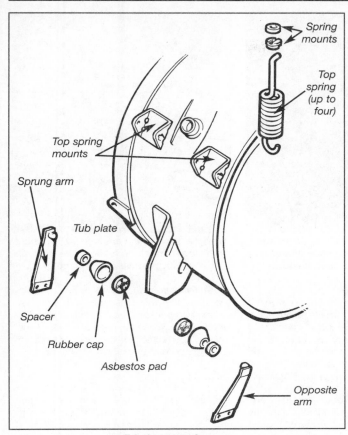

Friction type damper

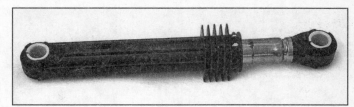

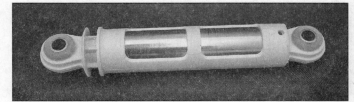

Typical air damper units

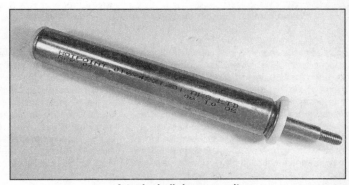

A typical oil damper unit

suspension via the dispenser or dispenser hose. This is best removed by a spray of lubricant/moisture repellent and an application of Molycote to the top bush and slides. The top and the guides of the suspension are the only parts that should be lubricated in this way.

When fitting top rubbers, the machine should be laid on its face, and the suspension should be held tightly with grips at the top end only. The top nut can then be undone. Do not hold the bottom of the shaft as any marks will quickly wear the plastic guides. When refitting, thoroughly clean the metal shaft and apply a smear of Molycote lubricant paste to the shaft and upper shaped washers. The plastic slides should also have the same paste applied prior to refitting.

The friction damper system

The friction damper system is not unlike the disc braking system on a motor car. Two support rubbers with asbestos (or similar material) pads are mounted on two spring steel arms. These rest either side of the flat plate attached to the outer tub. When the outer tub moves, the action is slowed down (damped) by the friction of the pads against the plate. This is a very cheap and very effective form of suspension.

When this type of damper is worn, the tub will move excessively and possibly emit a squeaking noise. The noise may be caused by the rubber pad mounts coming into contact with the moving plate, due to the friction material being worn. This is easily overcome by the renewal of the pads themselves. After isolating the machine it should be laid on its back or side to enable the steel spring arms to be opened. When opened, the pads can be prised from their ball and socket joint.

Note: *If the pads on this system become glazed and/or shiny on their contact faces, a 'chattering sound' will be noticed. It may be possible to avoid renewal, by slightly roughening the faces with sandpaper to remove the glazing and then refit. If unsuccessful, the pads will have to be renewed. Do not under any circumstances put oil or grease on friction damper systems. Do not inhale the dust from the friction pads as they can be harmful to the lungs. Moisten with water during removal and cleaning to avoid airborne dust particles. Do not blow them clean. Dispose of old pads safely and wash hands after contact.*

The damper and spring system

The damper type system is similar to the shock absorbers on your car, and they do the same job. If the smaller version of the system is used, the tub will not actually rest on the damper, but will be hung from springs at the top of the tub, using the dampers at the bottom for shock absorption only. In the larger systems however, the tub is held only by much larger dampers at the bottom of the tub, with retaining straps/springs at the top to limit movement fore and aft.

Faults found with this type of solid damper will have the same symptoms as the friction damper system. The only remedy in this case is the complete renewal of the faulty damper. This can be done by laying the machine onto its face or back, taking the usual care and isolation procedures. Access to the dampers can be gained by then removing the front or back panel, and unbolting the damper from the shell and tub mounts.

The air damper and spring suspension

Externally, an air damper looks similar to an oil damper, however it is much simpler in construction and consists of an outer casing with a movable inner piston. Movement of the outer tub is damped by restricting the escape of air through a small hole as the piston slides within the outer casing. The most common problem is that the seal between the casing and the piston wears and allows air to pass which greatly reduces the damping effect or renders it totally ineffective. This will require the renewal of the complete damper.

Note: *The left and right support springs of all systems are usually of different ratings. Be sure*

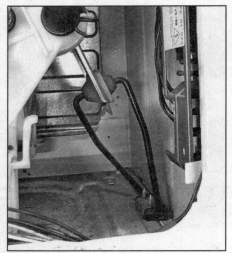

A typical friction damper system

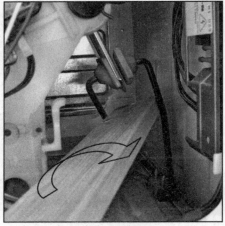

To remove a friction pad insert a suitably sized piece of wood within the spring arm and twist it to force open the jaws

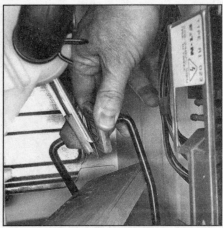

With the jaws of the suspension arm held in the 'open' position it should be possible to carefully remove and replace of the pads

Note: *Great care should be taken during this process to avoid the fingers from entering the gap between the friction plate and friction pad. When the pads are refitted and aligned correctly, turn the piece of wood in the opposite direction and remove it.*

to specify the required side when obtaining a replacement. Also, where two small springs are used for fore and aft support during repair, it is possible that they may become dislodged. It is essential that they are refitted correctly. Please examine the correct positions and make notes of all springs, etc., before you start.

It must be stressed that any combination of these systems may be found. A damper system may complement a friction damper system. Please read all sections thoroughly before starting any repair on the suspension system.

The purpose of suspension in the automatic washing machine, whether wash-only or combined washerdrier, is to damp the oscillations of the spring mounted outer tub and drum unit. Counterweights of concrete or in some instances cast iron, are used to help in the overall balance of the unit and to add weight to the appliance to further help in eliminating movement during use (especially spin). The suspension system works the hardest during the distribute (pre-spin) and spin cycles. Under normal load conditions the simple suspension and counterweight system works well and reduces tub oscillation as long as all components and connections are secure and in good order. However, if a severe out of balance condition occurs because of a mechanical fault, for example worn suspension, under loading e.g. one bath mat, one pair of jeans etc., overloading e.g. large duvet, or by washing unsuitable items, such as trainer shoes, excessive vibration and damage may result. Both the outer

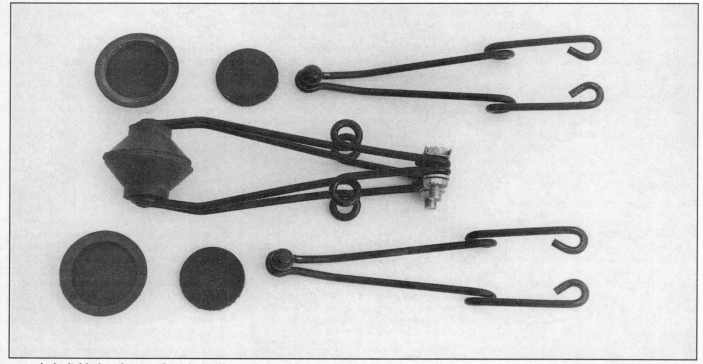

Indesit friction damper that shows the spring steel arms clearly. These support the rubber mounts with friction pad inserts

1 View of spring and slide suspension. This is prone to softening of the rubber mount at the top of the suspension leg
Note: If the top springs are removed, mark them so as to ensure that they are replaced in the same order. This is because the length and tension for the springs may differ for each position.

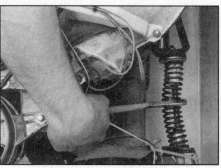

2 To renew the top rubber, the whole unit will have to be withdrawn. Grip the shaft through the spring at the top only, using adjustable pliers inserted through the spring

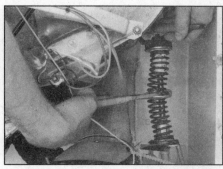

3 Whilst gripping the metal shaft tightly, the securing nut can be removed. (Right hand thread). Note the correct assembly of parts and pull spring downwards to remove top bush

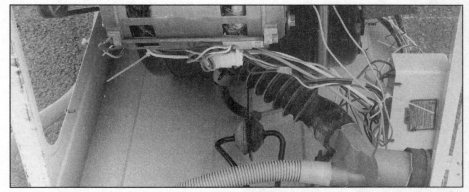

Friction style damper. Access is much easier with hoses removed. Do not lubricate this type of suspension

cabinet and internal parts may be damaged due to the suspension being unable to cope with adverse oscillations of the tub unit within the confines of the shell/cabinet.

All but the earliest of front loading automatic machines have a pre-spin speed or distribute as it is often called, the action of which is to balance out the wash load by rotating it at a pre-set drum speed. The centrifugal force created by the pre-set speed (usually around 83 rpm on the drum) arranges the wash load evenly over the inner surface of the drum prior to acceleration into the spin. However, this process can fail if:

1 A balled load occurs, i.e. the knotting together of items in a normal wash load usually as a result of poor loading by bundling all items into the machine together instead of separately. Stopping the machine, removing and replacing the items individually is usually all that is required for this problem.

Note: It is wise to reset the machine to a rinse position before the spin to allow correct distribution to take place.

2 Underloading occurs when insufficient clothes are in the drum to distribute evenly around the entire surface i.e. half drum surface covered but other half not; thus giving a flywheel effect when rotated.

Note: This is a common fault on some machines and aggravated by the user removing items in the hope of improving the matter when in fact extra items are required.

3 Overloading results in little or no free movement of the wash load therefore no distribute action is possible. This will also result in a poor wash.

4 An unsuitable wash load of, for instance, trainers, sleeping bags etc., will create severe out of balance situations and will subsequently damage the machine and/or its surroundings. Try to load the machine correctly.

New set of rubber sleeves and spacer washers. Do not be tempted to renew one side only – you must renew both sides!

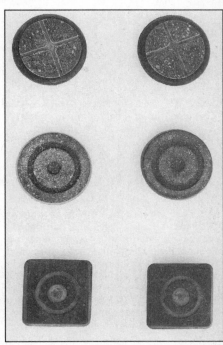

Friction pads from various machines. Top section is pad and mount for Zanussi, middle section pad for Indesit, and lower is square pad for Candy

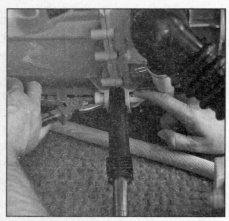

Dampers/suspension legs are often secured at both top and bottom with plastic push fit pegs – as in this instance. Removal is by depressing a small plastic barb and levering/pulling the securing peg free. To refit, simply line the damper with its securing point and tap the peg through and check that the barb has re-set. If you inadvertently break the barb during removal you must fit a new peg

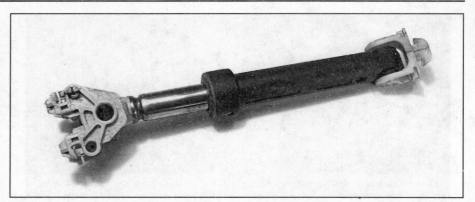

Dampers fitted to many Whirlpool, Ignis and Bauknecht models are held in place at the base by a simple slide system which is locked in place by a plastic retaining clip. Once the bottom of the damper is freed simply turning the unit allows the top to be disengaged from the outer tub bracket

Note: *Before removal make note of the fixing point as there are several options for different models.*

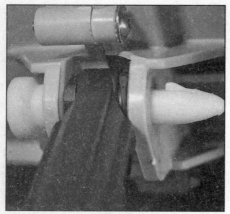

A close-up of a securing peg which clearly shows the locking barb

Out of balance protection

The best way to avoid out of balance problems is to load and use the machine correctly; although even having done this, an out of balance situation may still develop. Many modern machines, especially most computer-controlled models and many ordinary machines with microchip-based speed control modules, now incorporate means of detecting out of balance situations. When problems are detected steps can be implemented by re-balancing the load by extending the distribute phase or by terminating the acceleration up to full spin speed thus limiting or avoiding further vibration or damage.

How does out of balance protection work?

OOB detection as it is known can be detected two ways:

a) Electro-mechanically. This method uses light action microswitches strategically mounted on the edges of the outer tub or on the suspension legs. They may be actuated by a weight on the arm of the microswitch or by a contact bar, either of which will be adjustable for calibration of OOB movement. The microswitch is linked into the motor speed module control circuitry, see *Motors* chapter (speed control). Excessive movement or inertia resulting from an out of balance situation will actuate the micro-switch at a predetermined level. The impulse caused by the microswitch's operation terminates the build up to the spin speed selected and normally allows only the distribute speed to operate. After a period of time governed by the circuitry of the module, a spin sequence will be reinstated in the expectation that a second distribute has cleared the OOB problem. If this is not so, the process is repeated. With mechanical programme timers, this process may continue, dependent on the make and model of the machine, until the time allotted for spin has elapsed. Computer controlled machines are often programmed (See *Timers (programme control)* chapter), to accept only three OOB impulses before terminating the spin or remainder of the programme completely. The setting of the mechanical OOB detection microswitches differ greatly between the different makes and also between the different models from the same manufacturer, hence no specific adjustment details can be given within this text.

Note: *Ensure actuation of microswitches are free and all connections to and from them are in good order.*

b) Electronic only. The electronic OOB detection system is found on computer-controlled models and many machines with microchip-based speed control modules. It is only the detection process which differs from that already described in section a). Detection in this instance is by monitoring the motor speed reference voltage from the tacho coil, see *Motors* chapter (speed

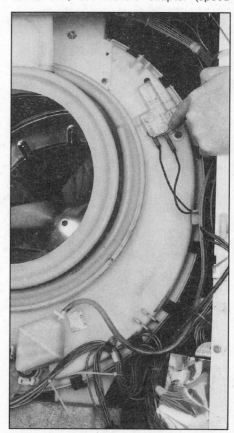

Mechanical out of balance (OOB) switch

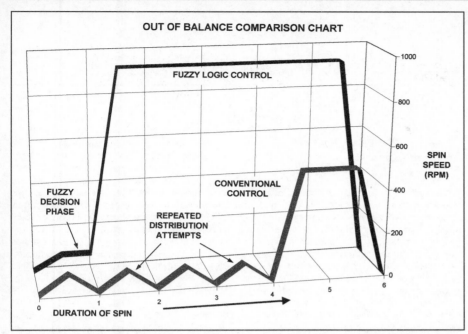

OUT OF BALANCE COMPARISON CHART

The above graph compares the operation of both conventional and Fuzzy Logic out of balance detection systems.
The lower trace shows the way conventional systems simply keep trying to redistribute the load with low speed distribute action each time an out of balance event is detected. After several failed attempts over a period of time the spin is simply reduced both in length and speed or in severe cases omitted completely.
The top trace shows how a Fuzzy Logic system assesses the severity of the initial out of balance and calculates the optimum spin speed for that particular load. The result in this instance is a faster spin over a longer period of time

Reference to OOB detection and implementation can also be found in the chapter Fuzzy logic.

Conventional electronic out of balance control

Many computer-controlled machines and the more sophisticated speed control modules (especially combined Hybrid timer systems) will have 'out of balance' spin limitation systems similar to the one described here. Prior to spinning the wash load a distribution sequence is implemented to balance the load. The distribute sequence will have a predetermined (by the manufacturer of the appliance) optimum drum speed, in this instance 90rpm. During the intermediate and final spin phases the optimum distribute speed of 90rpm will be monitored by the microprocessor from information provided by the tacho. Loads that fail to balance correctly will adversely affect the optimum distribute speed (in this instance 90rpm) and therefore the tacho output. If a load fails to attain the required distribute speed; further attempts at distributing the load will automatically take place. The ramp up to full spin speed will therefore not occur until a satisfactory distribute speed has been detected.

Note 1: *The figure of 90 rpm is used only as an example, reference to individual manufacturers will be required for specific makes and models.*

Note 2: *Only a predetermined number of re-balancing attempts will be allowed. Should a correct distribute speed not be attained, the drum speed will be limited to the distribute speed (90rpm) for the duration of the spin phase.*

Reference to Fuzzy logic OOB detection and implementation can be found in the chapter Fuzzy logic.

control). During an out of balance situation the motor speed will vary i.e. rise and fall on each revolution of the drum proportional to the degree of the imbalance. If this reference exceeds the pre-programmed tolerances for that particular programme setting or spin, a fault sequence similar to

that described in section a) is implemented and distribution occurs. As before, this may be limited to three or more such cycles before termination of the set programme and in the case of computer-controlled machines, the display of a corresponding fault code.

Chapter 24
Timers (programme control)

The programmer or timer, as it is more commonly known, is the unit located at the top of the machine, directly behind the selector knob on mechanically controlled machines, whereas machines that are controlled electronically may have the programmers split into two or more circuit boards (modules as they are usually known).

When a programme is selected, the timer follows a predetermined sequence switching components on and off (i.e., heater, pump, valves) for various lengths of time. Due to the apparent complexity of this component, it wrongly tends to be regarded as a 'no go' area.

The intention of this manual has been to show that the automatic washing machine is not so mysterious, and when broken down into its constituent parts, its simplicity of operation is revealed. To describe the workings of the timer in your particular machine would require the make, model number, date of manufacture and the timer number itself. These are needed to ascertain which variation of timer and associated variation of programmes that your particular machine has. In their most infinite wisdom, the manufacturers have seen fit to change their timers, numbers and wiring colours, etc., with regularity.

To provide detailed information about the particular unit that is in your particular machine, a book several times the size of this one would be needed. What follows is a general description of how timers function and some of the most common faults and their symptoms.

How an edge cam mechanical timer works

What follows is a description of how an electro-mechanical timer works, in this instance a Crouzet timer. This is one of the most common timers and is still to be found in machines sold today. The Crouzet is an edge cam timer, which means that each switch within the timer is operated by its own cam on a central rotatable barrel. This allows several switches to be dropped or lifted into different positions at the same time. This operation can be likened to that of the old style piano or musical box that played a tune with the aid of a cylinder. If the cylinder were to be changed, a different tune would be produced. The same principle applies to the timer. Although the external appearance of the timer may not change, a simple change of the central barrel will give the manufacturer a different switching sequence and therefore a different machine to put on the market. Because of this, when changing the timer it is important that the correct version is used i.e., one with the same central barrel. This is shown by the serial number on the timer.

On the central barrel there are several cams, with each cam having two corresponding switches. The barrel is rotated by the cam advance motor, which is energised by impulse commands such as that from the thermostat, i.e., if the selected temperature is reached, the thermostat closes, thus causing the cam advance motor to run. The motor will continue to run until a cam position is reached that open circuits the impulse path (advance motor circuit). The barrel is now in the correct position for the next sequence of instructions.

Most mechanical timers utilise a cam cycle of 60 steps. This means that on one complete revolution of the cam, it will have initiated 60 separate positions (60 'clicks'). The operating function of the cam may be split further into two or more separate stages or programme sequences. An instance of this is when half of the timer cycle is for robust washes and long fast spins and the remaining section used for cooler washes and short low speed spins. This may appear on the control knob as letters A–F for hot wash, rinse and long fast spin and G–K for delicate wash, rinse and short slow spin.

Note: *The letters used are an example only. The way in which programme sequences are laid out on any particular machine will depend upon the manufacturer of the appliance and the cam operating sequence may be split into more than two sections.*

There are two distinct variations in the way the cam barrel is advanced: a) timers with two drive motors mounted on the rear and b) a single motor drive system. A description of both types is as follows:

a) this style of timer is easily recognisable by the two small drive motors mounted in the rear of the timer. Each has its own function, one of which is dedicated to cam advance as described in the previous paragraph, and is called the cam advance motor.

Next to the advance motor is the timing motor, which times all of the functions of the machine, i.e., washing, spinning, etc. The

A typical mechanical timer

An internal view of a cam barrel. Each row is for one switch block and has three levels

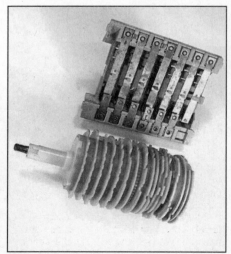

The internal view of a switch bank. Note switch movements and cam position

A hybrid timer and combined printed circuit board (PCB)

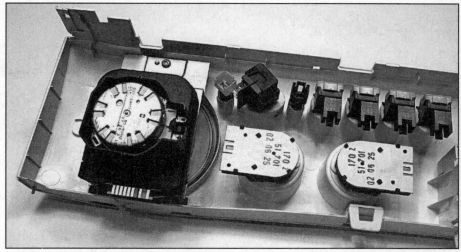

This small black unit mounted behind the appliance facia panel and connected to the programme selection knob is used to select the programme stored on a main power board PCB, situated on the lower left-hand shell of the appliance

timing motor drives a timing cam which, via internal gearing, turns one revolution every two minutes. Therefore a six minute wash consists of three, two minute timing requests. The rotational times may differ depending on the requirements of the appliance manufacturer.

Another function of the timing motor is that it is normally used to reverse the main motor on the wash action cycle.

Note: *Motor reversal on some machines may be controlled by the speed control module see* Motors *chapter.*

This is done by continually rotating two independent timing cams at the rear of the main barrel, on which two sets of switches are located. A combination of both main and timing (motor reversal) cam switches are used for motor control and direction depending on the type of wash programme selected. For instance, if a delicate wash is selected, the main wash motor receives power via the switches for five seconds (clockwise rotation), pause for fifteen seconds, then rotates for five seconds (anti-clockwise). The cam does this by continuous rotation in one direction but lifting the switches into three separate positions, ON, OFF, ON (reverse feed to motor). Delicate and heavy washes can be achieved by using different configurations of the same sequence. A heavy wash for example could be made up of the following sequence: wash for fifteen seconds clockwise, pause for five seconds, and wash for fifteen seconds anti-clockwise. The times of fifteen and five seconds are not random choices, but are directly proportional to the two minute timing cycle. The times of rotation and pause will differ between timer types and the requirements of the appliance manufacturer but will be proportional to the rotational time of the cam, e.g., 17, 3, 17, etc.

Switches resting on the main cam barrel controlled by the advance motor can also be moved into three positions by the cam they are resting on. For example, at the correct point in the programme; for instance after the

machine has filled with water and the pressure switch has activated, if the cam on which the heater switch rests is closed ('made'), the heater will be energised. At the same time the thermostat cam will also engage the correct thermostat switch for that programme. When the correct temperature is reached and the timer has timed out, the thermostat then impulses the cam advance motor onto the next step in the programme. In English, this is read as 'when filled to the correct level' allow heater to operate, when the temperature is reached, finish remainder of timing sequence and then impulse (move) onto the next cam position'. This means that both functions of the timing and cam advance

motors can sometimes be interlinked.

b) The alternative to the two motor Crouzet, is the one motor version, where the one motor carries out both functions of timing and cam advance. This version can be found in a wide range of machines. Timers with one motor for both timing and cam advancement fall into two further categories: the thermostop version and the temperature plus time version.

Single motor driven timers are required to provide the same wash programmes as their two motor counterparts. The main wash motor action is again governed by an independent cam to the rear of the main cam barrel. When power is supplied to the timer's

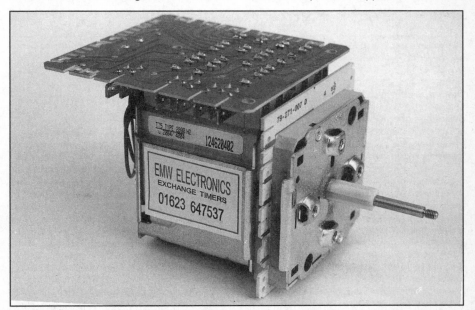

Shown is one of the easiest types of timers to replace. This type has Duotine block connectors and not single tags. Some later edge cam timers may be able to accept block connectors instead of tags. This makes timer removal and refitting a great deal easier

Timers with block connectors are much easier to fit. This timer has connections only on one side, a great improvement on its predecessor

This timer uses both block connectors and single amp tag fittings

Shown are early and late Hoover timers. The timer on the left has individual connections for each wire, whilst the later timer on the right uses block connectors

single motor, the timing cam rotates by internal gearing usually on either a 1 minute or sometimes 2 minute cycle depending on the make/type of timer. Once on every rotation a small 'pawl' located within the timing cam (so called because of its known rotation time), locates with the main cam barrel and moves it on one cam position thus giving the progression through the programme cycle.

However, some washes require the use of the heater to increase the water temperature and in some situations need a fair length of time to do so. If the programme barrel were to impulse, say, once every minute, it would move off the position that supplied power to the heater too quickly. Simply stopping the motor via a thermostat until the required temperature is attained would seem to be the answer, but in reality no wash action could take place as the timing cam upon which the wash action switching takes places would also stop. As mentioned previously,

there are two ways of avoiding these drawbacks.

Thermostop

To allow wash action to take place, i.e., rotation and counter rotation, during heating periods without impulsing the main cam barrel once every rotation of the timing cam, a solenoid (electromagnet) is used. The solenoid is normally located on the rear of the timer and when energised, pulls a metal plate or rod on to or in to the now magnetised metal core. This action mechanically lifts the timing cam pawl that would normally impulse the main cam barrel and, although the timing cam is free to rotate, the pawl is unable to locate and move the main cam barrel. The solenoid forms part of the thermostat circuit that relates to that particular wash programme temperature. When the predetermined temperature is reached, the thermostat in

series with the solenoid coil will go open circuit and sever the power to the coil. This in turn removes the mechanical retardation of the pawl which is then free to impulse the main cam barrel on to the next position. This combination of thermostats and solenoid coil is most often referred to as a 'thermostop' system for obvious reasons.

Note: *The thermostop coil may not be energised continuously throughout the wash and heat cycle. Often it is actuated by a control switch which rests on the rotating timing cam only engaging (if required) each time the pawl comes up to its impulse location point. If this did not occur, the coil*

This mechanical timer can be much smaller as motor reversal is controlled by the speed control module. Due to the 'badging' of products, timers such as these can be found in a wide range of makes and models

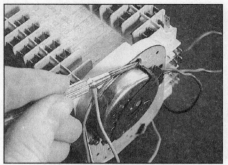

1 On many timers it is possible to renew the timer coil should a simple open circuit of the coil occur. First ease fixing clip latch

5 With care both halves will separate as shown

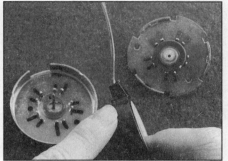

7 Ensure that the new coil is correctly fitted (identically to the original) and that the small plastic anti-reverse cam is correctly positioned prior to reassembly

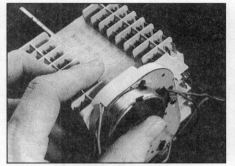

2 Slide clip sideways to free drive motor. Do not mix the motors if two are fitted as it is likely that each rotate in different directions

6 The motor coil can now be lifted free of the casing

8 When all parts are in position press both halves of casing firmly together and ensure free rotation of shaft in one direction only (as original).
Refit to timer in reverse order making sure that the securing clip is tight
Note: *Removal of the timer for this procedure is not normally required. It was removed in this instance for photographic purposes only.*

3 With motor free of rear of timer, further strip-down can commence

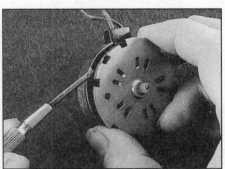

4 Carefully insert a small flat bladed screwdriver between the two halves of the motor and ease them apart at the three securing points

may overheat. Testing of the coil is a simple test for a closed circuit, testing for cam action within the timer cannot be easily verified. Confirm all other functions before suspecting internal mechanical timer failure.

Temperature plus time

This type of single motor timer does not use mechanical retardation of the timing cam pawl. The operation of this type of unit uses a fixed temperature thermostat as a reference point upon which a series of timed heat cycles will commence. A simulated wash may be as follows. A wash of 40°C is selected by the user. The inlet valve, governed by the main cam barrel selects a cold fill and commences to fill the machine with water at around 12°C, when full to the correct level, the pressure switch will transfer power from the valve to the heater, see *Water level control* chapter. Static heating will take place until 30°C is reached, i.e., no wash motor action due to the timer motor having the 30°C normally 'open' (NO) thermostat in circuit. The water temperature will soon rise and 'close' the 30°C thermostat completing the timing motor circuit. The timing motor and cam are now free to rotate and impulse the main cam barrel via the pawl. The next impulse of the main cam barrel would put into circuit the wash motor, and combined with the rotation of the timer and cam create wash rotation and counter rotation. The timer now also has a

reference temperature of 30°C. Normally water in a machine rises 2°C for every one minute of heating, therefore the next five cam positions would leave the heater in circuit thus attaining a 40°C wash temperature via a 30°C thermostat, i.e., temperature plus time. Controlling the type of fill (cold, mixed or hot only) along with a sequence of cam positions with the heater in circuit, a wide range of temperature variations can be achieved. In reality, a combination of fixed and variable thermostats is often used. The fixed thermostats giving set wash temperatures and the variable thermostats allowing the user to select their own setting if required (only on certain programmes). To avoid the selection of a temperature that is too high, the fixed thermostats usually override any incorrect setting of the variable thermostat. This usually allows the variable thermostat control over robust wash programme settings or cooler than normal selections for other programmes.

With a little imagination, it should be quite

Typical edge cam timer with thermostop system housed under rear black plastic cover

Thermostop timer with rear cover removed to expose solenoid coil and lever mechanism

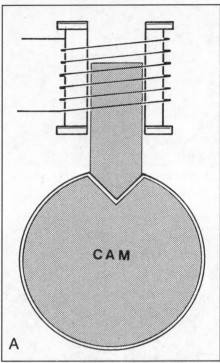

A

Diagram A. Shows the theoretical action of the thermostop, the action of which prevents cam advancement until the thermostop coil is energised, i.e., thermostat closes when correct temperature is reached

B

Diagram B. Shows thermostop coil energised i.e., thermostat closed (temperature reached) thus allowing main cam barrel to advance. Note: *The action of a thermostop system may also be the opposite of this sequence, that is to say locked when energised, free to advance when not. In such instances normally open thermostats would be used and a matching timer programme.*

clear how a programme actually works, not by some mysterious phenomenon, but by a sequence of simple movements that combine to form a complete operational programme.

How a face cam mechanical timer works

Although no longer popular with manufacturers a description of how face cam timers operate has been included in this book as it is still possible to encounter them.

Face cam timers are readily identifiable as all the connections are on the rear of the unit. This is because the face cam timer is much slimmer as only one disc is used to operate all of the switches.

The switching action is similar to that described previously, however the switches are operated by a single etched disc that allows the switches to drop in and out of the recessed positions on its face. Face cam timers are of the one motor variety with either thermostop or temperature plus time control.

The main drawbacks of mechanical timers

a) Units cannot normally be repaired. Complete unit changes are needed for internal timer faults (see *The alternative to buying a new timer* later in this section). However, on some timers, drive motor coils can be renewed if simple open circuit has occurred, see *Electrical circuit testing* chapter.

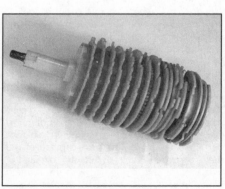

A mechanical timer cam barrel

(b) Without detailed information of the switching sequences of the faulty timer, internal faults are difficult to trace.
(c) Units can often be difficult to fit (unless a logical approach is used!).

The main benefits of mechanical timers

a) Modern timers are very reliable.
b) New units can be relatively low in cost,

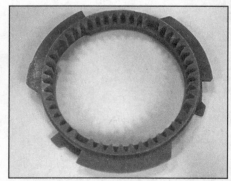

The profile of a typical cam barrel

although this differs from make to make of appliance. Having said that, the price variations for similar parts (e.g. only the cam barrel on some makes is different) between some brands can be extremely wide.

Timer replacement

It must be remembered that when a fault is suspected, it is not always the most complicated component that can cause the most trouble. If a process of elimination is used and all other parts of the machine are found to be working correctly, it is only then that the timer should be suspected. (Unless of course in the case of obvious failure, such as a burn out or damage to the timer.)

Note: *Ensure that the power is turned off and that the plug is removed from its socket at all times. Do not remove the timer from the machine at this point.*

The removal and subsequent exchange of the timer can be a long and tedious task on some machines, and should not be undertaken lightly. However, several of the more modern machines have improved the way in which the wiring harness is fitted to the timer. Multi-block connectors are now used on many machines making timer renewal much easier. Do not fall into the trap of replacing the timer because of the ease of the job. Correct diagnosis of the fault and a methodical approach to both fault finding and perhaps subsequent replacement of the timer is essential.

Do not remove any wiring as yet, but thoroughly check for any overheating of the connections to and from the timer spades (connections), i.e., if a fault is suspected in the heater switch, trace the wire from the heater to the timer. This gives the location of the heater switch and should be examined for any signs of burning or being loose. This would at least confirm your suspicions.

Having decided that the timer is at fault, a note should be taken of all of the numbers that are on the timer, together with the make, model, serial number and age of your machine.

Armed with this information, you can obtain an exact replacement. When the replacement has been obtained, visually check that they are identical, as timers will not usually be exchanged, once they have been fitted. (*You have been warned!*) Having confirmed that it is the correct replacement, and any accompanying documents have been read thoroughly, you can proceed to swap the wiring. The only way that this can be done is by placing the new timer in the same plane as the original, swapping the wires or block connectors on a one-to-one basis. Although very time consuming, this is by far the safest

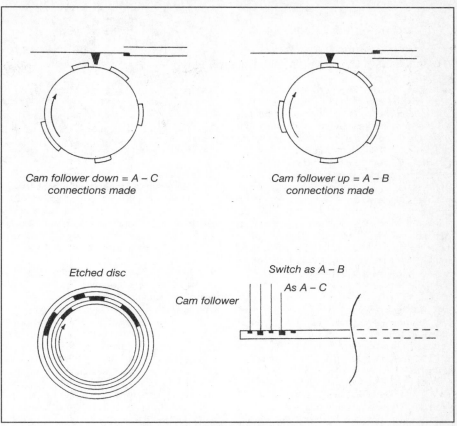

Cam follower down = A – C connections made

Cam follower up = A – B connections made

Etched disc

Cam follower

Switch as A – B

As A – C

Types of timer internal switches

method. A mistake at this point would be almost impossible to rectify without a wiring and timer diagram, therefore it is advisable to ask someone to supervise operations. When all connections have been successfully exchanged, the timer can be fitted into position ensuring that any parts that are connected to door interlocks, etc., are positioned correctly, then double check the work carried out and earth continuity. Once fitted into position, and the covers have been refitted, the power can be turned on, and a functional test programme can be implemented.

Note: *Some timers have small metal clips that join/link groups of terminals together. These generally do not come with the new timer. Ensure they are swapped from the original.*

Mechanical timer variations

The mechanical timers shown are only a small selection that can be found in today's automatic machines.

Note: *Information relating to 'Hybrid' mechanical timers appears later in this chapter.*

A manufacturer may have numerous variations of the same timer. For instance,

although your timer may be a Crouzet, your neighbour may have the same machine with seemingly the same timer in it, but in fact, it may be a variation of the same timer. These variations are identifiable by the slight difference in serial numbers shown on the timer. This illustrates the need to obtain the exact number of your timer and machine when a replacement is to be obtained.

Some machines have push buttons only to select the required programme and or a selector knob. The switch/button bank usually consists of an 'on/off' button, a series of selector buttons for various wash types and combinations, and a start button. Alternatively, a rotatable selector knob or wheel may be used in conjunction with a start button. On these types of machine, the timer is of a similar type to those described earlier and can be of the face or edge cam version.

The buttons/selector act as bypasses to unwanted sections of the programme, for instance, the selection of a pre-wash cycle will allow the timer to advance to that position missing out all the steps before and after it when the start button is pressed. Sometimes a combination of switches can be used but all act as 'impulse' or 'bypass' depending on the length and type of wash required by the user. In reality, the buttons select the required programme instead of the user manually turning the timer shaft via the programme knob.

Pre-selector/Jog-dial timers

Unlike the mechanical timers described previously where programme selection can only be made by turning clockwise, programme selection on these types of control can be made by turning the selector knob either clockwise or anti-clockwise. Such units are a combination of the mechanical timer and the electronic push button (electronic) programme selection units – a description of each is as follows.

Pre-selector controls are electro-mechanical. However, selecting a programme on this type of control does not directly turn the cam barrel of the mechanical timer as described earlier, it merely selects at which point the barrel should start from by closing a switch that corresponds to that point of the sequence. When the programme is then started the cam barrel advance motor is energized and runs until the cam barrel reaches the pre-selected point, which open circuits the selector switch and commences the programme from that point. In essence the pre-selector system turns the mechanical cam barrel to its starting position, rather than the user.

A jog-dial control uses a light-action dial to select the required programme, which is stored electronically rather than mechanically. As the dial is turned an electronic display panel indicates the various programmes and you simply stop turning the dial when the required programme appears. As the system is purely electronic the selected programme will commence as soon as the start button is pressed.

In addition to basic programme selection, both types of control will generally have additional selection switches/buttons for features such as half-load, spin speed selection etc.

As it is only the way in which the programmes are initially selected when problems occur, you will need to make reference to either the mechanical timer or computer controlled sections of this chapter.

Computer controlled machines
(electronic timers)

The functional parts of electronically controlled machines, i.e., motor, drum, pump, etc., differ little from machines with conventional selector knobs and mechanical timers. Microprocessor controlled machines are easily recognisable by their digital displays used to indicate the programme in use and buttons or touch pads for programme selection. Most have the ability to display an error code when faults occur which relate to a table in the handbook. Faults within

Unlike purely mechanical timers this programme selector knob (jog wheel) can be turned in either direction to select a programme and does not move on as the programme progresses. The programme position is displayed on a separate LCD or vacuum fluorescent display panel. Basic programme selection by turning the knob can be further enhanced by pressing various buttons on the facia of the appliance. These in turn actuate small, short-stroke switches (circled) on the PCB

microprocessor timer circuitry can be difficult to locate as the complex circuitry board components cannot be easily checked. It is best to eliminate all other possible causes of faults before suspecting either the power module or programme unit. If all the other checks prove satisfactory, then check all connections to and from the control boards (microprocessor machines generally have two – one low voltage board for the micro processor, selector panel and display, and one power board with transformer, relays and triacs to operate the mains voltage switching which the processor cannot do directly). The connections to printed circuit boards are prone to oxidisation giving poor electrical contact especially on the low voltages used by the programme boards. Check closely for poor connections.

If the fault remains after all other components have been checked and found to be satisfactory, the only option left is to change one or other (or in some instances, both) of the circuit boards. Due to the way in

which the power board functions (see following paragraph), it is most likely to be a failure in this circuitry or its components at fault. Do not touch the processor board's components at all as they are sensitive to static electricity and are easily damaged by careless handling. The power boards are more robust but care must still be exercised when handling them.

The power board is generally much bulkier than the programme board and may house a large transformer to drop the voltage to the processor. Electronic circuit faults occur more often with power boards as the mains switching operating the pump, heater, etc., is switched mechanically by relays or electronically by triacs operated by the lower voltage supplied from the programme board, i.e., processors themselves cannot directly switch mains power and use mechanical relays or triacs. Try to isolate if a mechanical fault is suspected (e.g. heater not receiving power, maybe a sticking/faulty relay, etc.)

Items that short circuit and blow fuses may

Like many such machines this computer controlled appliance has a wide range of options

also damage their respective control relay or triac. For instance, a simple fault such as the live supply to the outlet pump breaking loose during a spin cycle and touching the earthed metal shell of the machine would result in a direct short circuit. Such a fault on a machine with a mechanical timer would blow the appliance fuse in the socket and rectification would be straightforward. However, the same fault on a microprocessor controlled machine is likely to damage the components of the circuit board used to switch the pump supply, resulting in a much more expensive repair.

The programme board may also be referred to as the display board or module. It differs from the power module in that it is much slimmer (but often much wider) than the power board and lacks the larger components such as relays, transformers, etc. It is usually mounted behind the front facia of the machine although variations in positioning will be found between manufacturers and models within each range.

Obtaining individual board components from the machine manufacturers is not possible as only complete boards/modules are supplied as spares. The control micro-processor is normally located within the circuitry of the board but may, on some machines, be included within the power board circuitry. As explained earlier, the microprocessor takes the place of the cam barrel used in mechanical timers. The mechanical action of the cam barrel of physically switching components on or off is now carried out electronically by the solid state processor, i.e., no moving parts (although moving part relays may be required elsewhere), and the timing of each sequence is governed by a quartz clock chip, similar to that used in watches, within the board's circuitry.

The way in which the processor operates is very similar to the cam barrel of the mechanical timer in that it is programmed with unalterable predetermined functions, i.e., steps. The main difference is that the amount of steps can be (and usually are) much greater and the response from external sources 'feedback' can be utilised to monitor the processes being carried out, for instance to check the time of fill automatically, power consumption of motor, etc. Like the mechanical barrel, a predetermined set of functions are stored within the main chip in a similar way to the individual cam positions of the mechanical timer. The main difference being that a greater amount of 'positions' can be stored and accessed in any order unlike the fixed sequence of the mechanical version. The way in which a full wash programme is compiled is by electronically overriding or omitting the sequences not required. In this way an extremely variable and flexible wash programme can be built up with information obtained from the various wash selection buttons operated by the user and combined with fixed sequences to suit the type of wash load.

The various wash options finally selected

This large PCB shows damage caused by the short circuit of a connected component which damaged the printed circuit board track. Repair is not a matter of replacing the track as it is more than likely that damage has also occurred to components mounted on the board. Leave repairs such as this to specialised reconditioning/repair companies, or obtain a new replacement

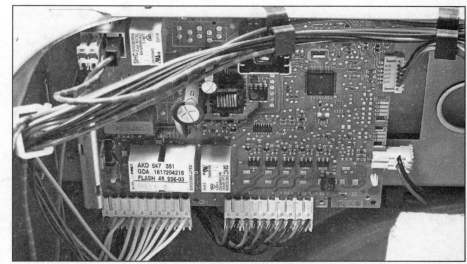

This large PCB has a series of edge connectors which are keyed to prevent incorrect positioning. However, as a precaution it is wise to mark all connections before removal as not all manufacturers key connections

A typical LCD panel with short-stroke selector buttons to the left and bottom of the display. Top right is where the larger On/Off button is positioned

This large PCB can be found on a wide range of machines in the Indesit and Ariston range. It is located on the base of the appliance and housed in a large plastic support. The one board is designed to fit a wide range of makes and models. This is done by inserting an EEPROM chip into a special socket during manufacture which configures the board to work in that particular model. The EEPROM can be seen just slightly to the upper left of the large rectangular processor chip. Many of the faults with this board are caused by a malfunction in this small chip which can be obtained as a spare part for a fraction of the cost of a whole new board. The EEPROM can be replaced easily as it is a plug-in device and does not require soldering. However, it is essential that the correct chip is obtained and fitted the correct way around (it has a location mark but is not keyed). Take static precaution when handling all such components and printed circuit boards

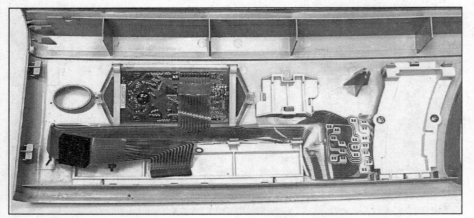

Ribbon cable is often used to connect the various electronic components

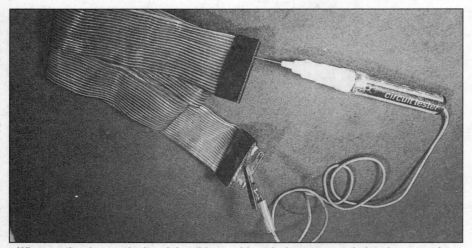

When testing for continuity of the ribbon cable only, insert a metal plate in one end to make contact with all connections as shown. Use a low voltage continuity tester to confirm continuity of each wire. Ensure the cable is moved during the test so as not to miss an intermittent fault

by the user and then held in volatile memory, i.e., held short term only for as long as the machine is switched on, but will be lost when turned off.

Note: *Some degree of memory retention is incorporated (approx 5 to 10 seconds) and varies from make to make. Most machines also have a set sequence of wash programmes plus the ability to store several user defined variations in a volatile memory that will only blank if the machine is unplugged for a long period of time.*

Faults within the components or circuitry of the board are extremely difficult to trace and as with the power board, only complete units are supplied by the manufacturer. Before contemplating a board fault, ensure all other components within the machine are satisfactory and that all connections to and from the printed circuit boards are in good condition and are firmly pushed into place. Check thoroughly all connections, wiring and all protective covers. With the machine isolated, look closely at all connections that carry mains voltage when in use, as loose connections can cause overheating and interference which can affect the processor chips. Include all earth path connections in the wiring checks and renew any that are loose, have cracked covers or show signs of damage, for example, overheating. Do not forget to include the plug connections.

With a persistent or unusual fault, e.g., intermittent operation, random displays, working for short periods and then blanking memory, etc., check the condition of the supply socket. If a poor connection exists between any pin of the plug and its supply connection, again interference will be present which may corrupt the processor, see *Basics – electrical*. Renew if suspect.

A faulty suppression unit may also be the cause of such random and difficult to trace faults. Ensure the unit is securely earthed, see *Suppressors* chapter.

With the need to prevent interference from particular components within the machine, items such as the main wash motor, may have small suppression units called chokes, see *Suppressors* chapter, which prevent any interference being transmitted along the wiring of the machine. Ensure that any chokes fitted within the machine are secure and in good condition (e.g., check continuity). If all the aforementioned checks prove satisfactory, then it is most likely that the processor chip is corrupted or the board has a fault within its circuitry. Such faults will require a replacement unit. Carefully note all connections to and from the unit and keeping in mind the paragraph regarding handling of the unit, remove it from the machine. Inspect it closely for dirt or debris which may be affecting the circuit or its components. If any dirt is present, it should be blown free (do not use metal items such as screwdrivers).

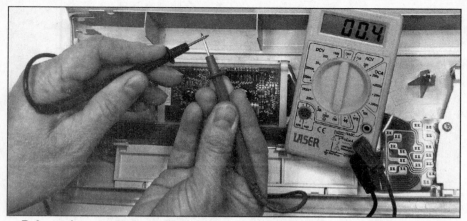

Before using your meter to check for low resistances – such as continuity testing a ribbon cable connection – touch the test leads firmly together and note the reading obtained, i.e. the reading of just the test leads (in this instance 0.4Ω). Deducting this reading from the reading obtained when checking for continuity will give the resistance of the item being tested

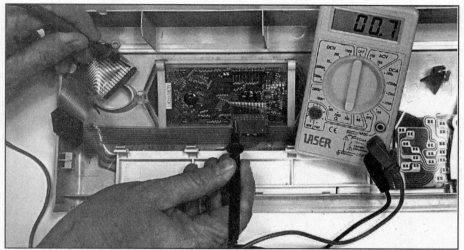

This type of ribbon cable can be tested by placing the test probes of the meter on the open connections immediately behind each connector block. In this instance a reading of 0.7Ω is shown, but the original reading of the leads on their own (0.4Ω) must be deducted from this figure to obtain the true reading of the cable itself (0.3Ω in this instance). When testing the continuity of electrical connections such as this, as low a reading as possible is required, but the quality/accuracy of your test meter will have a bearing on this. An open circuit is an obvious problem however, high resistances in cables and connections are also a problem especially on low-voltage connections within electronically controlled machines

Check the board for cracks or possible moisture damage due to faulty covers, etc. Before finally accepting that a new unit is needed, it would be wise to inspect the printed circuit board's soldered connections to verify that they are sound. Loose or poor connections (called dry joints) can often be easily rectified and if all these checks prove negative, a new unit will be necessary. Take care to fit the unit correctly on all its mounts and ensure all covers and connections are sound. Take particular care to avoid direct contact with the components of the unit.

Do not touch the processor board's components at all as they are sensitive to static electricity and are easily damaged by careless handling. The power boards are more robust but care must still be exercised when handling them.

Note: *All checks must be carried out with the machine isolated in the usual manner, taps off, plug out! Under no circumstances should you try to test the processor board even with a low 9 volt or similar tester because the microprocessor chip can easily be damaged. Use of the 1.5 volt tester shown in the photograph is recommended for continuity testing of the wiring between the module units. Try to leave the block connectors in*

place and using the probes of the tester, check for continuity between exposed printed circuit points close to the connector blocks. This will test both the wiring between the modules (usually ribbon cable) and the connection to the printed circuit board.

On computer-controlled machines faults that develop may be indicated by a code which is displayed on the front of the machine. Codes differ from machine to machine so refer to your handbook to ascertain the meaning of each code. For a range of popular fault codes refer to Chapter 26 – *Fault error and configuration codes.*

The alternative to buying a new timer

The cost of a new programme control (timer) unit can often be extremely high and this in turn often leads to the appliance being considered not worth repair. The other aspect of renewing the whole unit no matter what the fault is that of the sheer waste of materials when the old unit is simply thrown away. However, there is now an alternative to this expensive and wasteful practice, that of reconditioning. This is an interesting and welcome development not only in the significant reduction in the cost when compared with the cost of the new item but also in the 'green' aspect of recycling components and materials. If you choose the right company there are also other important benefits such as:
● Access to technical staff to help decide if it is a timer fault.
● The facility to return the unit if it turns out that it was not the problem.

Note: *This can even apply to timers that have been fitted and used for a short period as long as they are not damaged (a handling charge will normally be made for this service).*

● The ability to send your old unit for testing.
● All items supplied are thoroughly tested and guaranteed.
● A wide range of programmers/timers, all of which are available by mail order.

To avoid the problems that can so easily occur in removing the old faulty unit and waiting for the replacement to arrive, exchange reconditioned parts are supplied to you in advance. This allows you to do two very important things.
1 Ensure that you have obtained the correct part by comparing it with the original.
2 Fit the reconditioned unit to your machine on a one for one basis and return the old faulty unit back to the supplier when the job is successfully completed.

In addition to programmers/timers a wide

range of reconditioned speed control modules can also be obtained on an exchange basis. For further details see Chapters *Motors (Speed Control)* and *Buying spare parts*.

Hybrid electro-mechanical timers

Many modern machines have timer units that are a combination of electronic and mechanical programme control. Such units are often referred to as 'Hybrid' timers. Depending on the manufacturer, the timer, and the appliance, the combination may be one of two variations:

a) A simple combination of electronic speed control circuitry and mechanical timer (this may be one complete unit or made up of two separate units with block connections).

b) A combination of microprocessor and mechanical control in one unit.

Many of the major manufacturers such as Hoover, Hotpoint and Whirlpool to name only three, currently use this type of programme control. The hybrid is a middle option between the purely mechanical selection of programmes and fully computer controlled selection. When fault-finding, reference to both types of programme control mentioned previously will be required. A point to note is that fault-finding on machines with these types of control can be extremely easy. With both the speed control module and timer/programmer combined into one unit, fault-finding is a simple process of elimination. For instance if the drum fails to rotate and the belt is intact, motor continuity checks are all OK and the wiring to the motor from the hybrid timer checks out, then it's the timer at fault and needs replacing. Fault finding in other instances can be reduced to simple checking of components and wiring.

Fuzzy Logic

With the availability of microprocessor control systems, an extremely wide range of logic control options became available. However, in recent times another new option has emerged, that of Fuzzy Logic. An introduction to this relatively new form of processing is given in the chapter *Fuzzy Logic*.

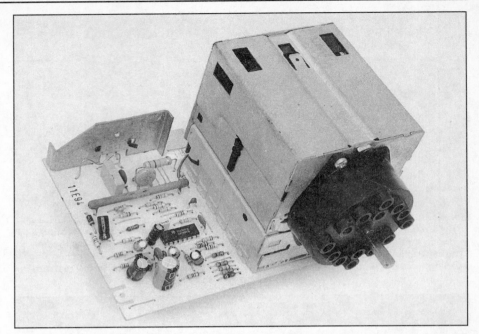

These two timers combine both mechanical programme and electronic speed control in one unit. Combined units such as these are often referred to as 'Hybrid' timers

Chapter 25
Fuzzy Logic

Although at present only a few manufacturers are currently using this technique of programme control it is envisaged that it will gain in popularity and become common place. This brief overview of Fuzzy Logic has been included to provide the reader with an insight into this latest technical innovation. It is not an in-depth study of this new science, rather an interesting insight at what the future holds. Reading this chapter should help complete your knowledge and understanding of machines past, present and future.

Most of today's front loading washing machines either mechanically or computer controlled, are based on simple logic. For instance, take the action of a fixed thermostat, it is either open or closed. The timer simply waits for the signal to proceed to the next step in the predetermined wash programme. As humans we know that the water being heated is not simply the right or wrong temperature (cold or hot) but warm, fairly warm, etc. When we wash clothes by hand we do not simply take the temperature of the water into consideration, we access a wide range of both precise and imprecise information such as – what type of material it is, the degree of soiling, what type of soiling is (mud, grease, etc.). All of these factors and more ultimately affect the way the garment is eventually cleaned, how warm and how much water, how much detergent will be required for the level and type of soiling and how much rinsing, etc. Unfortunately a thermostat cannot detect this range of imprecise approximations and the control unit can only respond to precise logical inputs.

However, with a combination of microprocessor control, additional sensors and a new way of programming, the purely logical approach may not be with us for much longer. This new way of looking at the washing process is called Fuzzy Logic and some makes and models already have varying degrees of this type of control system. The essence of Fuzzy Logic is to produce a machine that can react and adapt the wash process as a human would. To look at a wide range of variables and to make informed decisions based on all of the available information both precise and imprecise. To do this, additional sensors are required to supply the processor with the information for the decision process. The wash programme is therefore not just a series of predetermined sequences it has the ability to respond and react to information it receives, in essence Fuzzy Logic thinks the problem through and arrives at a solution based upon the whole range of both precise and imprecise information. In other words it has the ability to mimic the way we ourselves would react.

Some of the additional information the processor requires can be gained from existing controls such as water level switches and motor tacho generators. However, other sensors not normally associated with washing machines will be required to assist in the decision making process. The most common of these sensors is the optical sensor. This type of sensor is used to detect the turbidity (cloudiness) of the water passing through the sensor.

Opposed mode optical sensing is the most popular system used for this purpose and is often referred to as direct scanning. In simple terms this means that a light source and light sensitive receiver are positioned opposite each other and the wash water is allowed to pass between them – see diagram. The intensity of light reaching the receiver is dependent on how much soiling is in suspension in the water passing between the two points. This type of sensor can be used to provide information on the level and type of soiling. The way this can be done is as follows. The level of soiling on the wash load can be determined by how transparent (or not) the known volume of water within the tub becomes (a numerical value can be applied to this). What type of soiling is on the wash load can be ascertained by how long it takes to reach the transparency saturation value. Mud and other water-soluble soiling will reach its maximum saturation level fairly quickly whereas grease and other non-soluble soiling will take longer. In this way a relatively simple optical sensor can tell the programme two important factors.

The type of material can be gained by the use of more sensitive water level detection systems. For instance, cotton absorbs water and synthetic materials do not. When a machine fills and the level switch operates, a load of cottons will proceed to soak up some of the water and the level switch will reset to compensate for this loss (this happens on a normal machine as well). However, the second actuation of the level sensing device in this instance also informs the Fuzzy Logic system that the load is absorbent and is therefore cotton. The weight of the load can be

determined by spinning the loaded drum prior to commencing the wash. The energy taken to rotate the drum correlates to the weight of the load it contains and again this information can be used by the Fuzzy Logic programme. Quite simply a heavy load takes more energy to rotate it and the speed control module pulses the control circuit faster to compensate.

Note: *An important point to remember is that these sensor inputs are not a one-off event, they are continuously monitored and if circumstances/sensor output changes, then so will the programme.*

If the machine has the ability to dispense its own detergent then the exact amount required for that specific load can be dispensed.

The number of rinses can also be altered (increased or decreased) by optically sensing the rinse water.

Even the spin cycle can be fuzzy controlled and a maximum spin speed to match the load (or imbalance) applied at the end wash cycle.

Note: *The spin speed would be applied (or omitted) directly. With Fuzzy Logic the spin would not be the result of several efforts to spin as described in out of balance sensing in the Motors chapter.*

The application of this type of technology can give rise to both financial and ecological savings. The time when you can simply put your clothes in the machine and let it decide exactly how to wash, rinse, spin and dry them is not too far away.

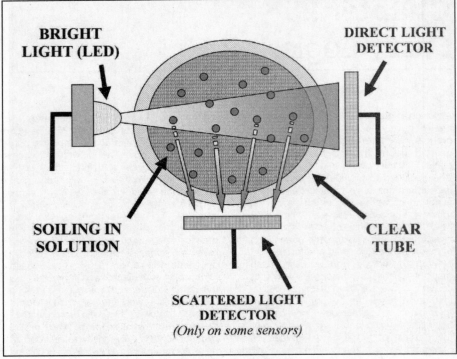

A turbidity sensor unit

Note: *Fuzzy Logic is not restricted to washing machines in fact it has been around in industry for several years and applications range from industrial processes to anti-lock braking systems. Only recently has it emerged on the domestic appliance front and can now be found in microwave ovens, domestic vacuum cleaners, cameras and many other mass market items. This trend is set to continue.*

A water inlet valve with a flow-control sensor

Electronic (analogue) water level sensors can detect even the slightest changes in water level. When combined with 'Fuzzy Logic' programme routines and circuitry the appliance can in effect think for itself

Chapter 26
Fault, error and configuration codes

Fault and error codes

Many washing machines have the ability to detect problems that affect the correct functioning of the appliance. When a problem is detected the appliance will abort the selected programme and display an error code which relates to the specific problem detected. Depending on the make, model and style of the appliance there are two ways in which error code will be displayed:

● Numeric (1, 2, 3 etc.) or more commonly, alphanumeric (E1, E2, E3 etc.) codes displayed by an LCD or LED panel on the front of the appliance.

● Where an LED or LCD display is not present on the front of the machine the error/fault code may be displayed by the flashing of a single light or a specific sequence of lights on the machine's facia.

The ability to assess and display a fault may appear to be an extremely complicated task to perform. However, as the appliance knows exactly where it is in the programme and exactly what is expected at that point (i.e. fill to a level, heat to a set temperature, rotate the drum) if the required action (i.e. pressure switch, thermostat/thermistor, tacho coil produce the required signal) is not detected then a fault must have occurred.

This in-built automated fault detection system is in essence the same as that described in Chapter 10 which can be used on appliances that can display error codes, and those that cannot.

The ability to indicate what the problem may be could be seen as a major benefit but for one major flaw – most if not all manufacturers of appliances choose not to disclose what the codes relate to other than the simple ones such are the taps turned on, is door closed? etc. The information is generally restricted to their own service network or appointed agents leaving the independent repair sector in the dark as much

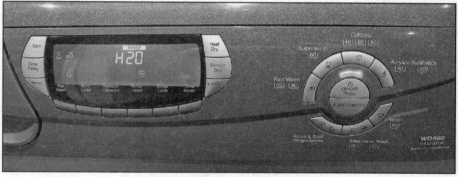

A typical error code display

as the customer when it comes to translating the fault code displayed. This apparently somewhat restrictive practice does not mean that anyone other than a manufacturer's engineer can diagnose faults in the product, but it does mean that you will need to treat the appliance as though it did not have the self-diagnosis feature. The information throughout this book has been produced to help those interested in appliance repair understand the practicality, function and technical depth to assist fault location and, if deemed necessary, repair of equipment whatever type is encountered.

The displaying of an error code is not a definitive fault-finding event and knowledge and understanding of the appliance, its correct installation and use will still be required to correctly identify the problem. Although helpful, at times they are not essential.

The basic range of faults that are detected differs little between the whole range of makes and models. Unfortunately, and for reasons known only to themselves, each manufacturer chooses to use a different coding system which may even differ between the models they produce!

The knowledge within this publication should help you diagnose faults without knowing exactly what a specific fault code means.

Although it is not possible to provide a definitive list of manufacturers' fault codes the following list has been produced to illustrate the diversity of systems, while at the same time showing the similarity of what they relate to. Surely this is an area where an industry standard code would be useful?

As mentioned, the following fault code list should not be viewed as definitive as it merely serves as a general guide to what may be found.

If your particular make, model or code display is not shown then you can still use the information gained from other areas of the manual to assist you in your fault-finding process. Alternatively, you may find additional information relating to specific makes and models error codes by using an internet search or by going to **www.ukwhitegoods.co.uk** which is an extremely detailed site for both users and independent service personnel.

Configuration codes

Many of the computer-controlled appliances (especially those in the Electrolux group – Electrolux, Zanussi, AEG, Tricity, and many more) not only possess the ability to self diagnose and display fault codes, but they also possess the ability to retain the information even after the appliance has been switched off and a repair carried out. This means that the appliance will not work until

This Hotpoint display panel indicates
1 *Door locked icon;* 2 *Water inlet problem icon;* 3 *Fault code H20 (water inlet fault)*

the stored error/fault message is cleared from its memory. The term for the clearing of such retained memory conditions is often referred to as re-configuring the control system, which is a little like pressing the Ctrl+Alt+Delete keys on your computer to create a hard break and clear the system ready for a re-boot back into Windows.

Configuration codes are also similar to the inputs required to set a digital watch, set up your video recorder, configuring a computer's dip switches or jumpers etc. These are all tasks that members of the public and engineers carry out all the time – once they are provided with the relevant information that is.

If they cannot carry out the required process themselves then instructional information is normally provided by the manufacturer of the product so that someone else can – be they the manufacturer's service personnel or a competent person selected by the customer who can read and apply the relevant information.

However, although manufacturers of other household equipment (computers, televisions, etc. often referred to as 'brown goods') readily provide such information, most if not all 'white goods' manufacturers choose not to do so. This leaves the customer and the independent service provider they may have chosen at a disadvantage, even after they have successfully identified and corrected the original problem. Without the simple configuration code the appliance will continue to display the original error and will remain unusable.

Retaining this vital piece of information means that you are effectively forced into calling out their own service personnel (or franchised agent) to carry out the work. Even when successfully repaired by you or an independent service provider you may still require a visit to simply re-set the control circuit memory and be charged a service visit. This restriction of vital information (yet not essential for the correct functioning of the appliance) means that you are effectively tied into their service system and range of fixed charges.

It can be viewed that the restriction of information in this way (especially to the independent repairers) poses a breach of your rights as a consumer to choose who repairs your machine. Although I am totally in favour of getting rid of the 'Cowboy' repairers that plague this trade I am equally in favour of a customer's right to choose one if they so wish. It could be considered by some, that not all 'cowboys' reside in the independent sector, as many may like us to think.

An apparent restrictive practice such as this which disadvantages the customer and the decent independent repairers alike is not the way to improve the image and operation of the appliance service industry. Such restriction of information is similar to the restrictive practices once used by other large businesses and organisations (but now outlawed). However, it took a very long time and pressure for a change to be implemented and I do not think that the general public or their guardians such as Trading Standards, Consumer Rights etc. even know that such a practice exists.

There is no easy way to get around this particular problem as the configuration codes and the way they are inputted into the various appliances differ between makes, models and variants.

However, searching the internet for specific information such as configuration codes can often uncover the required details – use your favourite search engine and a good website starting point would be – **www.ukwhitegoods.co.uk**.

Many modern machines have access panels like the one shown here, which allow service engineers to access fault codes and instigate test routines. Such equipment is expensive and more often than not restricted to use by their own service personnel
Note: *Although very useful such instruments are not essential for the correct diagnosis and rectification of a large percentage of faults.*

The test unit is plugged into the access point and can carry out diagnostic and test routines directly, or be connected to a suitable PC to enable modification to programme routines within the appliance's electronics

When the unit is correctly installed an automatic test routine can be selected. However, reference to the manufacturer's technical data will be required to interpret the results

Typical error codes

Typical AEG codes – German-made models 1997 on – (for Italian-made models refer to the Zanussi code list):

C1	No filling action/ too slow a fill
C2	No pump action/too slow pump output
C3	Aqua control activated, either overfill or leak in base or open or short circuit pump
C7	Not heating – may also be related to inlet valve failing to fully close
C8	NTC (thermistor fault)
C9	No tacho pulses (faulty) or no motor action
CA	Motor triac short circuit on PCB
CD	Door interlock fault
CE	Water distributor fault – some models have a small motor in the dispenser to select the required fill compartment which operates a microswitch inside the dispenser. If the switch is not triggered within two minutes, then the code is displayed, i.e. no movement of distributor
CF	EEPROM fault on PCB

Many of the above faults may remain stored in the processor even if the appliance has been turned off and the fault corrected. Running a test programme should clear the processor memory.

Typical Bosch Siemens codes

OE	Not draining – water not pumping out
IE	Not filling
DE	Door open or not locked
UE	Out of balance load
SE	No motor
CE	Current error – short circuit motor or triac on PCB
LE	Lock error – door interlock/wiring fault
FE	Overfill
TE	Temperature error – thermistor or heating element fault
PE	Pressure switch fault

Typical Brandt codes – (German-made models):

01	Slow fill/no fill
02	Drain circuit fault
03	Heater circuit fault
04	Short circuit triac
05	Temperature control circuit NTC thermistor
06	Motor tacho fault – Note, tacho may be OK but No motor action
07	Door interlock/latch fault
08	Unknown
09	Programme selector fault
10	Overfill detected
11	Heater circuit fault
12	Door latch fault
13	Incorrect spin speed
18	Incorrect mains frequency

Typical Hoover/Candy codes – current fault codes

Early Hoover (New Wave models)

E1	Timed out on fill, heat, or drain
E2	Open circuit thermistor
E4	Motor current exceeded
E5	Motor tacho fault
E7	Motor windings open circuit

Typical Hoover and Candy (2000 onwards)
These codes may apply to the flashing of an LED or an alphanumeric LCD display

0	Module fault
1	Door interlock/door switch
2	Filling time-out or solenoid valve etc.
3	Pump time-out – exceeded three minutes
4	Overfill (i.e. blocked air chamber/faulty water inlet valve)
5	NTC/heating element fault
6	Module fault
7	Motor jammed/drum shaft jammed/tacho generator fault
8	No motor action
9	Faulty triac on main board
11	Faulty dryer board or wiring (Interact models)
12	No signal between module's PCBs and wiring harness (Interact models)
13	Alternative to 12 above (Interact models)

Typical Hoover – alphanumeric codes

E0	Severe error on mother board
E1	Door interlock faulty or open circuit
E2	Water inlet problem, 3.5-minute time out on fill
E3	Water drain problem 3-minute time out
E4	Anti-flood device activated
E5	NTC temp probe faulty or open circuit
E6	Alternative to E0 (Severe error on mother board)
E7/E8	Motor or drum jammed, motor tacho faulty
E9	Faulty triac on mother board
EA	Processor did not encounter the expected component resistance as it advanced through the programme
EB	Faulty electronic drying module (W/Ds only)
EC	Faulty signal between PCBs
ED	Alternative to above EC

Typical Hotpoint/Creda codes

E10	No/slow cold fill – check taps are on/kinked fill hose
E11	No/slow hot fill – check taps are on/kinked fill hose
E12	No/slow mixed fill – check taps are on
E13	Check the water supply, inlet valve and hot and cold hoses
E14	Heating problem – check element and NTC thermistor
E15	Water draining problem/flood protection activated – check drain is fitted to recommended minimum height and the hose and fitment are free from blockages
E16	Too high a water level detected – turn off taps and check for inlet valve sticking open
E17	Door not closed – open and re-close door correctly
E20/1	Incorrect thermistor resistance detected (may occur if ambient temperature is below zero)
E30/31	Motor problem detected – check tacho, motor brushes etc.
E40	Water level below protection level during the heating sequence
E41	Incorrect water level detected
E50/51	Settings error i.e. language and wash programme have saved – this means the system will run with default conditions 1,000rpm max. and English language

Typical Indesit codes – these may apply to the flashing of an LED or an alphanumeric LCD display:

F01	Short circuit-motor triac
F02	Motor jammed or tacho coil/magnet problem
F03	Temperature probe o/c or s/c (open circuit or short circuit)
F04	Incorrect low water level detection
F05	Incorrect high water level detection
F06	Programme selector control error
F07	Heater relay stuck
F08	Heater relay cannot be activated
F09	Incompatible EEPROM
F10	Pressure switch not sensing correctly
F11	Drain pump problem
F12	Failure of LCD Display module and main module not communicating
E40	Door interlock problem

Typical LG codes:

IE 1	No fill or slow fill
OE	No fill even after 10 minutes
TE	Temperature control circuit/thermistor problem
CE	Over current detected from a component, i.e. short circuit
LE	Motor problem
PE	Pressure switch problem
DE	Door interlock failing to operate
UE	Unbalance error – out of balance load detected

Typical old Servis Quartz codes:

F1	Water temperature fault
F2	No/slow filling – check taps are on/kinked fill hose
F3	No/slow draining
F4	Motor problem – too fast, too slow or not at all due to worn carbon brushes or tacho coil fault
F5	Heating problem – check element for continuity

Typical Whirlpool codes:

FH	No water inlet
FA	Aquastop activated
FP	Drain problem
F05	NTC problem
F06	Tacho coil problem (no motor action detected)
F07	Triac short circuit detection (motor control module)
F09	Overfill
F10	Motor control PCB failure
F11	Communication error (control unit)
F13	Dispenser circuit error
F14	EEPROM failure (control unit)
F15	Motor control unit error
F16+F18+F20+F21+F22	Control unit failure
FDL	Door lock error
FDU	Door unlock error

Typical Samsung codes:

E1	Water supply – not filling in allocated time – check water supply
E2	Water drain – not emptying in allocated time – check pump and hoses for blockage etc.
E3	Overfill – water level too high – check for blocked pressure system
E4	Out of balance load detected – remove/rearrange clothing
E5	Water heating – water temp rising/falling too quickly – check thermistor
E6	As E5 above
E7	Pressure switch – abnormal water frequency. Pump may drain for up to three minutes – check pressure system
E8	Abnormal water temperature – temperature too high on low temp washes – check thermistor
E9	Water leak – occurs when water level reduces without draining taking place during the wash cycle i.e. machine leaking
EA	No tacho coil signal – check tacho circuit
EB	Triac short circuit detected – speed-control PCB fault
EC	Thermistor problem – component or wiring
ED	Door open – open and re-close door correctly

All error codes can be cleared by powering down the machine

Typical Zanussi codes:

E11	Fill problem
E13	Water level problem
E21	Draining problem
E23	Drain pump triac problem
E24	Problem with pump triac detection on main PCB
E31	Incorrect level detection – pressure switch, wiring or main PCB problem
E32	Similar to E31 above
E33	Inconsistency between level switch and anti-boil protection switch
E34	Similar to E33 above
E35	Overfill
E36	Problem with detection circuit for anti-boiling pressure switch – main PCB fault
E37	Similar to E36 above
E38	Pressure system blocked
E39	Main PCB fault
E3A	Main PCB heater relay faulty
E41	Door interlocking problem
E42	Similar to E41 above – try re-closing door
E43	Interlock triac on main PCB faulty
E44	Problem with interlock detection circuit on main PCB
E45	Similar to E44 above
E52	No tacho coil signals
E57	Three-phase motor inverter circuit is drawing too much current
E58	Motor drawing too much current
E59	No tacho signal for more than three seconds
E5A	Inverter heat sink too hot – may be due to ambient conditions – leave to cool and re-try
E5B	Low input voltage possible inverter PCB fault or mains too low
E5C	High input voltage possible inverter PCB fault or mains too high
E5D	Corrupted/no signals between module PCBs – faulty wiring, PCBs, main board
E5E	Corrupted/no signals between inverter and main board
E5F	Inverter PCB fails to start motor
E61	No/low heating problem – check element and NTC thermistor, main PCB
E62	Overheating problem – check thermistor and main PCB
E66	Heater relay on main PCB faulty
E71	Detection circuit on main PCB for thermistor fault
E74	Similar to E71 above – check position of thermistor
E82	Programme selection error – reselect programme
E83	Similar to E82 above
E85	Pump triac detection circuit on main PCB faulty
E91	Corrupted/no signals between main board and display board
E92	Similar to above if incompatible parts fitted
E93	Main board configuration problem
E94	Similar to E93 above
E95	Corrupt/no signals between microprocessor and EEPROM on main board
E97	Similar to three previous codes
EB1	Power supply outside fixed parameters
EB2	Power supply voltage too high
EB3	Power supply voltage too low
EBE	Lack of parity between sensing circuit and safety relay
EBF	Faulty safety sensing system
EC1	Faulty inlet valve – flow meter working when valve should be closed – faulty inlet valve
EC2	Parameters of turbidity sensor out of specified range – check sensor (clean)
EF1	Slow draining – check filter, drain hoses and connections

Chapter 27
Low insulation

What is low insulation?

Low insulation is best described as a slight leak to earth of electricity from the wiring of one or more of the components or wiring in an earthed appliance. If very slight, this will not harm the appliance but is an indication of faults to come and should be corrected immediately for safety reasons. A gradual breakdown of the insulating properties of a normally electrically leak proof system which will eventually result in a short circuit to earth if the root cause is left unattended.

How is it caused?

This can be caused by normal wear and tear over a long period, resulting in a breakdown of the insulating coating on wiring, motor windings, heater elements, etc. Such a breakdown of insulation may not result in a failure of the part at this point and the appliance may still function as normal. However, this is no excuse to ignore low insulation as failure to trace and rectify it is foolhardy and in the long run can be costly in both money terms, and above all safety. Faults such as leaking/weeping shaft seals can give rise to water penetrating the motor windings and resulting in low insulation. If not corrected, this could lead to a complete failure of the motor, or worse. A simple

renewal of the shaft seal and careful cleaning and drying of the T.O.C. and windings may be all that is needed to save money and improve safety for all concerned. It is important not to compromise on safety by ignoring such symptoms.

How can it be detected?

When a service engineer tests for low insulation, he will use an instrument called a Megger/low insulation tester. The law requires repair engineers to test for low insulation, and there is a low minimum allowable level and the following tests should be made by commercial repair engineers.

Earth continuity

Between the earth pin on the plug and all earth connection points within the appliance, the maximum resistance should be 1 ohm, i.e., very low resistance, a perfect connection.

Insulation test

With the appliance turned on, but unplugged, test between the live and neutral pins joined at the plug and the earth pin on the plug. The minimum resistance should be 2 megohm (2 million ohms), ideally the reading should be much higher than this minimum figure, i.e. very high resistance, no discernible

connection at all. Repeat this test at various programme settings.

In practice one test lead of the meter should be connected to both the live and neutral and the other to the earth pin. This avoids the possibility of inadvertently passing the high test voltage through the normal live-neutral circuit and simultaneously tests both supply conductors.

Note: *For best practice connect the red lead to the earth pin and use the black lead to bond (join) the live and neutral pins.*

Testing of individual components can be carried out easily by removing connections to the suspect item and connecting one lead to one of the free terminals and one to the earth terminal and testing, minimum resistance should be 2 megohm, then repeat the test using the other connection.

Note: *Items controlled by double pole relays will also need to be tested in this way.*

These tests are carried out using a meter designed to test insulation by applying a high voltage (500V DC) at a very low current for safety to test the insulation quality of the part to which it is connected. It is an unfortunate fact that many engineers do not possess such a device, and therefore do not check for low insulation. This does not mean that you should not!

A professional meter to test for low insulation would cost upwards of two

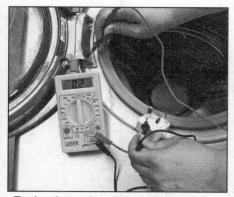

Testing the earth path from the plug pin to the metal door hinge fixing gave a reading of 0.2Ω. Prior to testing the earth path test leads of the meter were touched together to find the resistance of the test leads which, in this instance, was 0.07Ω. This figure was then deducted from the combined reading (leads and earth path) indicating the earth-only reading to be 0.13Ω and therefore within the required limits

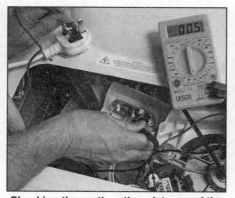

Checking the earth path resistance of the heater on a Hotpoint machine. Remember to deduct the reading taken of the leads joined together to obtain the reading of just the earth path

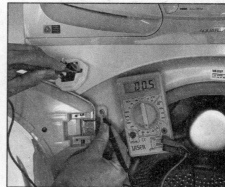

The door hinge securing screw on this Hotpoint machine was chosen to check the earth continuity of the shell of the appliance. Remember to deduct the reading taken of the leads joined together to obtain the reading of just the earth path

Low insulation flowchart

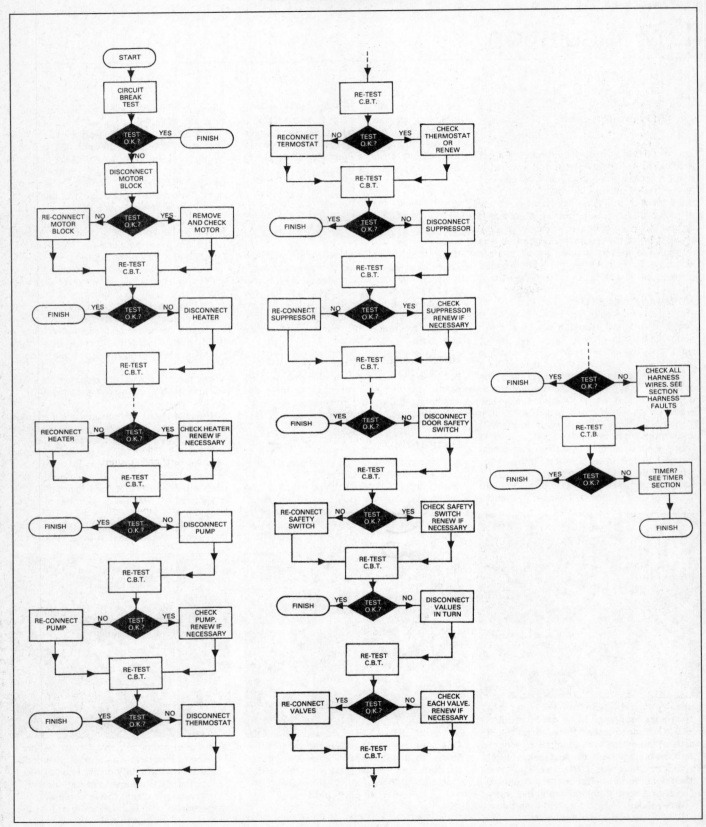

hundred pounds and is therefore out of the reach of most DIY enthusiasts. However, low priced insulation test meters may be found in mail order outlets such as Maplin.

An alternative (rather than no test at all) is to utilise an in line circuit breaker (see *Low insulation flowchart*). The appliance is plugged into the circuit breaker, which is then plugged into the socket, unless an RCD already protects the circuit or socket. As mentioned in *Basics – electrical*, the purpose of the device is to detect low insulation or leakage to earth and turn off the power to the appliance. Although this is not the ideal way of testing for low insulation, it will help in locating more severe cases of it (well below the 2 megohm level) and provide additional safety for the appliance and its user.

It is wise to test RCD systems on a regular basis to ensure they function correctly and are fully operational when needed. Follow the instructions shown on the unit or on the leaflet accompanying the adapter. If a fault

with the unit is suspected it will need to be tested and possibly recalibrated for maximum performance by a skilled electrician using a special RCD test meter. If a fault is suspected in an RCD unit, have it checked as they are there for your safety.

The use of an RCD in this way is to aid those who do not possess a low insulation test meter. It must be remembered that the units have a wide range of uses and are designed to ensure safety when using appliances or equipment such as lawn mowers (where there is a danger of cutting through the cable), irons, washing machines, etc. (where water and electricity are in close proximity).

If any appliance trips an RCD (or similar) system, do not use the appliance until the fault has been rectified. If tripping occurs with no appliances or load on the system, then a fault within the house wiring is indicated and the trip switch should not be reset until the fault is found and corrected.

Have your RCD tested regularly by an approved electrician to ensure that it functions correctly and safely at the right speed of no more than 0.4 of a second. Such tests require an RCD test meter that calculates the trip time of the unit. On simple tests the unit may trip but take too long for it to be classified as safe.

Points to remember about low insulation

Ensure that any disconnection or removal of wires is safe and not earthing via another wire or the metal case of the appliance, etc.

Whilst disconnecting any wires during the testing for low insulation it should be remembered that the machine must be isolated from the mains at all times and the panels or covers must be replaced before the appliance is re-tested, i.e. do not test with exposed wiring.

Before testing for low insulation, using a circuit breaker all earth paths of the appliance should be tested. This is done by connecting a meter between the earth pin of the plug, and all other metal parts of the appliance in turn. Maximum resistance should be 1 ohm. See 'Using a meter' in the *Electrical Circuit Testing* chapter.

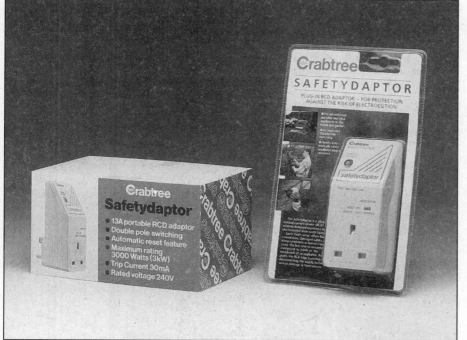

Two popular RCD adaptors. An essential item for all households that do not have RCD protected supply circuits or socket outlets see *Basics – electrical* chapter

Chapter 28
Motors

There are three types of main wash motor used in today's machines, the universal AC brush motor, permanent magnet (PM), DC brush motor and induction motor.

Where is the main motor located?

On most machines the motor is bolted to the underside of the outer tub. The exception to this is the early Hotpoint front loader where the motor can be found bolted to the top left-hand side of the outer tub (viewed from the rear).

What types of motor are there?

The following text is a brief introduction into the various types of motor found in use throughout machines in general. Each type of motor is described in greater detail later in the chapter.

Brush motors

These normally consist of two sets of electromagnets. An outer fixed set called the field coil and an inner set which are free to rotate called the armature. The armature is made up of many separate windings and is configured in such a way that power is only supplied to one set of windings at a time via moving contacts called a commutator. Rotation of the armature is produced due to the energised field and armature windings being slightly out of line to one another. The corresponding movement induced in the armature continuously brings a new set of windings into circuit, whilst the previous winding circuit is broken. The windings are out of synchronisation, therefore inducing continuous rotation of the armature whenever power is supplied. Reversal of the motor is normally achieved by reversing the power flow through the armature windings via a set of reversing switches in the timer. This type of motor can be used with alternating current (AC) from the mains, or with direct current (DC) from a battery, and is often used for the main drive motor in washing machines, especially on machines with drum spin speeds above 1000 rpm.

Induction motors (capacitor start)

Two versions of main wash induction motors can be found in today's appliances – 'single-phase' and 'three-phase'. The latter category was until recently only found in commercial situations where three-phase power supply is available (as opposed to the standard single-phase supplied to our homes). However, due to advancements in technology it is now possible to convert the domestic 'single-phase' supply into three-phase to power a new breed of induction motor. Further information on each version of motor can be found later in this chapter.

Both types of induction motor use a capacitor to 'kick' the rotor into action by putting a delay into the motor's start windings. The resulting imbalance (called phase displacement) creates rotation in the direction of the 'run winding' current flow. A reversal of power in the run winding reverses the motor. On basic single-phase induction motors, variations in motor speed are governed by the amount of windings. However, it is more common for speed control to be a combination of winding selection (poles) supplied with variable power (voltage) provided by a speed control circuit (PCB). Appliance three-phase induction motor windings are generally of two-pole configuration and speed is governed by both the voltage and the frequency supplied to the motor windings by a special speed control circuit board (PCB).

IMPORTANT SAFETY NOTE: *Voltages in the components of this type of motor system can be in excess of 300 volts. It is extremely important that prior to any inspection or servicing the appliance is isolated from the mains supply – switch off – plug out.*
IN ADDITION *to the standard isolation safety*

This type of unit normally requires renewal if faulty, although some brushes and patterned armatures are available separately

precautions above, a minimum period of 5 minutes must be allowed to pass before removing any panels. This is to allow potentially charged components within the motor control circuitry to automatically discharge as designed.
DO NOT *attempt to discharge three-phase control circuits by any other means.*

Induction motors (shaded pole)

This type of motor is associated with pumps. It has a low starting torque, i.e., this style of motor is easily impeded from starting, as the initial rotation is only from copper segments bound into the stator. When power is applied to the stator coil, the copper segments create a permanent imbalance in the magnetic field produced. This induces rotational movement of the rotor.

Induction motors (permanent magnet rotor)

This extremely simple style of motor is used to drive all versions of mechanical timers, both for timing and cam advance. Consisting only of a wound circular coil fixed around a permanent magnet rotor and supported at both ends by simple sleeve bearings, this motor can be made extremely small and at a low cost. As with all induction motors, its simplicity of construction limits it for use to AC supply only. A larger version of this principle is also used to power outlet pumps in many modern machines. The PM rotor is housed within a sealed plastic chamber but is still free to rotate by the alternating current (AC) supplied to two externally mounted stator poles. The rotor drives the impeller of the pump in the normal way, only the motor of the pump differs.

Brush motors

A brush motor can be readily identified by its shape, as its length is normally greater than its width. Owing to their continuous switching device, the commutator brush motors can be designed to operate on AC from the mains or DC from a battery. The switching device (the commutator) is made up of many copper segments. Each segment is connected to a winding in the armature and is supplied with electricity through two stationary pieces of carbon/graphite, called brushes. These are pushed onto the commutator by springs.

When power is applied to the motor, current

flows to the field coil and through the brushes to the commutator. This creates magnetic fields in both the field and armature coils, inducing rotation due to the magnetic fields in both items being slightly offset from one another. As the armature moves to align the magnetic forces created, the next two segments of the commutator come into contact with the brushes as the first set go open circuit. This operation is repeated many times per second for as long as power is supplied to both parts.

Speed control of this type of motor is achieved primarily by 'pulsing' within the speed control module circuitry which varies the voltage supplied to the motor, i.e., if the pulse is slowed, the motor slows or vice versa. This is not as straightforward as it may seem, as the pulse has to be in the form of a lower voltage and smooth enough to eliminate any jerky action at low speeds. Full control is achieved by timer switch selection in conjunction with the speed control module, which is dealt with in the section: Speed control in brush motors.

In addition to electronic speed control, universal series wound brush motors can be made to rotate faster by means of a feature called 'field tapping'. In a standard motor the wiring connections are as follows: two for the tacho coil, two for the armature (via the brushes), and two for the two field winding coils. Some motors may have two wires for a T.O.C. while others have the T.O.C. in the motor's brush wiring circuit. This in essence means that depending on the configuration brush motors used in washing machines would have either six or eight terminals in their respective connector blocks.

Although six and eight terminal motors are the basic configuration it is possible to encounter motors with seven or nine. Such a combination indicates that the motor has the ability to be 'field-tapped'.

In the diagrams relating to this section it can be seen that the additional (field-tapping wire) connects between the two field winding coils. Under normal circumstances the two field coils are connected by the timer/programme control unit in series with

Typical commutator wear. Ridges such as this can cause problems unless the new brushes are fitted correctly

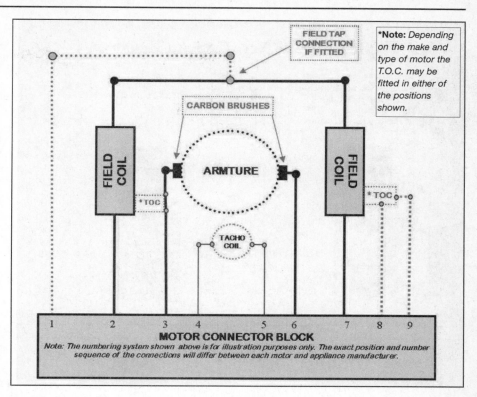

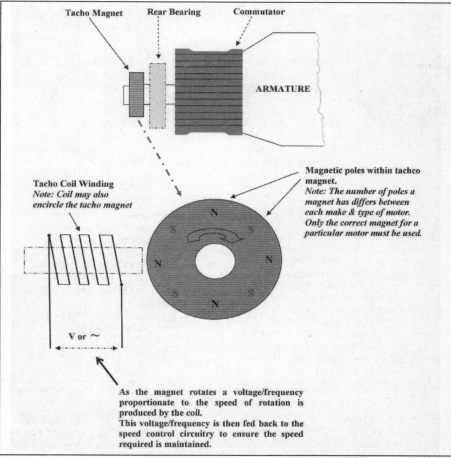

Bedding-in New Carbon Brushes

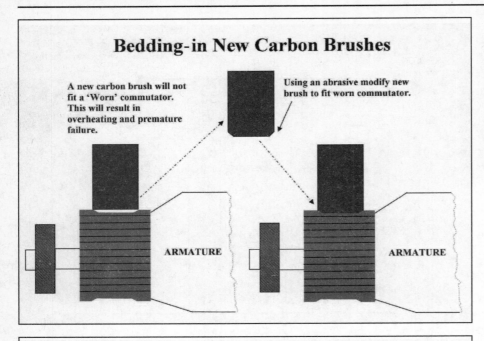

A new carbon brush will not fit a 'Worn' commutator. This will result in overheating and premature failure.

Using an abrasive modify new brush to fit worn commutator.

ARMATURE

ARMATURE

Bedding-in New Carbon Brushes

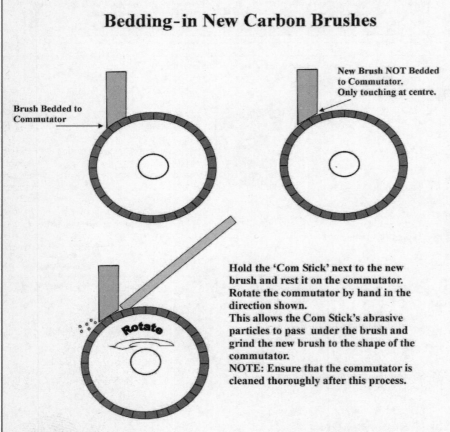

Brush Bedded to Commutator

New Brush NOT Bedded to Commutator. Only touching at centre.

Rotate

Hold the 'Com Stick' next to the new brush and rest it on the commutator. Rotate the commutator by hand in the direction shown.
This allows the Com Stick's abrasive particles to pass under the brush and grind the new brush to the shape of the commutator.
NOTE: Ensure that the commutator is cleaned thoroughly after this process.

The new carbon brushes will have flat profiles and prior to use it is best if they are 'bedded in' (shaped to match the circular commutator of the armature). This can be carried out by applying a 'com-stick' as shown and rotating the armature by hand to draw the grinding material between the two parts
Note: *It is important that the resulting abrasive dust is brushed free from the motor before placing it back into the appliance.*

Sandstone-like 'com-stick' is available from spare parts retailers

the armature resulting in a maximum motor speed when the full voltage is applied for the spin sequence. However, if the field tapping connection is used in place of the normal circuit only one field coil will be used and this action results in a dramatic increase in the rotational speed of the motor (as with induction motors, less magnetic poles, more speed) and can be likened to fitting a 'turbo' or super-charger to a standard car engine. The 'field-tapping' feature is used to provide an increased spin speed with minimal changes to existing components and wiring. However, the resulting increase in motor speed produced by this method also creates a higher current draw and therefore the motor will get much hotter if it is used for long periods. This is why models that have this feature will only use it at the very end of the fast spin cycle and usually for a short period of time (often for only around 20 seconds). However, this short period of very fast motor and drum speed does allow the manufacturer

Shown is a typical Hoover motor. Many variations of this motor are currently available and are very similar. The motors look identical in every respect, except for the block connector at the rear. Although they look similar it is essential that you obtain the correct replacement unit for your machine. This motor is fully repairable and each component is available separately. When obtaining replacement parts or replacement motors, ensure that you always quote the make, model and serial number of your machine

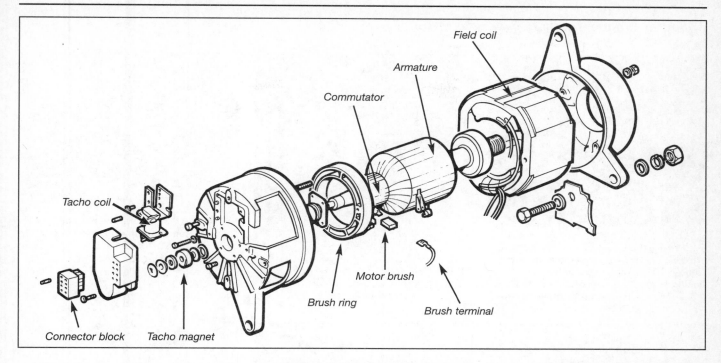

Field coil

Armature

Commutator

Tacho coil

Motor brush

Brush ring

Brush terminal

Connector block   Tacho magnet

to indicate that the model has a spin speed faster than others in the range, albeit for only a short period of time!

Main drawbacks of brush motors

a) Generally noisy in use, especially at high spin speeds.
b) Brush wear.
c) Commutator wear/burning. Two or more segments incorrectly linking together. This would cause sparking and overheating, resulting in poor running and eventual failure.

Shown is a popular brush motor manufactured by CESET. Many variations of this particular make of motor are used by a wide range of appliance manufacturers. Although they may look similar, it is essential that you obtain the correct replacement unit for your machine. Only the carbon brushes are available as spare parts, for all other faults will require a complete replacement motor. When obtaining replacement parts or motors, ensure that you always quote the make, model and serial number of your machine

d) Complete unit change needed if fault is other than brushes. This is true of most makes, however, it is wise to check to see if parts are available separately, as some manufacturers of appliances may supply armatures and other components as separate items for their motors.
e) Prone to low insulation due to carbon dust build-up created by brush wear.

Main benefits of brush motors.

a) In general, much cheaper than induction motors.
b) Infinitely variable speed control available.
c) Small in size.

Brush motor repairs

The main aim of this photographic sequence

As with many modern motors, only the carbon brushes are available as spare parts for this particular type

is to show the removal of the motor from the machine, and the detailed removal and refitting of a new armature and brushes.

The motors shown are of the universal type to be found in many popular makes and models produced by companies such as Creda, Hotpoint, Hoover, Servis and Zanussi. As many producers own a range of brand names it is common practice for appliances to be 'badged' with various brand names whilst the internal components remain the same. Externally, components such as the facia, door and control knobs will be cosmetically changed but the appliance will retain the basic structure and the internal components. There are also appliance manufacturers who make machines which other manufacturers and retailers can buy and badge as their own brand hence the similarity of many components such as motors.

The carbon brushes on this motor produced by SELNI are a simple screw fit

Armature change – early Hoover type motor

1 Ensure the appliance is fully isolated prior to removing panels to access the motor fixing bolts. In this instance a 'low insulation test' disclosed the motor fault. Remove the motor bolts and withdraw from the machine

4 The four end rivets can be drilled out or removed with a sharp chisel, as in this instance

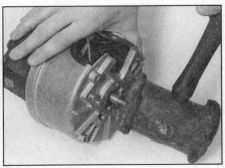

7 Knock the armature tacho end shaft free. Remove armature and inspect for faults

2 After noting the motor block colours, positions and connections, remove the plastic cover to reveal the tacho coil

5 Mark the position of the end frames, by marking with a pencil. When marked, remove the four securing bolts

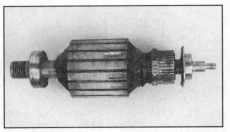

8 Check copper segments on armature for damage, i.e., burnt looking or loose/raised segments, and for carbon build-up. (This one is badly damaged)

3 The tacho coil and magnet can be removed carefully. (The clip on the shaft can be lifted with a small screwdriver)

6 When the end bolts are removed, use a hide mallet (or similar) to free and remove the front end frame

9 Check the bearings for free and quiet running by spinning them on the shaft. Also check for tight fit to shaft. (This one had damaged the shaft)

10 Old brush ring inspected for damage. Carefully check for smooth brush slides. Also check that no carbon deposits have caused low insulation. Change if in any doubt. (This one has burnt slides)

11 New armature ready to fit. Note screw plates and screws instead of rivets to aid fitting. Fit replacement unit if in any doubt as to condition of old unit

17 Adjust tacho setting (if necessary). Screw centre up to the magnet and turn back 1½ turns only

12 Fitting of new brush ring. If original unit is cracked or damaged due to bad brushes, replace this unit. Slides should be smooth

14 New armature fitted to rear end frame

18 Refit front end frame and reassemble motor, lining up the marks made in step 5

15 Hold plate on inside of end frame with finger. Insert and tighten the securing screws

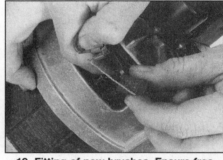

19 Fitting of new brushes. Ensure free movement of brush in slide. Make sure all connections are tight and do not foul metal body of motor

13 Shown are new and old brushes. The left lines show tagged and non-tagged type of brushes. The right lines show split and worn brushes

16 Refit tacho magnet and clip. Ensure that when fitted the magnet will not turn on the shaft, i.e., it should be locked to the armature

20 Ensure insulation strip is fitted to brush opening. It will fit easily if warmed first. The motor is now ready to fit to the machine for functional testing when all panels have been refitted

Brush change – GEC type motor

1 This is a very popular style of motor which can be found in a wide range of makes and models in the early Hotpoint and Creda ranges

4 With the latch depressed the holder complete with carbon brush can be removed

7 With your finger tip, check the profile of the commutator and if new brushes are being fitted, modify them as required. Refer to the diagrams relating to the bedding-in of new carbon brushes

2 Prior to removal ensure the position and orientation of each holder and brush are clearly marked. This is essential if it is found that the original brushes and holder can be refitted as this must be to their original location. Marking will also ensure a new set is fitted correctly

5 Using a suitable brush and if required, a cotton bud, remove all traces of carbon dust build up from the motor. Pay particular attention to the commutator segment spaces, the rear of the commutator, the carbon brush holders, and their fixing positions

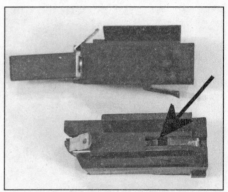

8 To prevent damage during transit the brittle carbon brushes are retained within the holder. To release them you will need to fully raise the small brass tag at the base of the plastic 'V' section. Failure to fully raise the tag can result in the brush not being fully released which can cause it to stick in the holder which will cause the motor to stop after only a short period of use

3 This type of carbon brush holder is removed by inserting a small, flat-bladed screwdriver to lift the small plastic latch on the inner edge of the holder

6 If the copper commutator segments are severely oxidised due to poor carbon brush contact this can be removed using a glass-fibre pen which is designed to remove only the oxidisation

9 Ensure that the carbon brush is free to slide back into its metal sleeve and carefully press the plastic holder into position until the latch clicks into position
Note: *You may need to place a finger between the commutator and the end of the carbon brush to ensure that it slips back into its sleeve as you press the holder into position. Failure to do so can result in breaking of the brush as it is fitted.*

Popular carbon brush sequence – screw-fit type

1 This motor is typical of those fitted to many of today's machines as only the carbon brushes and tacho coil are available as spare parts. As with most motors of this type, the carbon brush and holder are replaced as one unit

4 Remove the securing screws

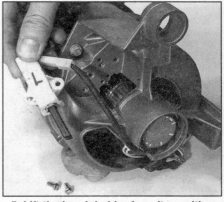

5 Lift the brush holder from its position
Note: *When the holder is removed from its position the carbon brush will become visible. In this instance it can be seen that there is a good amount of carbon protruding – indicating that wear is not a problem.*

2 Various types of fixing methods are used. In this instance the carbon brushes and holders are secured to the rear-end frame by two hex-head self-tapping screws

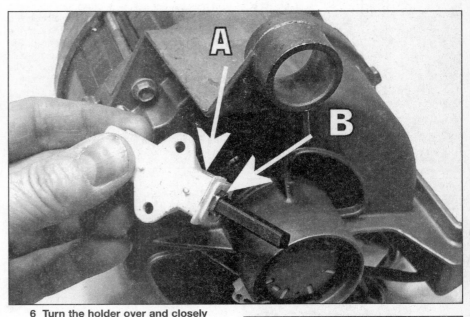

3 Prior to removal, ensure the position and orientation of each holder and brush are clearly marked. This is essential if it is found that the original brushes and holder can be refitted as this must be to their original location. Marking will also ensure a new set is correctly fitted

6 Turn the holder over and closely inspect the underside. A common problem of motor 'low insulation' is a build-up of carbon dust between points A and B. This can create an unwanted electrical path between B – live brush connection and A – the earthed metal body of the motor. Thoroughly clean the holder and its fixing point and renew if need be

7 Using a suitable brush and if required, a cotton bud, remove all traces of carbon dust build-up from the motor. Pay particular attention to the commutator segment spaces, the rear of the commutator, the carbon brush holders and their fixing positions

8 If the copper commutator segments are severly oxidised due to poor carbon brush contact this can be removed using a glass-fibre pen which is designed to remove only the oxidisation

9 Carbon brushes should only be renewed as a pair and when fitted should be bedded in using a com-stick

10 With the com-stick inserted in front of the carbon brush and in contact with the commutator rotate the armature several turns in the direction of the brush. Repeat the process for the other brush

11 Ensure that all traces of the dust produced during the com-stick bedding process is removed. Pay particular attention to the commutator segment spaces and the rear of the commutator

12 Refit all electrical connections ensuring that they are correctly routed and are a secure fit

Permanent magnet main motor (DC)

An unusual but reliable motor found on some appliances (mainly Philips/early Whirlpool) is a permanent magnet main motor (similar to the smaller pump and timer motor versions) or PM main motor for short. It is an extremely compact and versatile motor and due to its construction, runs on DC (direct current) only.

How does the DC (PM) motor work?
The DC motor, as the name implies, runs only on direct current (as opposed to normal household AC alternating current). The operation of the motor is similar to the brush gear motor described in the previous section. DC power is supplied to a wound armature via

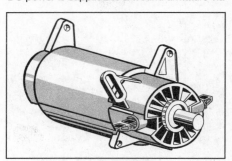

A PM motor

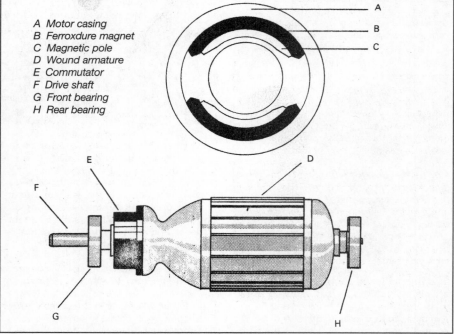

A Motor casing
B Ferroxdure magnet
C Magnetic pole
D Wound armature
E Commutator
F Drive shaft
G Front bearing
H Rear bearing

Permanent magnet motor (DC)

a commutator and carbon brush system. However, there is no corresponding wound field coil. The motor has a permanent magnet field requiring no electrical supply, see diagram. Power (DC) is supplied only to the brushes. This induces rotation of the armature within the permanent magnet poles. Such motors are easily reversed by simply reversing the supply voltage to the brushes. Care must be taken when dismantling the appliance because if the terminals are accidentally reversed, the motor will run in the wrong direction during the distribute and spin cycles causing severe problems. As always make notes when stripping down the appliance for repair or inspection.

Why are they used?

This type of motor is used because it is much smaller in size, lower power consumption, greater reliability, smooth running and low cost. Failure, other than brush wear, requires complete motor renewal – make sure only the correct replacement is obtained.

How does it get DC when appliance receives only AC?

Within the motor speed control module there is mounted a bridge rectifier. AC power supplied to the module is rectified (changed) to DC voltage and supplied to the PM motor. The DC voltage supplied to the wound armature induces rotation. The speed of rotation is directly proportional to the voltage supplied, i.e., the lower the voltage the slower the motor turns, conversely, the higher the voltage the higher the motor speed. By using resistors within the module (and often a variable potentiometer mounted on the facia as a spin speed control) the motor can have infinite speed control. In practice, during wash action, i.e., slow rotation, the module – via resistors controlled by timer switching may only supply the motor with 16 volts DC but due to its efficient design and operation, it works extremely well and has good torque. During spinning, the DC voltage supplied to the motor can be as high as 240 volts DC. No extra tacho system is required as the motor itself is an excellent generator of power. When running free the back EMF can be used as a reference voltage for the module circuit.

Note: *When using a test meter on the motor (checking for continuity/worn or sticking bushes), do not rotate the drum pulley or the motor quickly as the voltage generated may damage your meter. Remember all tests are to be carried out only when the machine has been isolated. On no account should you test for supply voltages to the motor. The voltages quoted do not represent those that may be found and are given only to emphasise the flexibility and operation of this type of motor.*

Main benefits

Easily reversible. Small and compact in design. Extremely versatile. Cheap.

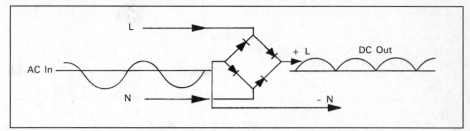

Full-wave bridge rectifier (both halves of wave rectified)

Drawbacks

Only motor brushes can be renewed.

The need to control the PM motor via a resistive circuit led to some machines within the range using a section of the heater as a motor circuit resistor. This system can be easily detected by a dual wash heating element being fitted. Therefore, when investigating problems with motor speeds on such machines, the element should also be checked.

Note: *It is the smaller of the two elements that is used but a fault (open or low insulation) can give rise to motor problems. A fault with either element will require the fitting of a new complete unit.*

Speed control in brush motors

It must be remembered that not all motor speed faults are directly attributable to the motor. The fault could be caused by a piece of electronics often referred to in the trade as the 'module', which is connected between the timer and the motor and controls the speed of the motor. There is no standard location for the module but it is easily identified by its distinct printed circuit board (PCB) and large heat sink. Computer and hybrid-controlled machines normally integrate the speed control into the power module and mechanical timer unit. See *Timers (programme control)*.

How does it work?

On the rear end of the motor's armature is a circular magnet that revolves in unison with it. Close to this magnet is a coil of wire (this may be encased in plastic), which is called a tacho generator. If a magnet is rotated next to or inside a coil of wire a voltage/frequency is produced which is proportional to the rotational speed of the magnet. Therefore, the faster the motor is running the more voltage is produced or the higher the frequency. This voltage/frequency is fed to the module as a reference voltage/frequency and is used to monitor the performance of the motor by comparing the relative speed of the motor with a known voltage/frequency via a comparator circuit. If the reference voltage/frequency is found to be lower than the comparator, the module will increase the pulse rate, therefore increasing the speed of the motor. If the voltage/frequency is found to be high, the pulses are slowed, therefore

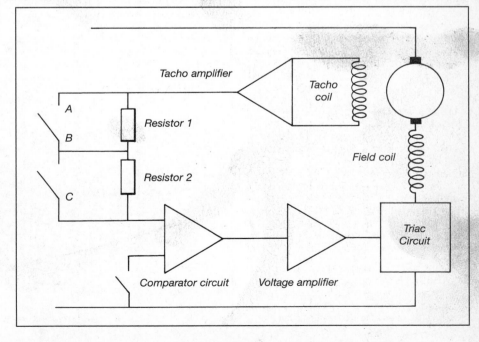

decreasing the motor's speed. This happens many times a second, and is undetectable.

The rotating magnet of the tacho unit produces an alternating voltage and frequency both of which are proportional to the speed of rotation. The speed control module can be designed to respond to either the voltage or the frequency produced. Early modules operated predominantly on the voltage output whilst most modern modules and computer controlled machines operate on the frequency. Visually they can look very much the same, however it is essential that the correct replacement is obtained.

The speed control module obtains electrical information from both the timer and the motor. If the timer requires a wash speed it supplies power to the motor via the module whilst simultaneously switching in an appropriate resistor circuit in the module. There are two resistors in the example shown, therefore three speeds can be achieved, i.e., no resistors, one resistor, both resistors.

Wash speed – A-B and B-C closed: therefore bypassing both resistors.

Distribute speed – A-B open, B-C closed: therefore one resistor in circuit.

Spin speed – A-B and B-C open: therefore both resistors are in circuit.

Note: *Some machines have a means of varying the spin speeds via a control on the front of the machine. This is simply a potentiometer (variable resistance). The inclusion of the potentiometer in the circuit will vary the switching of the triac over a wider range than the fixed resistors. Some machines have an off position on the switch, see* Machine will not empty *chapter.*

How to check if the module is at fault

If any of the internal components of the module have burned out, i.e., charred or burnt looking, the motor should be checked for any shorting, loose wires or low resistance, as these may be the probable cause.

Checks on the tacho magnet and tacho coil

a) If the magnet is loose or broken, this would result in incorrect speeds at lower motor speeds.

b) Severe damage or complete loss of the magnet would cause the motor to spin on all positions.

c) A break in the coil would result in a spin on all positions. This is because a 'good' coil is usually about 200 to 1600 ohms resistance. If there is a break in the coil, the resistance is infinity. The tacho generator is not returning any voltage or frequency, therefore the module speeds the motor up. The increased speed is not transmitted back to the module, so the process is repeated *ad infinitum.*

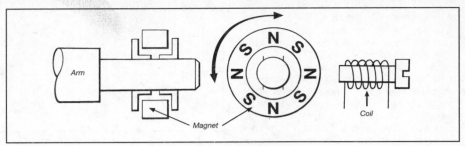

Tacho generator

Note: *Most modules fitted to modern machines have an in-built tacho test-circuit and will not operate if the tacho circuit is open.*

d) Breaks and/or poor connections of the wires leading to and from the tacho can have the same effect. This is especially true at the connection block with the motor, and the connection at the module.

It should be remembered that any loose connection will be aggravated by the movement of the tub on the suspension, and this should be taken into account when testing for such faults. The following chart can be used to help locate the module faults and assist in establishing the correct course of action. Do not attempt to adjust the tachometer other than as shown in the armature section.

The modules shown are a small selection of modules that are fitted to today's machines. Their appearance and function differ very little from one another but are strictly non-interchangeable. Always ensure that the correct replacement unit is obtained by quoting the make, model and serial number of your machine when ordering spare parts.

If the fault persists the module is probably at fault. This should be replaced with a new unit, ensuring that the correct type is purchased. To fit, make a note of the connections, remove them and replace them on the new unit. It is important that the 'Duotine' (edge) connector fits tightly on the module (the connections can be closed slightly by inserting a small

screwdriver between the back of the tag and the plastic Duotine. Care should be taken not to close it too far as this may result in the tag not making contact by being pushed back into the connector).

The machine must be isolated from the mains. Turn off at the wall socket and remove the plug.

Warning: *The large metal back of the module is used as a heatsink. This means that it is live when in use, and therefore should be fitted correctly and securely to its plastic mounts. Even when testing, any contact with the earthed shell of the machine will render the unit useless.*

The alternative to buying a new speed control unit

As with timers and programmers the cost of a new speed control unit (PCB) can often be extremely high and this in turn often leads to the appliance being considered not worth repair. The other aspect of renewing the whole unit no matter what the fault, is that of the sheer waste of materials when the old unit is simply thrown away. However, there is now an alternative to this expensive and wasteful practice, that of reconditioning. This is an interesting and welcome development not only in the significant reduction in the cost when compared with that of the new item but also in the 'green' aspect of recycling components and materials. See – *Buying spare parts* chapter.

The top left-hand terminals of this module show signs of overheating/burnout. Loose connections can cause such problems but in this instance it was caused by the breakdown of insulation of a component connected to the board leading to a short circuit to the earth path of the appliance. The resulting surge of current which blew the fuse in the plug unfortunately also damaged the tracks (and very likely components) of the circuit board

Incorrect Drum Action	Check Operation		Interlock — Check Interlock and Latch	Motor — Check Complete Motor Circuits	Tacho — Check Circuit Late M/C's	Module — Fit New One	Module — Replace Original	Tacho — Fit New One or Adjust	Timer — Check Timer moves on at all
	Spin	None	●	●	●	●			
		Slow		●		●			
		Cont	●	●	●	●			●
	Distribute	Cont	●			●			●
		None			●	●			
		Fast		●	●	●	●	●	
		Slow		●	●		●	●	
	Tumble	None	●	●	●	●		●	
		Fast			●	●	●	●	
		Slow		●	●	●	●	●	
		Cont		●		●	●	●	●

A Merloni module found in many 'badged' models

Electrolux

An Ariston-Indesit module

Note: *The connectors to this module are 'keyed' the same, so ensure you mark them clearly before removal. The top left connections are mains voltage while the top right are low voltage. Accidentally swapping them will irrevocably damage the module.*

Zanussi

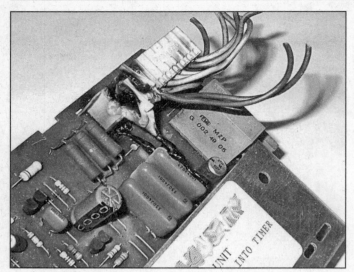

The IDC connector to this module shows clear signs of overheating and charring due to poor connection to the board or internal wiring in the connector block. Always ensure that all electrical connections are sound and in good condition

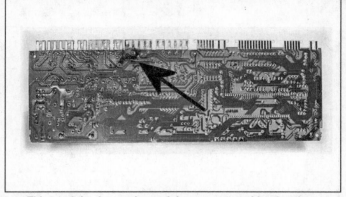

This module shows signs of damage caused by the short circuit/short to earth of a component connected to it. The excess current drawn by the faulty component melted sections of the tracks on the PCB. This was due to them being weaker than the mains fuse and ruptured through excessive current draw. Simply attempting to renew the tracks is not the answer as damage to other board components may have occurred. Obtain a repaired/reconditioned guaranteed replacement unit, or purchase a new PCB

The induction motor

Most people seem to understand a little about series-wound universal motors (motors that require a wound armature and brush gear, etc.) but very little about induction motors of any type.

The synchronous induction motor is in fact quite simple and uses the absolute basic principles of electricity. Its apparent complexity stems from the need to use extra windings to control its speed. Although modern electronics have allowed for variable control, we deal here with the basics of the two types of synchronous induction motors found in domestic washing machines – single-phase and three-phase as well as those used without module control. For speed control, see later section.

Capacitor/relay start

Unlike brush motors, induction motors can only operate on alternating current (AC mains), and are technically called synchronous induction motors.

Single-phase induction motors consist of two main items, an outer wound coil called a stator and a rotatable core called the rotor, made of high grade cast aluminium with internal metal laminations which are slightly askew to aid torque for starting purposes (see diagram 2). The rotor is isolated from the windings and receives no power at all.

The most simple stator would consist of two sets of windings 180 degrees to one another (see diagram 1). Two windings are needed to induce the rotor to turn by their magnetic fields when power is applied. One coil would not induce movement, though if the motor were started by mechanical means, it would run up to

maximum speed and continue to turn as long as power was supplied to the stator coil. In reality, the motion/starting is induced by placing one set of the windings 90 degrees out of phase with the other. This can be with the use of a relay, but more usually by the use of a capacitor, the rating of which is matched to the windings and is given in microfarads (µF) on its casing. Being out of phase due to the delay caused by the capacitor/relay, a rotating magnetic field is created, causing the rotor to turn up to speed at which point the start windings, as they are

known, could be switched out if required. Reversal of the motor is quite simply a reversal of current flow through the start winding or the run winding, but not both. Speed reduction is obtained by the use of more wound poles of the stator being employed (see diagrams 1A and 1B).

When a motor is supplied with 230V at 50Hz (i.e. mains voltage) a 2-pole motor will mimic the supply phase cycle and rotate at 50 revolutions per second, i.e. 50 x 60 seconds = 3000rpm. Variations in speed can be made as follows: 4

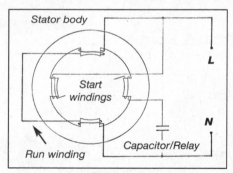

Diagram 1

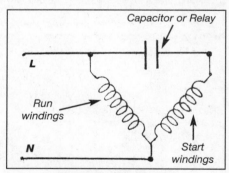

Clockwise Diagram 1B

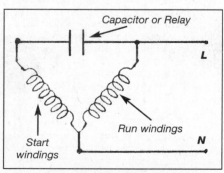

Anti-clockwise Diagram 1A

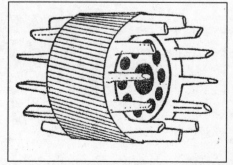

Diagram 2

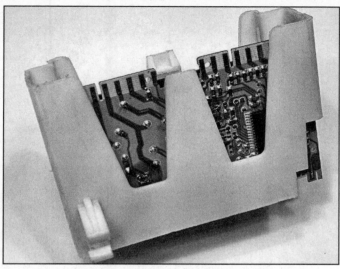

A speed control module within housing

Modern induction motors are often only available as a complete item. However, some makes and model may supply tacho coils and magnets as spare parts. It is often possible to renew worn or damaged bearings by obtaining the correct sizes required from bearing suppliers and carefully dismantling the motor and renewing them

poles 1,500rpm, 8 poles 750rpm, 16 poles 375rpm, varying speed in this way results in complex stator windings and expensive motors. Ensure that faults with motors are checked and rectified promptly. A loose motor block connection may allow power to one winding only and cause overheating and failure of the whole motor. A faulty capacitor or a malfunction of the programme switches or internal T.O.C. of the motor can also have the same result.

Main drawbacks of induction motors

a) As all of the work is done by a complicated set of windings in the stator, this motor is generally not repairable and must be changed for a new unit.
b) Capacitor failure often results in the motor failing to run. This can result in burn out as the rest of the motor windings are receiving power but no rotation is possible. Overheat is inevitable, even when TOC (thermal overload cut-out) protected.

Main benefits of induction motors

a) Generally reliable.
b) Quiet.
c) Can be run in both directions.

Warning: *When checking for faults, the machine must always be isolated from the mains. Turn off at the wall socket and remove the plug. The capacitor(s) will still contain a charge although the mains has been isolated. This must be discharged by using an electrically isolated screwdriver. Do this by 'shorting' the terminals of the capacitor with the shaft of the screwdriver ensuring that you are only in contact with the insulated handle. It is not safe to proceed further until this has been done.*

If the stator windings of an induction motor are faulty, it may continue to run although appearing sluggish and getting

extremely hot even when used for a short time. Therefore, if you have been running the machine to determine the fault, proceed with care as the motor will remain hot for some time. If the motor appears to be very hot, the motor winding may be faulty and the unit should be replaced.

In an effort to retain the benefits of the single-phase induction motor such as low noise while avoiding the draw backs of low spin speeds, manufacturers of appliances have

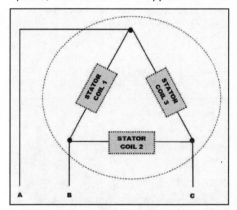

A typical three-phase washing machine motor configuration. The premises' single-phase electrical supply is fed to a phase converter speed control module which in turn feeds the three-phase motor with power via connections A, B and C. The phase shift between the three coils is 120° (360 divided by 3 = 120). Varying the frequency and the amplitude of the power supplied to the motor directly affects the speed

Note: *In order to gain the most benefit from this system the maximum amplitude (voltage) supplied to such motors can be in excess of 310 volts. When checking this type of motor all three windings should be the same resistance i.e. A to B, A to C and B to C.*

resorted to using three-phase induction motors within domestic washing machines.

Appliance three-phase induction motor coils are generally of two-pole configuration with all speeds being governed by both the voltage and the frequency supplied to the motor windings by a special speed control circuit board (PCB). Combining three-phase configuration with the ability to change both voltage and frequency results in a motor that is fast, quiet and reliable.

To do this the speed control module (PCB) has a phase converter incorporated in the circuitry. This part of the module converts the single-phase house supply into a three-phase output for the motor. A microprocessor within the speed control module controls the complex switching routine required to produce the rotating magnetic field within the motor windings while changing the voltage and frequency applied to them. As with other motors the instructions for speed and direction required for the various parts of the programme are provided by the timer/programme while tacho feed back is used to confirm that the required speed is maintained.

A three-phase motor as used in single-phase washing machines
Note: *Due to their high rotational speeds these induction motors have 'Multi-V' drive pulleys and a tacho coil system and may at first glance be mistaken for universal motors. However, as can be seen here, a three-phase induction motor will NOT have carbon brushes.*

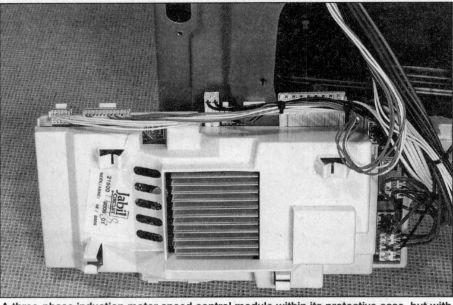

A three-phase induction motor speed control module within its protective case, but with an exposed heat sink

A three-phase induction motor speed control with protective cover removed

Module control

Most modern machines that use single-phase induction motors use electronics to help control the selected pole speed more precisely and help smooth the transition from one speed to another. Such induction motors will only have internal pole configurations which, when selected by the timer/programme unit, produce two basic speeds – slow, which will be a 12- or 16-pole configuration and fast which will be a two-pole configuration. The 12- or 16-pole configuration will be used for low speed high torque wash actions and the two-pole lower torque for all other speeds i.e. fast speed

selected but reduced by the speed control module to attain the desired speed. For models that use three-phase induction motors refer to Appliance three-phase induction motors in this chapter.

The module works by ramping (slowly increasing) the voltage to the pre-selected (by the timer) stator windings. This achieves a smooth operation of the main motor. The tacho magnet and coil produce a small voltage/frequency proportional to the rotational speed of the motor which is used as a reference to the electronic module. This simply means that speeds can be increased gradually, for instance, allowing a slow build up to spin from distribute. This minimises the jump in speeds as the windings are simply switched in and out causing the excessive vibration normally associated with early induction motors.

Ramping in this way allow the clothes in the drum to balance out more evenly by centrifugal force, resulting in a much smoother spin and less vibration of the machine. Another benefit of the electronic speed control is that a small potentiometer linked to the module and fitted to the facia panel of the machine enables the user to vary the spin speed to their own desired level (usually between 500–1,000 rpm, with a switch facility on the potentiometer for no spin at all).

Faults in either motor or module would require a complete change as no internal components are available, except for the tacho coil. For faults and symptoms, see *Speed control in brush motors*.

Speed and combined programme control

When combined with mechanical timers the electronics of some modern speed control

*IMPORTANT SAFETY NOTE: Voltages in the components of three-phase motor systems can be in excess of 300 volts. It is extremely important that prior to any inspection or servicing the appliance is isolated from the mains supply – switch off – plug out. **IN ADDITION** to the standard isolation safety precautions a minimum period of five minutes must be allowed to pass before removing any panels. This is to allow potentially charged components within the motor control circuitry to automatically discharge as designed. **DO NOT** attempt to discharge three-phase control circuits by any other means.*

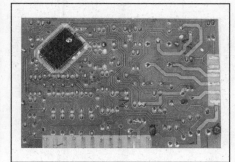

This small motor control module has an extremely wide variety of motor speeds and complex OOB control, it also carries out motor reversal and timing functions normally carried out by the timer. The ability to carry out this wide range of tasks comes from the use of a surface mounted microchip (clearly seen on the top left of the photograph)

Chart A (right)
This chart shows the variable agitation sequences that are applied throughout the various wash and rinse cycles. The motor has a 'soft' start action and ramps slowly up to the selected speed during the timed sequence. Refer to chart B for drum speed variations

Wash cycle	Drum Rotations Per Minute	Timed Rotation Clockwise	Timed Pause Seconds	Timed Rotation Anti-Clockwise Seconds
Woollens	35	12	9	12
Delicates Wash	45	8	7	8
Delicates Rinsing	55	12	7	12
Normal Wash	45	12	65	12
Normal Wash Rinsing	55	15	6	15
Drying Cycle	35	20+20	3	20+20

	WOOL WASH	DELICATE WASH	NORMAL WASH	VIGOROUS DELICATE WASH	VIGOROUS NORMAL WASH	DISTRIBUTE AND O.O.B.	SLOW SPIN	FAST SPIN
DRUM → SPEED (rpm) WASH ↓	35	45D	45N	55D	55N	100	500	1200
CODE 1 Switch A	X		X			X		
CODE 2 Switch B					X		X	X
CODE 3 Switch C		X				X		X
CODE 4 Switch D	X			X			X	

Chart B
This chart shows the wash codes and the 4 timer switches A,B,C,D. A cross in the box indicates what function is selected when that switch is closed and the corresponding drum speed. Refer to Chart A for timing details of how long the rotation is for that particular wash. For instance – a woollens wash has timer switches A and D closed. This results in a drum speed of 35rpm on this chart and rotational timing of 12 seconds clockwise, a pause of 9 seconds followed by anti-clockwise rotation for 12 seconds

modules may also include other functions such as temperature and basic programme control. As can be seen in the *Timers (programme control)* chapter, the trend towards electronically controlled machines is increasing and this combination is a further step in the process. The inclusion of a microchip within the speed control circuitry opens up a wide range of control options. What follows is an overview of a system currently in use and one, which many manufacturers will surely follow in the future. Transferring control of functions such as motor reversal and rotation times, etc., greatly reduces the complexity of the main programme unit. The motor control is by simple basic switch commands called wash codes supplied by the timer (i.e. wash at code 1). These basic switch commands actuate a series of complex predetermined sequences stored within the integrated circuit (IC) within the module circuitry. With the predetermined sequence selected the module then controls and monitors all functions such as motor speed, direction of rotation, wash action i.e. length of time for rotation and pause, normal, delicate, wool, distribution speed and both spin speeds. A tacho generator like the ones described previously is used as a reference for the module control unit. Simply by varying the combination of 3 or 4 timer switches a whole range of wash variations can be achieved. The two charts A and B show the way in which a typical system of this type works and the range of variation possible. It would be very difficult and complex to achieve this level of control and variation with a purely mechanical timer. The system also has OOB capabilities details of which can be found in the chapter on *Suspension*. When used on combined condenser washerdriers the module may also be used to control the intermittent timing sequence of the drain pump during the drying cycle.

The alternative to buying a new speed control unit

The alternative to buying a new speed control unit is to purchase a fully reconditioned replacement on an exchange basis. This is a welcome development in the field of repair work not only in the significant reduction in the cost when compared with a new item but also in the 'green' aspect of recycling components and materials. In addition to speed control modules a wide range of reconditioned programme/timer units can also be obtained on an exchange basis.

For further details see chapters *Timers (programmer control)* and *Buying spare parts*.

The capacitor

What does a capacitor look like? Capacitors used for motor starting can have either metal or plastic outer casings with an insulated top with two terminals, see photo.

What follows is a simplified version of what happens within a capacitor in an AC circuit.

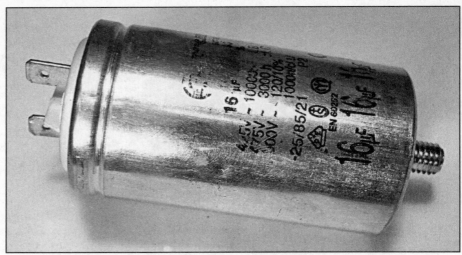

Typical capacitor for use with induction motors. Do not confuse capacitors with suppression units. They may look similar, but their functions differ
Note: *Capacitors can be found in many different sizes and ratings and may have plastic or aluminium casings.*

The two terminals of the capacitor are in fact completely insulated from one another. Internally they are connected to two sheets of metal foil and between this foil is an insulator. This package of large surface area is rolled into a tube formation which fits into the shell of the capacitor. If the two terminals and their connected sheets of foil are insulated from one another, you may ask, how do they pass a current when in use? The answer is that as the voltage supplied to one terminal is in fact alternating (i.e. at 50 times per second: 50Hz) so does the polarity of its connected foil. An opposite movement of electrons is produced in the other foil even though they are insulated electrically. This effect causes a delay in the electrical path at this point, and this, in the case of an asynchronous induction motor gives the out of phase feed to the start winding.

The storage capacity of a capacitor is measured in microfarads (μF) and is displayed on the casing of the capacitor. Any replacement must be of the same μF rating.

If the motor fails to run on wash, but runs on spin and there are two capacitors fitted, it is possible that one of them is faulty. Change the capacitor with the lowest μF rating and re-test. If only one capacitor is fitted then the motor should be checked, see *Motors* chapter.

If the motor runs on wash but fails on spin and there are two capacitors fitted, there are two possible faults. Change the capacitor with the highest μF rating and re-test, remembering the previous warning about an isolated capacitor retaining an electrical charge. If the door interlock is connected directly to the motor spin circuit, and the door is not closed properly, then the spin will be prevented from operating. A fault within the interlock would also prevent

the spin, refer to *Door switches (interlocks)* chapter.

The relay

What is a relay? A relay is an electromechanical device used in this particular instance for induction motor starting in place of a capacitor.

The most common relay consists of a plastic moulding with three terminal tags, two at the top and one at its base. On the centre section is a wire wound coil (see photo).

The main aim of the relay in the context of asynchronous induction motors is to cause a delay in the start winding supply, similar to the capacitor. The main difference is that the relay achieves this operation mechanically. The wound coil section is connected in series with the run winding. When power is supplied to the motor, the current to the run winding passes through the coil and on to the motor run winding. This current induces a magnetic force in the coil which in turn attracts the metal core of the

Typical relay

relay. The metal core is linked to an internal contact switch and when 'made' allows current to pass to the start winding (see diagram). This operation gives the required delay to induce starting of the induction motor.

When power is switched off, gravity resets the relay core. It is, therefore, essential that the relay is in its correct position and the machine upright for this item to function correctly.

The relay may also be matched to the run winding of the motor, i.e., as initial power draw of the stationary motor is high the magnetic attraction of the relay coil is great enough to attract the core. When the motor is running, the initial high power draw drops and weakens the magnetic pull of the coil, the core drops and open circuits the start winding allowing the motor to continue running more efficiently. Always make sure that the correct replacement is obtained by quoting model numbers and manufacturer when ordering.

Faults to watch for are: open circuit of the coil, metal core sticking (in either position), and contact points failing. Renew any suspect relay immediately as the failure of this item, like the capacitor, can lead to motor failure.

If you have to renew a damaged stator coil or motor and it is relay started, it is wise to change the relay at the same time as it may:
a) have caused the original motor fault or
b) have been subsequently damaged by the motor failure.

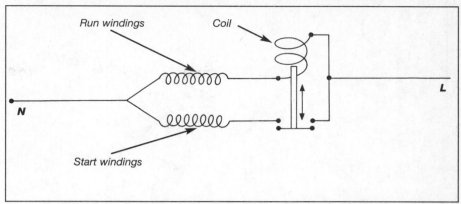

A relay may be placed in circuit to cause the phase displacement necessary to start the induction motor. This is a mechanical delay as described and it is essential that the relay is upright when energised

Main drawbacks of shaded pole motors

a) Can be used in one direction only. This is governed by the positioning of the shaded pole.
b) Due to the permanent imbalance described previously, excessive heat would result if used for long periods.
c) Low starting power.
d) If subjected to overheating for long periods, the motor will eventually fail, even if T.O.C. protected.
e) Generally not repairable.

Main benefits of shaded pole motors

a) Very cheap.
b) Very reliable.
c) Very quiet.

Note: T.O.C. = Thermal Overload Cutout. This means that if the safe working temperature is exceeded, this device will sever the power supply to the motor. Most T.O.C.s are now self-resetting, resulting in constant heating up and cooling down of the motor. If the fault is not spotted quickly, the

The shaded pole induction motor

The shaded pole motor is one of the most simple of all induction motors and is similar in basic format of rotor and stator (see diagram). However, only one stator coil is used to create the magnetic field. Obviously this alone would not induce rotation of the rotor, only a constant magnetic field. To start rotation, an imbalance in the magnetic field is required and created quite simply by copper band inserts at the pole ends of the stator laminations. The copper bands within the mild steel stator laminations (dissimilar metals) distort the magnetic field in a given direction, therefore inducing rotation in the stator. Reversing the supply to such motors does not effect any change in motor direction as this is governed by the direction of the fixed shaded poles. These motors do not have a high starting torque and because of the magnetic imbalance being fixed, heating of the stator occurs which, under normal conditions creates no problems, but most stator coils are protected by T.O.C.s for safety.

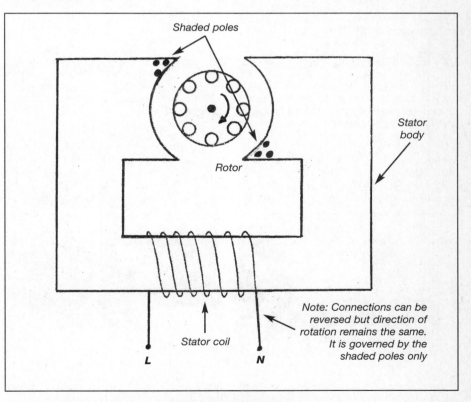

Shaded pole diagram

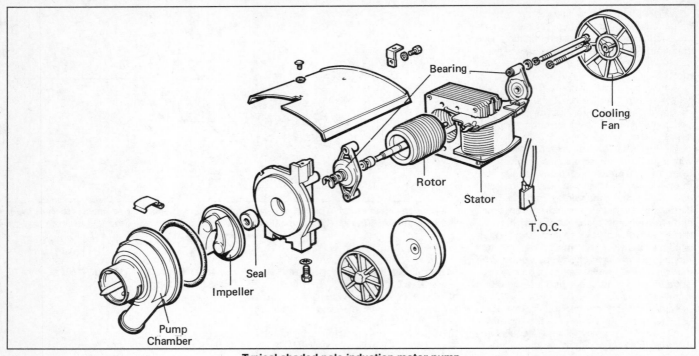

Typical shaded pole induction motor pump

T.O.C. itself will fail, resulting in complete motor failure.

Induction motor – permanent magnet rotors

This extremely simple style of motor is used to drive all versions of mechanical timers, both for timing and cam advance. Consisting only of a wound circular coil fixed around a permanent magnet rotor and supported at both ends by simple sleeve bearings, this motor can be made extremely small and at a low cost. As with all induction motors, its simplicity of construction limits it for use to AC supply only. A larger version of this principle is also used to power outlet pumps in many modern machines. The PM rotor is housed within a sealed plastic chamber, but is still free to rotate by the alternating current (AC) supplied to two externally mounted stator poles. The rotor drives the impeller of the pump in the normal way, only the motor of the pump differs.

This type of motor has been used for many years to power the timing and advance mechanism of washing machine programmes. As mentioned previously, they are now used to drive the outlet pump of some machines. It is the most simple of electric motors, quiet to run and cheap to produce. It also avoids some of the more common pump problems.

A circular multi-pole permanent magnet forms the rotor of the motor and its construction is similar to that described in the module control section relating to the tacho. Within the casing of timer motors a finely wound coil encased in plastic surrounds the permanent magnet rotor. Permanent magnet pumps have two coils wound on to a laminated steel stator. In both instances, supplying A/C power to the coil(s) induces rotation of the magnetic rotor. However, rotation could start in either direction and this, in the case of timer motors, would be most unwelcome. To ensure that rotation occurs in the required direction, i.e., clockwise or counter-clockwise, a small plastic cam is positioned within the casing (seen as a small plastic pip on the rear of the motor casing), which allows rotation in one direction only. Should the motor try to start in the wrong direction, it hits the plastic cam which flicks it back, thus inducing correct rotation.

The ability to run in both directions is utilised to its full extent when this style of motor is used to drive an outlet pump impeller. Should the impeller of the

This dismantled pump shows the component parts of a PM pump unit. However, only complete units are available as replacement items

Motors with permanent magnet rotors have been used for many years to drive the timer units. See *Timers (programme control)* chapter

For many years, small, permanent-magnet motors have been used to drive mechanical timer units. The knob connected to this programme selection unit is advanced through the cycle by this small PM motor which simply clips into and out of its location
Note: *This particular timer is only a selector and indicator switch which provides and responds to information from a larger electronic control unit situated elsewhere in the appliance.*

pump come into contact with an item such as a button (this would normally jam/stall a normal shaded pole motor) the motor may be nudged into revolving in the opposite direction and clear the blockage or continue to pump whilst running in the opposite direction.

The construction of the permanent magnet pump helps alleviate the problem of shaft seal leaks and bearing failure which are common to shaded pole versions.

Centrifugal pulleys

The centrifugal or variomatic pulley is the large pulley that can be seen on some induction motors on the Candy, early Ariston, Indesit and Philips washerdriers.

A three-phase motor as used by Hotpoint. Due to their much faster rotational speeds three-phase induction motors have 'Multi 'V' drive pulleys

An induction motor with centrifugal pulley used to maintain belt tension. This type of motor can be found in models in the Zanussi range which are also 'badged' under other popular brand names such as Electrolux, AEG, Tricity Bendix etc.

Note: *Some early Candy machines also utilise a centrifugal drum pulley.*

What does it do?
It is fitted to help increase the drum speed when the machine spins.

Why have complex pulleys?
The reason for having adjustable pulley drives relates mainly to the need for faster spinning at the end of the wash cycle. Adding a large pulley to the motor to create an increase in drive ratio to the drum pulley for the spin, causes problems for induction motors. The low speed wash action would require extra windings to slow the rotation whilst high spin speeds would be affected by lack of torque as the number of poles are reduced to increase the motor speed. In the past when spin speeds were much slower (500–800rpm) the induction motor was the ideal choice. However, the need for ever faster spin speeds has outstripped the capabilities of the normal induction motor. To compensate for this inability to comfortably reach higher drive speeds, further mechanical additions have been made to the drive pulley and in some instances (Candy) to both drive and drum pulley. Some Zanussi machines use

This Zanussi motor is visibly similar to the Bendix motor, except for the round control block. This can also be found with a centrifugal pulley (as with the Candy)

Shown is a Fagor motor, typical of the new style induction motors that are capable of variable speed build up via a module. Note the tacho connector at the rear of the motor

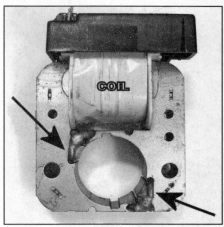

Shown is the induction stator of a pump. The shaded poles are clearly visible by the two bands of copper inserted in opposing poles. Note the orientation of the copper bands before removing the stator from the pump. If the stator is refitted back to front, the pump will run in the opposite direction and not pump at all

a gear and clutch arrangement to help in increasing the drive speed of their induction motor. Both of these systems are still limited to a drive ratio that produces a maximum spin speed of 1,000rpm (of the drum). However, with modern electronics some Italian produced

This Candy motor has a centrifugal clutch/pulley system that increases the spin speed

Operation of a centrifugal pulley system

Centrifugal weights

Small belt drive point

Slow motor speeds (spin)

Sliding rear of pulley

Larger belt drive point

Fast motor speeds (spin)

Fixed front pulley

An early Ariston motor with centrifugal pulley system. The motor is only supported at the rear by two large rubber mounts. This allows the weight of the motor to automatically tension the belt as the pulley size increases and decreases in relation to the motor speed

machines now have induction motor spin speeds of 1,200rpm.

Universal brush motors are normally used for machines with spin speeds that exceed 1,000rpm (many modern machines now attain spin speeds in excess of 1,500rpm).

How does it work?

Weights within the pulley are 'pushed outwards' by centrifugal force when a fast motor speed is selected. As the pulley is constructed in two halves, the outward movement narrows the gap between the front and back plate of the pulley, therefore increasing its diameter.

This increase in diameter increases the drive ratio between the drum pulley and the motor pulley. When the motor speed slows, the reverse occurs, i.e., the back plate moves away from the front plate, and the belt rides on the smaller diameter of the

pulley. This can be seen in the photograph of the motor at rest.

Similar clutches can be found on early Ariston and Philips machines. Early Candy machines also have a similar centrifugal pulley on the drum, although this opens at the higher speeds, thus giving a smaller drive ratio. This produces an increase in speed with a constant belt tension, without having to resort to expensive motor windings. **Do not** over-tighten the drive belt on machines with a centrifugal pulley.

Note: *Some are self tensioning by the weight of the motor, i.e., motor only supported by rubber mounts on the rear end frame, allowing weight of the motor to tension the belt and the motor to rise as the pulley size and drive increases during the spin.*

The addition of a mechanical pulley system to an otherwise simple and reliable motor increases the risk of faults. In addition to the normal induction motor faults, problems occur with the mechanical action of both centrifugal motor pulleys and drum pulleys (if fitted). Due to the belt being constantly squeezed along its edges, belt wear is accelerated and regular checks are advised. Renew if suspect as spin efficiency will decrease and/or excessive noise will occur.

Pulleys are made either of plastic or cast aluminium and as such, wear ridges form on the belt contact faces. This may lead to restricted movement of the belt resulting in poor drive (poor wash, spin or both), noise, excessive belt wear or jamming and finally, possible motor failure.

The early Zanussi geared systems are similar, with noise and internal gear wear being the most common problems. There are no individual spare parts available for these types of drive pulleys, therefore if faults do occur, complete pulleys will be required. However, it is not uncommon for some manufacturers to supply the pulley and motor as one unit, no matter what the fault.

This Zanussi induction motor has a large metal drive pulley with internal gearing and a centrifugal clutch system

Access to some makes and models can be quite restricted as in the later Hotpoint range of appliances. With the rear panel removed you can access B – speed control module; C – main motor; D – heater; E – pressure vessel, and F – drain pump. Item A is the cover for the speed control diagnostics connection – see *Fault, error and configuration codes* chapter

Chapter 29
Suppressors

What is a suppressor?

A suppressor is a device designed to eliminate the formation and transformation of spurious radio waves that may be produced by the operation of the motor and switches within the appliance during normal operation. When switching occurs within the appliance and it is not suppressed, small sparks at the contact points or brushes may produce interference on radio and TV channels or audio equipment plugged into the same electrical circuit, i.e., not only through air waves, but also down the mains cable.

Why should all appliances have them?

By law, all domestic appliances must be suppressed to conform to the regulations on radio interference, and it is an offence to use an appliance that is not suppressed to these standards.

Where are they located?

Suppressors vary in style, shape, position, size and colour. Sometimes individual parts are suppressed, but more often the mains supply is suppressed at or just after the entry point into the appliance. This is called 'in-line' suppression as both the live and neutral supply goes through the suppressor and on to supply the whole of the appliance with power. Do not confuse the suppressors with capacitors, which may be used in the appliance for induction motor starting. They may look very similar, but carry out distinctly different functions. Suppressors may also be called 'mains filters' because of their ability to remove spurious radio transmissions.

An alternative version of suppression unit can be found in addition to those described above. This is an induction coil, fitted in series between the neutral position at the terminal block and the shell of the machine. As an induction coil is of a far heavier gauge, it only passes suppression current, whereas the two earlier versions carry the full voltage load. Some machines have a combination of both in-line and induction coil types of suppressor. All versions require a good earth path on both plug and socket, see *Basics – electrical*.

An in-line suppressor unit

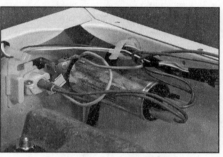
A suppression unit in situ

Faults with suppressors

The main fault is one of short circuit to earth usually resulting in the unit 'blowing' both the main fuse and itself. This is often accompanied by a pungent burnt smell. Renewal is a straightforward one-for-one replacement.

Open circuit problems can occur and the unit will fail to allow current to pass through as normal. The suppressor can easily be checked for continuity using a meter, see *Electric circuit testing* chapter. When checking, inspect the top insulation closely and if cracked or at all suspect, renew complete unit.

It is common for in-line suppressors to use the earth path as part of their filtering circuit (although very little power passes through it). It is essential for all appliances to have a good earth path. If an appliance with an in-line suppressor/filter has a break in its earth path (due to cable, plug or socket fault) small electric shocks may be experienced when the user touches metal parts of the appliance, especially if they are in touch with a good earth path themselves, e.g., holding metal sink or work top, etc. It is essential that such faults are traced and corrected immediately,

A suppressor with an overheated terminal connection – ensure all electrical connections are in good condition and are a tight fit

The motor in this computer-controlled machine has additional motor suppression components attached to the connector block

see *General safety guide* and *Basics – electrical* chapters.

Although the continuity of a suppressor (lead through type) can be checked easily, its function of suppression cannot be so easily checked. If all other checks, i.e., good earth connection (check for loose/poor connection to shell of the machine) no cracks or loose/heated terminals, etc., prove to be satisfactory, and interference to other equipment persists, renew the suppressor.

An additional means of suppression may be found, especially on micro-processor controlled machines. This is a choke type and may be fitted in series between live and neutral positions or individually in-line on both live and neutral supplies to individual components such as a series wound main wash motor. A choke consists of a ferrite core or ring around which the conductor is wound. The aim of the choke is to prevent interference within the brush motor (commutator/brush arching, etc.) from being

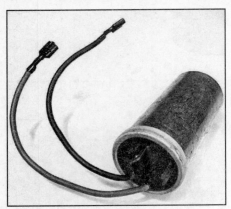

Check suppression units closely for cracks or expansion, etc. If in doubt, renew it. This unit has a small crack across the top but otherwise it looks OK. However, internally it is a direct short circuit and potentially dangerous

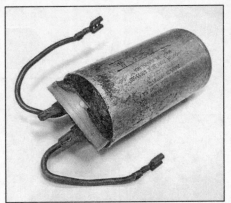

Some suppressors give clear indication of failure

Some models may be found with an induction coil fitted in series between the neutral position at the terminal block and the shell of the machine

transmitted directly to the microprocessor mounted on the control board. Interference of this nature can corrupt the current programme resulting in random crashing of the programme. This can be an annoying intermittent problem requiring resetting of the programme, which may or may not complete the cycle. In severe cases the microchip may be permanently damaged.

Some appliances use a combination of different types of suppressor. Suppressors of any type should not be bypassed or omitted, as to have an unsuppressed appliance is an offence owing to the interference that it may cause to others. In the case of 'chokes' failure or omission of this device may cause damage to or corrupt electronic circuits within the appliance, see *Timers (programme control)* chapter.

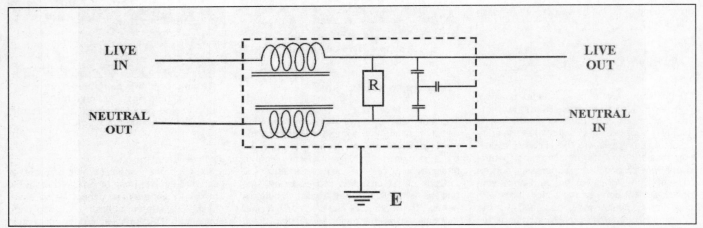

With the appliance isolated from the mains supply and the suppressor removed from the appliance wiring, the readings obtained using a simple multi-meter should read as follows

Between **Live** and **Neutral** – very high resistance – you are effectively testing the resistor 'R' in the diagram and this usually has a resistance of around 470,000Ω or more.
Between **Live In** and **Live Out** – very low resistance (continuity through the suppressor).
Between **Neutral In** and **Neutral Out** – very low resistance (continuity through the suppressor).
Between **Earth** and **Live** – infinitely high resistance (effectively no circuit detectable).
Between **Earth** and **Neutral** – infinitely high resistance (effectively no circuit detectable).
NOTE: *Although the above diagram shows a circuit between Live and Earth and Neutral and Earth the circuit is through a series of small internal capacitors. When testing a suppressor with a battery powered multi-meter (DC voltage) no circuit should be detected. However, the capacitance suppression circuit will conduct under AC (mains) supply. An earth path in both appliance and supply is therefore essential not only for the safety of the product but for the correct functioning of this type of suppression unit.*
Replace the filter unit if incorrect readings are obtained.

Chapter 30
Bearings

This chapter deals predominantly with the main drum support bearings, although many of the associated problems also relate to other areas such as main motor bearings and pump motors (on machines which use ball race or roller bearings in these items). For items which contain sleeve bearings, see *Pumps* and *Motors* chapters.

Types of bearing

Basically, there are four types of bearing used in washing machines.

1   The sleeve bearing. This is simply a phosphor bronze bush in which the motor shaft is free to rotate. It is most commonly used in shaded pole pump motors and reference to that section will give further detail.

2   Ball race bearing. This type of bearing consists of an outer ring in which a small inner ring is supported by circular ball bearings and is free to rotate.

3   Taper roller bearing. The taper roller bearing uses rollers in place of the ball bearing in (2) and as its name implies, the design angles the rollers to give a tapered appearance. The outer ring (shell) is not fixed as with the ball race type, and is fitted into position separately. It is essential that taper bearings are fitted as a matched pair, i.e., inner and outer. If this is not done, then the result will be early failure.

4   Needle bearings. A needle roller bearing is similar in looks and construction to the ball

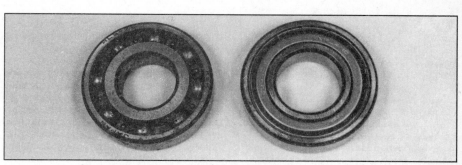

Shown are both unshielded and shielded ball race bearings

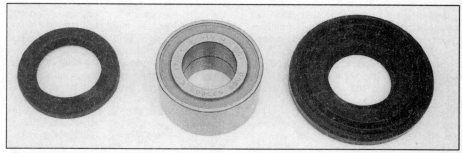

This large ball race bearing has one large outer but two inner races. It is often referred to as a conical bearing and can be found on models in the Zanussi and Ariston ranges

race bearing but uses roller (long thin rods) in the inner cage in place of balls.

The type of bearings used on the main drum bearing assembly will differ not only between manufacturers, but also between models from one manufacturer, i.e. one range may use ball race bearings when a similar model from the same manufacturer will have taper roller bearings. Although there are only two types of bearing used, the variations in size of both outer and inner are vast, so therefore it is essential to fit identical bearings when replacing old or damaged ones and ensure that all shaft seals and

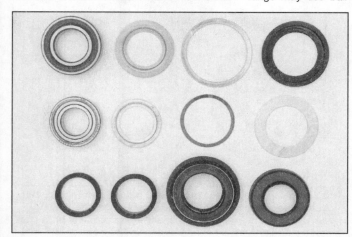

This early Creda bearing kit uses the cup seal system. Two shaft seals are provided as changes were made during production. Use the seal that matches the one already fitted and discard the other

Shown are widely available patterned bearing kits for two popular makes of washing machine. Genuine kits are also available but are generally of higher cost. Both types of kit are supplied with front bearing, rear bearing and shaft seal. However, neither is supplied with the tub joint seal which is also required when changing the bearings. Ensure you obtain all the relevant items to carry out the task correctly

This drum support shaft (spider) had an unusual fault. The machine exhibited signs of bearing failure (very noisy). However, when stripped down for repair the bearings, shaft seal and phosphor bronze bush at the base of the shaft were found to be in good order. Closer inspection revealed that the mild steel support shaft inserted in the aluminium support was working loose and was the cause of the noise problem

Note: *The support shaft shown was cut away to illustrate how the mild steel shaft is secured to the cast aluminium support member.*

spacers are renewed at the same time. If possible, obtain a bearing kit to make sure that all relevant parts are renewed. Do not cut corners by replacing only one bearing in a set of two or fitting a new taper roller inner to an existing outer shell because the old outer shell is difficult to remove. These short cuts will lead to premature failure and further damage. Be warned!

Why do bearings fail?

There are several reasons why bearings fail, apart from the normal wear and tear over a long period of time. What follows is a list of the most common causes and points to watch out for:

a) The most common failure of both ball and taper bearings is the ingression of water and detergent into the bearing housing. This is usually due to wear or premature failure of the shaft seal. Two types of seal are used. The first one is a simple shaft seal which is pressed into the bearing housing on top of the front bearing. When assembled, the lower section of the drum shaft locates within the seal, usually a raised metal shoulder or collar of mild steel or more commonly phosphor bronze, and is fixed to the base of the drum shaft. The seal has either one or two spring-loaded lips which press firmly around the collar to create a watertight seal. Normal wear, fluff or scale may break this seal down and allow water and detergent into the bearings quickly resulting in failure. Ensure that the collar is secure on the shaft and clean and that both seal and bearings are renewed at the same time. The second type of seal is a carbon face seal. This system relies on two smooth 'faces of carbon' (or ceramic) that are pressed firmly together when assembled. One face is free to rotate, being fixed to the base of the drum shaft, whereas the other, as before, is fixed on top of the front bearing and is spring-loaded. The two smooth surfaces held under the pressure of the spring within the seal creates the movable watertight seal. Again, fluff, scale and normal wear will lead to water ingression. Ensure that the fixed carbon

Some makes and models may have a bearing housing (often referred to as a 'boss') which contains the drum bearings and shaft seal – this particular version is from a Whirlpool machine. The unit is secured to the outer tub with a series of large screws/bolts. This type of bearing arrangement allows for much easier bearing replacement as a full strip down of the outer tub is not required. The housing is supplied as a complete replacement by the manufacturer, but as usual, there are size differences between the various models so ensure you obtain the correct version for your machine. If you wish to eliminate the need to replace the whole unit it is possible to obtain replacement bearing and shaft seals and fit them to the existing housing ('boss'). To avoid leaks ensure you replace the large 'O' ring that seals the 'boss' to the outer tub. Also when refitting any item with an 'O' ring, it is wise to wet the ring slightly to allow it to slip into position and avoid damaging it. Do not use detergents or any other type of lubricant, but just a little smear of water around the sealing ring

This new bearing set is shown to emphasise what the severely damaged bearing in the accompanying photograph should look like

This photograph shows the remains of a drum bearing set. Due to the user continuing to use the machine despite it being extremely noisy the front bearing finally collapsed. It is both false economy and potentially dangerous to use any equipment that has problems of any kind. In this instance the drum was so loose that it damaged the heater and the collapsed front bearing damaged its support shaft which essentially trebled the cost of parts required for the repair

ring is smooth, not cracked and securely fixed to the base of the shaft. Check the new spring loaded face seal in a similar way and make sure that it seats correctly into the bearing housing. Application of a little sealant is recommended to make certain of a watertight fit to the housing. Do not allow any sealant or dirt on either of the faces of the seals when assembling them.

b) Bearings will also fail if incorrectly fitted. Do not hammer in the bearing (or shell, if taper roller type) directly with a hammer as this may crack or chip it. Do not force the bearing or shell into distorted or dirty housings as this will distort the bearing and create overheating resulting in failure. Inspect the drum shaft closely for ridges or rust which again will distort the inner race of the bearing, resulting in overheating or if worn, create a loose fit. Take care to clean all areas and fit only the correct size of bearings carefully.

c) Inspect failed bearings closely for they will have sizes stamped on them which can be used to ensure the new bearing is of the same dimensions. Failed bearings may also give an indication as to why they failed. Rust would indicate that the seal had failed and prompt closer inspection, cleaning or renewal of the shaft, collar or carbon face. Bearings that are dark blue in colour are usually the result of overheating. Check the shape of the housing and shaft and do not over-grease. Flakes of metal from the bearing also indicate some form of distortion or ingress of dirt during assembly.

d) Do not over-tighten bearings (especially taper roller types) hoping that it will help seating. The result is usually overheating and premature failure.

Recognising bearing failure

Noise can be a good guide to early recognition of bearing problems. Simply removing the drive belt should help ascertain if the faulty bearing is in the motor or the drum shaft support bearings. A selection of noise faults are given overleaf together with possible causes.

Tips on fitting

To gain maximum life from any bearing, care must be exercised when handling and fitting

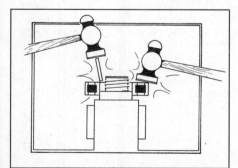

DO NOT hammer directly on the bearing

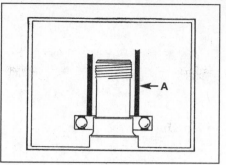

When fitting a bearing only apply force to the non-moving part of the bearing. If bearings cannot be pressed into position, use a metal tube (A) of similar diameter to drive the bearing evenly

it. Prior to stripdown and removal of the old bearings, ensure that a note/drawing is made of the position of seals, clips and washers, etc. Inspect both the shaft and housing closely for defects. Ensure the shaft, housing, work area and hands are clean. Remove the new bearing from its protective packaging only when you are ready to fit it.

Ideally, bearings should be pressed into position, but in reality however, this is not always possible and some means of drifting the bearing into place will be required. Great care must be taken if this method is used as damage can easily be done to the bearing at this stage. Endeavour to use a tube when fitting the bearing to enable an equal force to be applied. The tight fitting part of the bearing should take the force only, i.e., if fitting to a shaft, contact should only be with the inner race and when fitting a bearing into a housing, only the outer race should take the force. Do not apply any force to the part of the bearing that is free to rotate during fitting. To assist in fitting bearings, expansion and contraction with heat can be used, although excessive heat must be avoided.

Fitting a bearing or taper roller bearing outer shell into its housing can be assisted by simply putting the bearing or shell into the household freezer for a while and warming the housing with the aid of a light bulb for an hour. This simple technique can help enormously. When fitting a bearing to a shaft, a reversal is required – cool the shaft and warm the bearing, but be careful not to overheat the bearing (especially sealed bearings) as this may create problems. Do not exceed 100°C.

Many ball-type bearings are greased during manufacture and sealed on both sides. Such bearings do not require any extra lubrication prior to assembly. Roller bearings (and some open cage ball bearings) do require packing with grease. This should be done sparingly as over-greasing results in churning of the grease and heating occurs which results in loss of

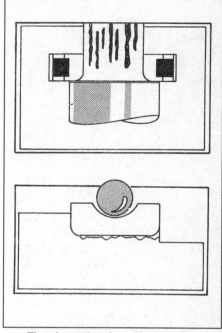

The above drawings illustrate the problems that occur if a bearing is fitted to a scoured shaft

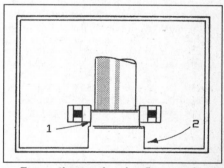

Ensure the new bearing fits up to its locating point and does not leave a gap as shown in (1). Always ensure that the collar (2) is secure and clean

Typical cast iron bearing housing. This type of bearing housing is used on many different makes such as Ariston, Zanussi, Electrolux, and AEG

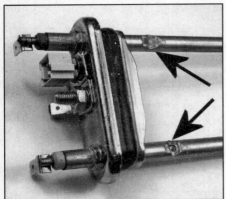

Due to excessive bearing wear the drum of this machine dropped low enough to come into contact with the heater located beneath it. Despite the noise caused by worn bearings and the grinding of the metal drum contacting the heater during both wash and spin actions the owner continued to use the appliance. Eventually, the outer metal sheath of the heater was worn away completely and water penetrated the heating element resulting in a leakage to earth which tripped the consumer units RCD. If the appliance had not been on an RCD protected supply the direct short to earth would have resulted in additional damage to the heater at the break point. It is false economy and potentially dangerous to continue to use any appliance that exhibits faults. In this instance, in addition to the cost of the drum bearing repair, the user had to pay an extra £50 for the new element which, had the problem been addressed earlier, would not have been needed

Noises	Possible cause
Loud rumbling especially on spin	Collapsed front drum bearing or seized front bearing. This often results in shaft damage if not attended to quickly
Rattling with intermittent knocking	Ball or roller of bearing defective
Rattling/knocking proportional to speed	Inner or outer of bearing faulty
High pitched metallic noise	Common on worn motor bearings at high speed and on new bearing if it has been forced on to a damaged or over-sized shaft
High pitched ringing noise	Indication that bearing has been fitted to a damaged housing or fitted carelessly
Grating and crunching noise	Collapsed bearing cage or dirt between inner and outer race
Squeaking	An old bearing, usually due to lack of lubrication or ingress of water past shaft seal. May also occur when new bearings are fitted to machine with carbon face type seals if care was not taken to keep both surfaces clean, or if check was not carried out for cracks or scouring on carbon faces

lubrication. Pack the bearing with grease and rotate both inner and outer with the fingers to allow any excess to be pushed out from the moving parts.

Typical tapered bearing change

The sequence of pictures overleaf shows the renewal of a set of drum bearings. It was found that the main drum support bearings were water damaged which was caused by the shaft seal failing and allowing water and detergent to enter the bearing and housing.

This was suspected because of the noise of the machine, especially on spin and was confirmed by removing the drive belt from the motor to the drum pulley, spinning the drum slightly by hand and listening for any grating noise. If this had been quiet, the motor would have been spun in the same way to test its bearings.

To confirm severe drum bearing failure, a simple method is to open the door of the machine and move the bottom of the door

seal so as to see the inner drum and outer tub gap clearly then try to lift the top lip of the drum only. At this point, the gap between the outer tub and inner drum should not increase nor decrease in size and no movement should be felt other than that of the outer tub on its suspension. This applies to all machines irrespective of bearing types.

The removal of the drum and back half assembly on this style of machine is quite straightforward. This style of drum and backhalf are fitted to many of the leading makes including early Hoover, Hotpoint, Creda and Servis although in each case the size of bearing and type of carbon seal differ slightly between machines. As the bearing kits are complete matched sets, no problems should arise.

After isolating the machine and laying it face down on a suitable surface, the removal of the back panel will reveal the back half and outer securing nuts. All of the nuts and bolts securing the back half and tub should be removed. If necessary the top of the machine may be removed to gain access to the top bolts.

When this is done, mark all of the connections to the heater and thermostat and disconnect them. The back half assembly can now be manoeuvred from its position and removed from the back of the machine. The back half is made watertight by a rubber seal located on its outer edge. If the back half sticks

to the tub, and all of the necessary nuts and bolts have been removed, gently prise the back half from the tub ensuring that no excessive force is used. The drum and back half can now be manoeuvred free of the machine.

The removal of the pulley and bearings can now proceed.

If the bearing set for your machine is of the ordinary ball bearing type, the job is much easier as the old bearing should knock out in one piece. Should this type of bearing 'collapse' or leave its outer shell, the shell can be removed by drilling two grooves on either side of the inner of the soft aluminium bearing housing which will allow access to the bearing shell. A small diameter rod can then be used to drift (knock) the outer shell of the bearing from the housing. Care must be taken not to go too deep with the drill into the soft aluminium housing.

When greasing the new bearing (this is obviously not necessary on the sealed bearing type) take care not to over-grease them, as this will not help lubricate it and in fact will considerably reduce the bearing life.

A new taper bearing kit will come complete with an odd shaped aluminium washer that fits between the rear bearing spacer and pulley. This is known as a torque washer and is essential for the correct operation of the bearing. Always fit a new torque washer to this type of bearing if the pulley is removed for any reason. The torque washer is a simple way of putting the taper bearings under a known pressure without the use of a torque wrench.

When fitted together, the torque washer collapses at a given pressure and dispenses with the need for a torque wrench for tightening the pulley bolt.

A full set of instructions for the torque washer will come with the new bearing kit, however I have included a typical bearing change below.

If your machine is of the type with ball bearings, please disregard the paragraph concerning torque washers, as this type of bearing assembly does not require a torque setting. Renewal of this type of bearing is a simple reversal of the stripdown procedure.

Instructions for early tapered bearing change

Dismantle the pulley and bearings

i)   Remove the bolt (1) and washer (2 & 3) securing the tub pulley and remove the pulley (4).

ii)   When removing the back half gasket, you will notice that it is compressed. It is advisable to replace this item to ensure a true watertight seal between the back half housing and outer tub.

Extraction of old bearings

i)   The existing bearing sleeves (9 & 11) will be found inside the tub backplate (10). Extract the bearing sub assemblies and then apply heat to the area containing the sleeves.

The sleeves can then be gently tapped out with a small chisel, drift or old screwdriver.

Renewal of bearings

i)   Push the new sleeves into place, ensuring that the inner surface of the tub backplate is thoroughly cleaned.

ii)   Insert the first (larger) bearing and washer (12).

iii)   Gently push the seal (13) into place. It is advisable to use a waterproof adhesive around the seal to aid fitting and prevent leaking past the outer edge.

iv)   Clean the new carbon face seal thoroughly to remove all traces of grease, oil, etc.

v)   It is advisable to fit new washers to the front and rear (12 & 7) as it is likely they have been scoured by the faulty bearings. Many bearing kits do not contain items 12 & 7 and these may have to be obtained separately.

vi)   With the drum face down, fit the back half with the new front bearing spacer and carbon seal fitted, to the cleaned and inspected drum and shaft.

vii)   The rear bearing race can now be fitted.

Inserting the torque washer

i)   Reassemble the remaining parts in reverse order to that in which they were removed. Do not use the old torque washer (6) – only use the new spacer supplied with the kit.

ii)   Fit the shim washer from the kit under the torque washer in the position shown in (6a).

iii)   Tighten the bolt (1) against the pulley as far as possible without locking the tab washer.

iv)   Complete the tightening operation until the 'D' washer fits firmly against the shoulder of the spider unit (5).

v)   The spacer is now correctly pre-set. It is essential to do this, in order to ensure the correct loading pressure on the bearings.

Complete reassembly

i)   Remove the bolt (1), washers (2 & 3), pulley (4) and spacer (6). Discard the shim (6A).

ii)   Reassemble in reverse order again. This time locking the tab washer against the bolt.

iii)   If this procedure on taper roller bearings is not followed correctly, the life of the new bearing set could be considerably shortened.

Refitting assembly

Below are a few helpful hints on the refitting of the assembly back in the machine.

a)   It is advisable to remove the heater from the back half before refitting the back half and drum into the machine. The subsequent refitting of the heater in this fashion ensures the correct location of the internal heater securing clip, see *Heaters* chapter.

b)   A thermostat pod (if applicable) and the heater grommet can be smeared with sealant to help slide them into position. If the thermostat grommet looks perished, it should be changed.

c)   Remember to reseal any hoses on the pressure system if they have been disturbed.

d)   Always remember to fit a new tub back half seal.

e)   Check the tension on the main drive belt and adjust the belt if necessary. This is done by moving the motor up or down to slacken or tighten the belt (like adjusting a fan belt on a motor car). Do not over tighten the belt, see *Main drive belts* chapter.

Bearing changes requiring outer tub removal

Often, the restricted rear-access type of bearing housing or shell/cabinet construction will not allow for the renewal of the bearings or drum in the manner previously described. In such instances, for repairs to, or renewal of the drum bearings, tub seals or outer or inner drum renewal, it may be necessary for the whole of the outer and inner drum unit to be removed from the shell of the machine before further stripdown can take place. There are three main reasons why this course of action may be required.

1 Access to the rear of the outer tub is restricted because of the very small access panel on the rear of the shell of the machine. However, on machines with external cast-iron bearing holders, it is usually possible to manoeuvre the whole bearing unit out through the opening after first laying the machine face down and removing the securing bolts and pulley. Several AEG, Electrolux, Zanussi and Ariston models may have bearings fitted in this way, but for inner drum removal/renewal, the whole unit would need to be removed as can be seen in some of the following sequences.

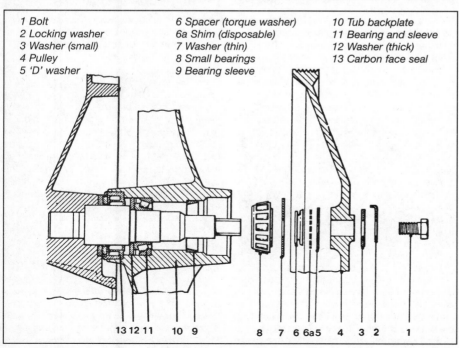

1 Bolt	6 Spacer (torque washer)	10 Tub backplate
2 Locking washer	6a Shim (disposable)	11 Bearing and sleeve
3 Washer (small)	7 Washer (thin)	12 Washer (thick)
4 Pulley	8 Small bearings	13 Carbon face seal
5 'D' washer	9 Bearing sleeve	

13 12 11   10 9   8   7 6 6a 5   4   3 2   1

Bearing renewal – split tub – front service type

1 With the appliance fully isolated (switched off, plug removed from supply socket and taps turned off) remove the rear access panel securing screws

2 After noting the position of the drum drive belt on the motor pulley grooves, remove it by gripping the centre of the free section and pull it towards you while lifting it upwards. This will cause the belt to ride free from the large pulley

3 Prior to attempting to remove pulley securing bolt strike it two or three firm blows with a plastic hammer or better still, a dead-blow mallet as this will help free the locking compound used in production. DO NOT use metal-to-metal contact

4 Lock the drum pulley to the tub rear using a mallet shaft or wooden block. This should allow you to safely apply the force required to undo the bolt. The use of leather gloves to protect your hands is recommended

5 With the securing bolt removed waggling the pulley will help remove it from the drum shaft. This particular drum has a splined shaft and pulley fixing

6 Next, replace the securing bolt and strike it two or three firm blows with the plastic hammer or better still, a dead-blow mallet as this will help free the shaft from the grip of the old bearings Only a slight movement is required and DO NOT use metal-to-metal contact

7 Clearly mark the position of all connections prior to carefully removing them

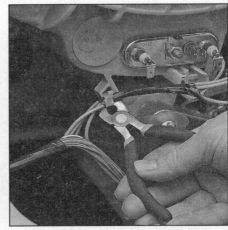

8 This cable tie needed to be cut to free the wiring harness from the outer tub unit Note: It is important that all such fixings are replaced during re-assembly.

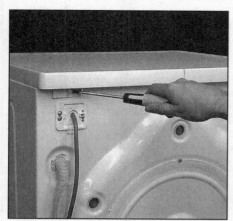

9 Remove the lid securing screws and the lid of the appliance

12 Clearly mark all electrical connections prior to removal. On this make of appliance they are 'keyed', but were marked anyway as a precaution (a wise working practice to adopt)

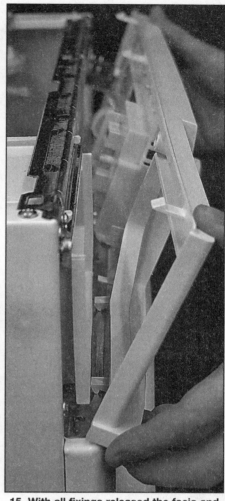

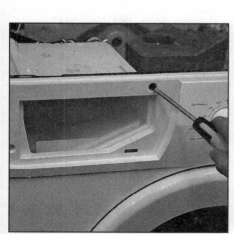

10 Press the dispenser drawer retaining latch and remove the drawer

13 Ease the connections free – pull only on the connector NOT the wiring and avoid waggling the connector as this can result in damage to the PCB and IDC wiring connections as used here

15 With all fixings released the facia and control circuitry can be removed
Note: DO NOT touch the connections or circuit board as the electronics on the PCB can be easily damaged by static discharge.

11 Remove the recessed facia securing screw(s)
Note: Screw fixings in this area of an appliance are generally stainless steel so keep them separate to ensure they are replaced correctly.

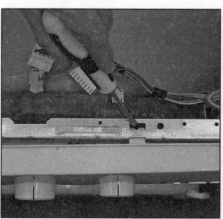

14 Carefully release the plastic latches holding the facia in place
Note: Do not exert undue force – some plastic latches can be released by finger pressure only.

16 Note the position of the hidden spring fixing. Use a small, flat-bladed screwdriver to ease the door seal's front clamp band free from its recess

17 Remove the two screws holding the door interlock in place
Note: *Some makes may use bolts and recessed nuts that are not captive – use your free hand behind the interlock to capture them.*

20 Using a suitable low dish to catch any residual water, remove the filter

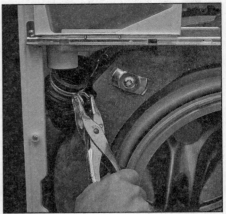

23 Next remove the clip securing the detergent dispenser hose to the detergent box. In this instance a large 'Corbin' clip was found and 'Corbin' pliers used to remove it

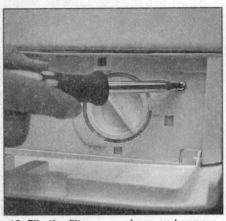

18 Flip the filter cover down and remove the single securing screw

21 Remove the metal front panel fixing screws exposed when the plastic kick plate cover was removed

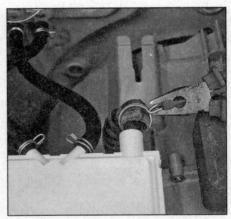

24 A smaller 'Corbin' clip that could be removed by normal pliers was used to secure the steam vent hose to the detergent box

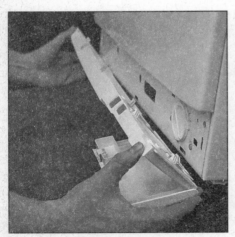

19 With the fixing screw removed – slide the whole of the bottom kick plate slightly to the right to release the plastic 'L'-shaped pegs from their slots on the metal shell

22 Hold the front panel firmly and press downwards to release the metal front panel

25 Remove the screws securing the detergent box to the front support rails

26 Next, mark the position and orientation of the top support rails, remove the screws from each end and lift them free of the machine

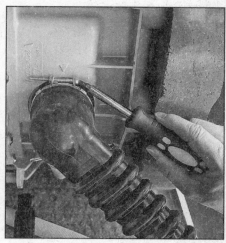

31 Remove the clamp securing the sump hose to the outer tub

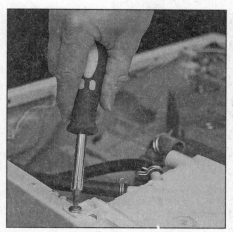

27 Remove the large headed screw used to secure the rear of the detergent box to the shell of the machine

29 Remove the two nuts securing the top outer tub weight and lift it free from the machine

Note: *The weight is very heavy, yet once free of its mounting it can easily be damaged by careless handling – handle it with care.*

28 Carefully lift the detergent box away from the work area

30 Remove the screw securing the pressure vessel to the outer tub and disconnect the pressure tube

32 Next remove the screws securing the large circular tub weight in place – the fixings used in this instance were large Torx-headed self-tapping screws which simply expand the plastic securing studs to secure the weight. When all the fixings are removed invert the door seal into the tub and carefully slide the weight forwards and free from the machine **Note:** *The weight is very heavy yet once free of its mounting it can easily be damaged by careless handling. Handle it with care.*

33 Depress the locking barb on the peg securing the top of the suspension leg to the outer tub unit and carefully pull it free

34 Raise/support the whole of the outer tub unit on a suitable size block (a solid piece of polystyrene was used in this instance

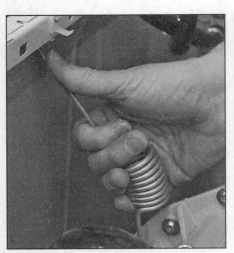

35 Ease the outer tub support springs from their top shell support points

36 When all items are disconnected from the outer tub carefully lift it free from the outer shell of the appliance
Note: *This is a very heavy item so ensure that you have help available if you need it.*

37 With the outer tub free from the shell, the self-tapping screws holding the two halves together can be removed

38 When all the fixings are removed the two halves can be eased apart

39 The inner drum can now be removed
Note: *If the machine has been run for some length of time with faulty bearings it may be necessary to use the plastic dead-blow mallet to knock the drum shaft through the old bearings.*

40 The shaft seal can be levered free using a seal removal tool like the one shown or carefully eased free using a large-blade screwdriver. Look closely to see if a large 'circlip' is fitted in front of the bearing

41 From the inside of the tub use a suitable drift to remove the rear bearing first as this will allow better access to remove the front bearing which may have more damage to it

43 If you do not have access to a bearing press or suitable large bolt and washer to press the bearings into place you will need to carefully tap the new bearings and seal into position using a plastic-headed hammer or mallet. DO NOT use metal to metal

44 Prior to reassembly check the phosphor bronze bush at the base of the drum shaft for damage and clean it with a non-abrasive pad. If the shaft or bush is damaged it may be possible to obtain a replacement support and shaft

42 With the rear bearing removed use the drift to remove the front bearing
Note: *When removing bearings in this way knock the bearing alternatively at the 12 o'clock, 6 o'clock, 9 o'clock and 3 o'clock positions until it comes out.*

Reassembly is a reversal of the strip-down procedure with the following points:-
- *Ensure that a new tub joint seal is fitted in addition to new bearings and a shaft seal.*
- *Check that all components and electrical connections are refitted correctly.*
- *Renew any wiring harness securing ties that were removed during the stripdown process.*
- *Use a thread-locking compound such as Loctite when refitting the pulley securing bolt.*
- *Carry out an earth continuity and insulation test (Chapters 3, 4, 26 and 31).*
- *Double check all work carried out prior to running a functional test sequence (Chapter 10).*

45 Refit the drive belt by locating it on the motor pulley in the position noted before removal. Then feed it around the larger drum pulley while slowly turning the large pulley. This will allow the belt to ride smoothly back into the correct position. The position of the belt and grooves on the motor pulley can be adjusted by pressing on the belt while slowly turning the shaft. This will make the belt jump the grooves until the correct position is attained

Early Hotpoint drum bearing removal

1 With machine isolated, open door and remove the securing screws for the plastic surround for the door seal

4 Remove the screws holding the timer knob in position. Later models are secured by a screw between the knob and the timer. Remove the top to acess it

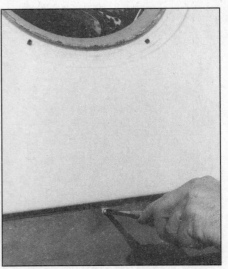

7 Remove the screws securing the bottom of the front panel. Hexagonal headed bolts may be found on early models

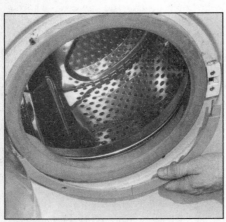

2 Next, remove the door seal surround carefully. This one is in two halves (top and bottom)

5 Pull to remove the soap drawer and remove the exposed screws. This allows the front facia to be removed

8 With front panel off, remove the door catch and interlock (if fitted)

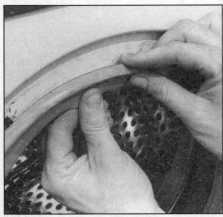

3 Free the door seal from the outer shell lip of the machine and allow to rest on the inside of the front panel

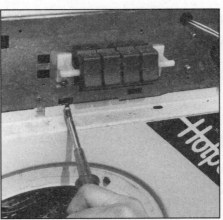

6 Remove the screws securing the top of the front panel

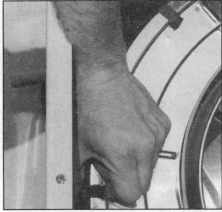

9 Note the position of the clips securing the front of the outer tub and remove carefully

10 With the clips removed, the tub front can be removed completely. Take care not to damage heater or connections

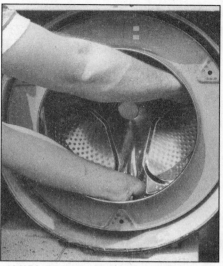

13 With the pulley securely wedged, grasp inner paddles of the drum and turn anti-clockwise. This will unscrew the pulley

16 This machine also had severe drum damage as indicated

11 Remove the screws securing the rear panel to expose the drum pulley

14 With pulley removed, tap the drum shaft free from the bearings using a soft-headed mallet

17 This style of machine has a catch pot style filter in the sump hose. When removed a large amount of coins, metal screws, curtain hooks and various other household items were found

12 Remove the pulley lock nut (right-hand thread) and chock the pulley against the tub with a wedge of wood

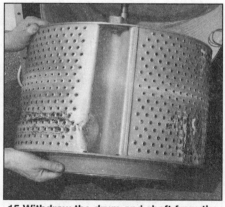

15 Withdraw the drum and shaft from the tub. This will allow ample room to drift out the ball bearings and shaft seal. Bearing replacement for this type of drum is quite straightforward, using a soft drift, knock the new bearing home, taking care not to damage the new seal. Reassembly of your machine is a reversal of the previous procedure

18 These items should not have been allowed to enter the machine. They have damaged the drum severely. What would have been a relatively inexpensive bearing only repair, has now required the renewal of a costly drum. (The £1.44 that was found did not cover the cost of the new drum!) This could have been avoided with a little care and attention to pockets, etc., when loading the machine

Popular split outer tub drum bearing sequence

1 This make and model has a typical split outer tub

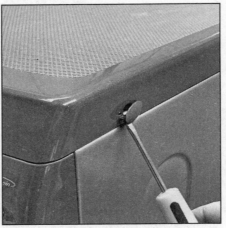

4 Use a small flat bladed screwdriver or thumb nail to remove the plastic covers at either side of the lid

7 The lid is held in place by plastic pegs and slots on both the lid and the top edge of the shell of the appliance

2 Pressing the plastic lever at the rear of the detergent dispenser allows the drawer to be removed

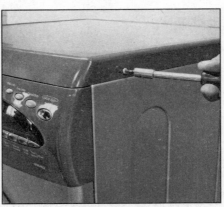

5 Removing the covers allows access to the lid securing screws (in this instance Torx-headed screws were used)

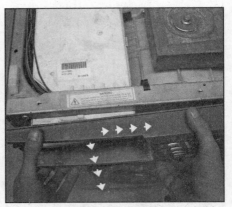

8 Next – carefully ease the left-hand side of the facia slightly forwards and then slide it gently to the right to release the captive slots and latches on the right-hand side of the plastic facia

3 Removing the detergent drawer allows access to the recessed facia fixing screws which need to removed
Note: *These screws are normally stainless steel to avoid rusting.*

6 To release the lid on this particular make and model it needs to be raised and knocked backwards

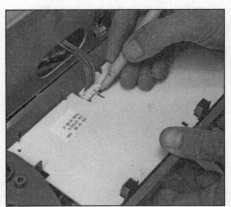

9 Before the facia can be completely removed the wiring to the programme board needs to be marked and then disconnected

10 Removing the facia creates the access to continue with the stripdown

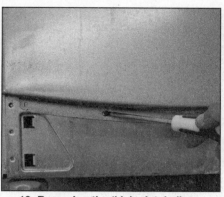

13 Removing the 'kick plate' allows access to the front panel fixing screws which need to be removed

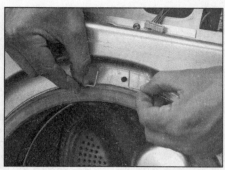

16 The two plastic parts of the latch hold the two ends of the clamp wire under tension **Note:** *To aid refitting lubricate the wire band with a little fabric conditioner to ensure it fits deeply into the door seal recess.*

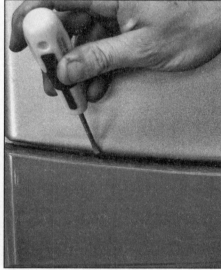

11 Next remove the plastic 'kick plate' at the base of the front panel by inserting a flat-bladed screwdriver and releasing the catches

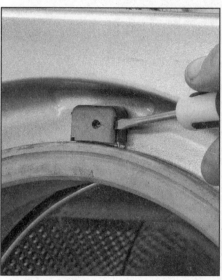

14 Release the door seal front securing clamp band by carefully inserting a small flat-bladed screwdriver into the recess of the plastic latch and gently easing it forwards

17 With the clip and clamp band removed grip the door seal firmly and pull it free from the shell lip

18 Next remove the top securing screws exposed when the facia was removed

12 When all the catches are released the 'kick plate' can be removed from the appliance

15 The previous action releases the plastic latch

19 When all fixings are removed lift the front panel to release it from the retaining slots and posts on each side

20 Shown are the post and slot securing system similar to those used by many manufacturers

25 Removing the tub weight allows greater access and lightens the outer tub to make removal easier

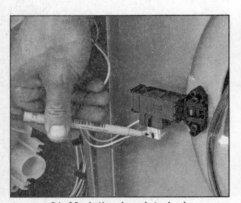

21 Mark the door interlock wires/connector block

23 Next remove the top tub weight fixing (in this instance large self-tapping screws are used)

26 Remove the front tub weight fixings and lift it free from the appliance

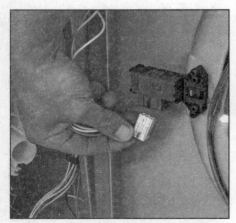

22 When a note of the connection's position has been marked it can be disconnected. This allows the front panel to be completely removed from the appliance

24 With all fixings removed the top tub weight can be carefully lifted free
Note: *This can be quite heavy and you may need assistance.*

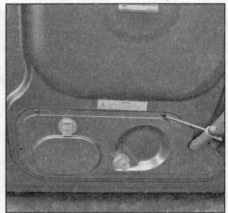

27 Next remove the rear access panel fixing screws

28 Limited access is obtained by completely removing the access panel

31 The plastic cover and bolt are an important safety item and must be replaced correctly during the refitting process

34 Some of the cable ties may be hidden or difficult to reach

29 To remove the outer tub unit you will need to cut the series of cable ties that secure the wiring harness at various points **Note:** *Any ties removed MUST be replaced.*

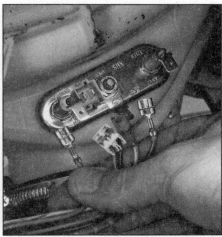

32 Next make a note of the heater wiring and then remove it

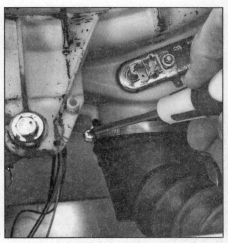

35 Unscrew the sump hose securing clamp and free the hose from the outer tub

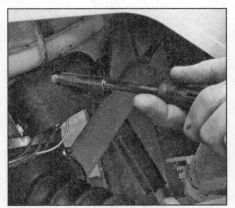

30 Using a thin walled 10mm 'deep' socket remove the plastic bolt holding the heater terminal cover in place

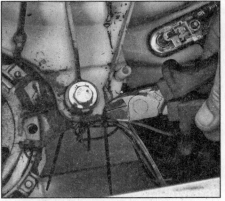

33 Cut the cable ties that secure the wiring harness at various points

36 On this model the sump hose has an internal plastic filter which contains an eco-ball valve system **Note:** *In this instance the hose and filter contained several coins which should not have been left in pockets.*

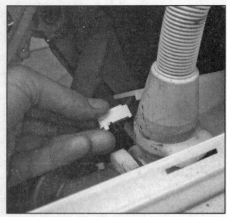

37 Mark and remove the drain pump wiring connector

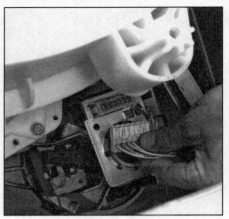

40 After making a note of its correct position remove the motor wiring connector block

43 Next remove the screws securing the metal facia support plate

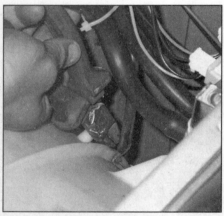

38 Cut the cable tie securing the pressure hose to the outer tub unit at the top of the outer tub and any others that may have been added during construction. Any such cable ties that are removed must be replaced during rebuilding

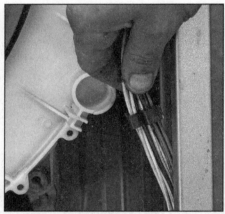

41 Next release all the wiring harness to shell securing clips

44 With all the fixings and clips removed gently lift the metal plate and its components and place them safely behind the rear of the shell

39 Remove the clip securing the dispenser hose to the outer tub

42 It is recommended that you release the wiring harness rather than disturbing the connections to the main power board

45 With most of the components freed and placed safely you can proceed to get the outer tub ready for removal

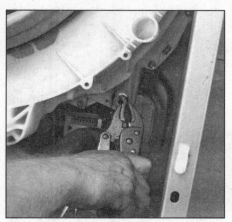

46 Lock a pair of adjustable grips to the plastic peg securing the suspension to the outer tub and turn it so that the split is pointing to the top and press the latch whilst pulling on the peg

49 When both left and right-hand pegs are removed, position the suspension legs away from the outer tub as this helps prevent damage during the next section

52 Having disconnected all the relevant hoses and fixings the whole outer tub unit can be lifted free of the shell of the appliance
Note: *The unit will still be heavy and you may need assistance to remove it in this way.*

47 You may need to waggle the peg as this can help removal
Note: *Great care must be taken to avoid slipping off and hurting yourself.*

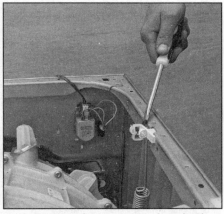

50 Remove the two top spring plastic securing clips

53 With the outer tub unit positioned on a suitably protected floor, chock the pulley and undo the drum pulley bolt

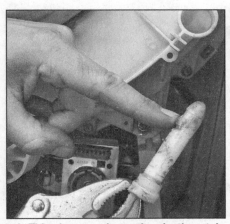

48 This close-up shows the plastic catch that needs to be depressed at the same time as the peg is pulled free. Failure to fully depress the catch will prevent the peg from being removed

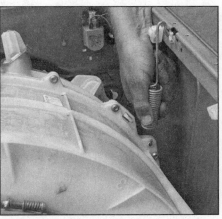

51 With the clip removed the spring can be lifted to free it from its position

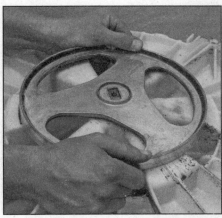

54 With the fixing bolt removed the pulley can be 'waggled' to help free it from the drum shaft

55 Lift the pulley free from the drum shaft

56 While the outer tub is still in one piece refit the pulley bolt and strike the bolt a couple of sharp blows to help free the shaft from the grip of the old bearings

57 Next carefully ease the spring fittings that hold the two outer tub halves together

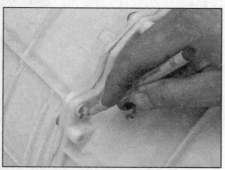

58 Now mark the two plastic inserts into which the support springs fit
Note: *These are fitted differently on each side so ensure you make a clear note of the correct position.*

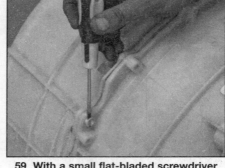

59 With a small flat-bladed screwdriver ease each peg out of position

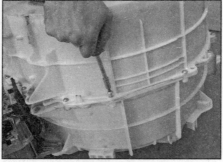

60 Next remove the series of screws holding the two halves of the outer tub together. Torx-headed screws were used in this instance

61 When all of the fixings have been removed use a large flat-bladed screwdriver to lever the two halves apart

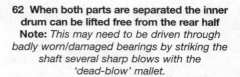

62 When both parts are separated the inner drum can be lifted free from the rear half
Note: *This may need to be driven through badly worn/damaged bearings by striking the shaft several sharp blows with the 'dead-blow' mallet.*

Special note: *There are models produced by this manufacturer that are fitted with outer tub units that are heat welded together in manufacture (no clips, screws or fixing holding the two halves of the hub together). This renders the outer tub, drum bearings and inner stainless steel drum unserviceable and means that no matter what the fault a complete outer tub will be required even for a relatively simple fault such as bearing/shaft seal failure. Various models within the Ariston and Indesit ranges may also have welded outer tub construction. Such construction techniques obviously lead to higher than needed repair cost (having to replace a lot of parts you simply do not require) and cannot be good for the environment with such a high degree of wastage*

63 Support the outer tub rear half and place a suitable metal drift through the front bearing and knock the rear bearing out. Keep changing the position of the drift during this process

66 Obtain new bearings and shaft seal
Note: *In this instance the new shaft seal differs slightly from the original as the design was improved.*
Alternatively, and for a much higher price a new back half with bearings already fitted could have been purchased

69 An alternative method of fitting is to use a correct size bearing drift tool like the one shown. These may be available from local tool hire outlets or a local garage

64 The rear bearing is removed first as this allows greater access to the front bearing which is often the most difficult to remove

67 Ensure you clean your hands thoroughly prior to handling the new bearing set and carefully tap the new bearing into position
Note: *Ideally it is best to have the bearings pressed into position with a bearing press if available.*

70 Carefully fit the shaft seal

65 With the rear bearing extracted place the drift through the hole and remove the front bearing. This action will also remove the shaft seal at the same time
Note *On some makes check to see if a circlip has been used to hold the bearing.*

68 Next fit the inner bearing ensuring that contact is only made with the outer bearing
Note: *Ideally it is best to have the bearings pressed into position with a bearing press if available.*

71 As the user of this appliance had left it some time before deciding to have the repair carried out, water had penetrated the bearings for quite some time. This resulted in a great deal of noise, and discharge from the bearings

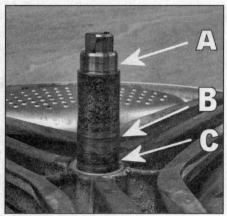

72 Prior to being refitted the drum shaft required both cleaning and inspecting for damage at the key points of contact

A. Rear bearing position and shoulder – no damage in this instance.

B. Front bearing position (no shoulder used on this model) – although slightly discoloured there was no damage.

C. Point where the shaft seal rests – although slightly discoloured and marginal.

Note: *This particular model does not use a phosphor bronze bush and the shaft seal rests on the mild steel shaft. It is essential that this area of the shaft is both clean and smooth for a watertight seal to be created. If in doubt, as in this instance, it is recommended that a new shaft (drum spider unit) is obtained.*

73 Prior to reassembly it is essential that a new tub joint seal is fitted. All split outer tub systems must have new joint seals fitted as a matter of course during bearing renewal

Refitting is a reversal of the strip-down procedure

Note: *When refitting the outer tub securing screws they must be tightened in alternate sequence i.e. left-hand – right-hand, right-hand – left-hand etc.*

servicing the drum bearings, outer tub and seals which entails the removal of the outer tub unit from the machine via the top of the machine's cabinet as a complete unit. These should be unscrewed and the components laid over the front facia of the machine. If possible do not disconnect any wiring, but detailed notes of all connections and fixings should be kept in the event of items getting misplaced or dislodged. Release the screws securing the dispenser unit to the cabinet and remove the dispenser hose from the dispenser unit. Lay the dispenser unit over the front of the machine. Remove the top tub weight (if fitted) and release the front fitting of the door seal. To help slide the tub unit out of the machine, two pieces of wood 5mm x 2½mm x 120mm (2in x 1in x 4ft) can be inserted down the left-hand side of the machine between the tub and cabinet to support the tub during its removal (see Diagram 1). **Note:** *If your machine has the timer on the opposite side to that shown in Diagram 1, the wood should be inserted down the right-hand side and the machine laid over correspondingly.*

Now lower the machine onto the left-hand side after making sure that the cabinet side and floor are protected, and release the shock absorber or friction damper mountings. Now disconnect the sump hose, pressure hoses, heater connections, thermostat connections and motor block connections. Remove the drive belt and drum pulley and check that all connections are free from the outer tub unit. At the top of the machine, release the suspension springs by pushing the tub unit towards the top of the machine. It will now be possible to slide the tub assembly out of the cabinet. At this point a little help may be useful as the unit will be quite heavy and needs manoeuvring

2 The construction of the outer tub is jointed at the front of the machine and not the rear, and the inner drum can only be taken out by first removing the front of the outer tub. Unfortunately, the front shell of many machines is not detachable and so the whole unit needs to be removed as described. However, many manufacturers now produce front serviceable machines with removable front panels. Check the model you have to see if it has a detachable front panel. **Note:** *The way in which the panels are secured differs greatly between the manufacturers. Look for tell-tale signs such as hidden screws, side joints in the shell of the machine (indicating separate front panel construction). Refer to the various bearing renewal sequences within in this chapter, as they give an insight into front panel fixing techniques.*

Many makes and models of machine now require tub unit removal for both bearing and inner drum problems.

3 The outer tub unit is made up of two large plastic mouldings with a centre joint secured by screws or clips and the shell/cabinet of the appliance is of rigid construction.

It is not uncommon for manufacturers to buy in products from another company and then 'badge' them as their own. This leads to a mix

of model designs throughout the range. Until fairly recently, the current production machines were merely updated variations on a basic design, and therefore some continuity and standard format existed. However, this is not always the case nowadays, which means that each machine has to be assessed prior to carrying out repairs, e.g. are the bearings mounted in a detachable housing? If access requires removal of the front of the outer tub, can the front of the machine be removed to allow the unit to remain in situ? (See photo sequences.)

If no other option exists, then the outer tub unit complete with drum and bearing will have to be removed to allow for complete strip-down. The removal of this large unit is via the top of the machine shell. The following text describes the removal of the outer tub unit after removing such items as the top/bottom tub weights, pulley, all connections and hoses and electrical connections to the unit. (A photo sequence is not used for this as it would tend to mislead rather than help, as each machine will have distinct variations, depending on the original manufacturer.)

It is advisable to remove all knobs from the front of the machine to reveal the fixing screws of the items behind them. This will help when

This picture shows a machine with the front panel removed, illustrating the excellent access that can be found with this type of machine

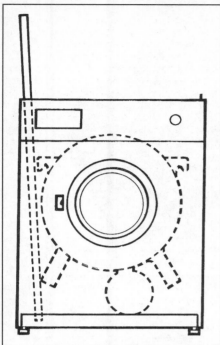
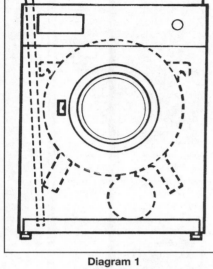

Diagram 1

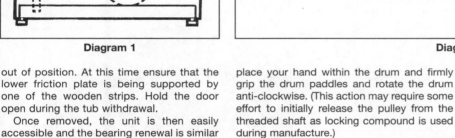
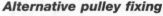

Diagram 2

out of position. At this time ensure that the lower friction plate is being supported by one of the wooden strips. Hold the door open during the tub withdrawal.

Once removed, the unit is then easily accessible and the bearing renewal is similar to that shown in the previous photo sequences. Make a note of all clamp positions, tub front and back positions, etc. It is advisable to re-seal and check all hoses and their fixing points prior to refitting the unit. It is important to do this when the tub is out of the machine as this may be difficult when the unit is replaced.

Refitting is a reversal of the removal procedure. After refitting, ensure that all electrical and earth connections are replaced correctly and securely and an RCD protected socket is used when the functional test sequence is carried out. **Remember:** *Many manufacturers now have machines on the market with detachable front panels. With this type of machine, the drum and bearing assemblies can be removed and changed with the outer tub in situ, or the tub unit removed through the front of the machine – see photo sequence.*

Pulleys

With the early Hotpoint machines, the pulley was threaded to the shaft and secured by a locknut. To remove the pulley – first remove the large securing nut. Next chock the spokes of the pulley to the recesses in the outer tub with wood – from the front of the machine

place your hand within the drum and firmly grip the drum paddles and rotate the drum anti-clockwise. (This action may require some effort to initially release the pulley from the threaded shaft as locking compound is used during manufacture.)

When refitting, apply a little locking compound to the shaft thread. This can be

obtained from any good DIY or motorists shop.

Alternative pulley fixing

As can be seen from the various photographic sequences, the way most pulleys are secured to the shaft are relatively simple and with a little thought and reference

Prior to starting the removal procedure strike the pulley bolt two or three sharp blows to help loosen the thread-locking compound used during production

Prevent the pulley from turning and remove the pulley bolt. A Torx bolt secured the pulley on this model

Remove the drive belt prior to freeing the pulley from the drum shaft

Insert a suitable ball-joint wedge or similar wedges between the centre of the pulley and the rear bearing inner. Several sharp blows may be required to free the pulley from the drum shaft
Note: *The wearing of protective goggles is recommended during this process.*

Check the pulley for damage when it is free of the shaft

to this chapter most can be worked out. However, a not-so-obvious method of securing the drum pulley to the drum shaft is by means of a tapered cone and pulley. Two popular makes that use this method on some of their models are Ariston and Creda and when the securing bolt is tightened the pulley and cone are forced together. This reduces the diameter of the cone which grips the circular drum shaft. When fitted for some length of time the separate parts can become very tight.

Prior to removing the securing bolt strike it several firm blows with a dead-blow mallet or hide/plastic hammer as this will help free the locking compound and grip of the bolt. **Note:** *Do not use a metal-to-metal blow, i.e. a metal hammer.*

It is likely that even after removing the centre securing bolt the pulley will remain firmly attached to the shaft and cone, so loosely refit the centre bolt and once again strike the bolt with the dead-blow mallet or hide/plastic hammer to help shock it free. If this fails it may be necessary to insert opposing metal wedges or a ball-joint separator (available from good tool shops/car part suppliers) between the rear bearing inner race and the thick base of the pulley to apply pressure. (It is not recommended to use pullers on the aluminium pulley.) When handling the metal pulley, gloved hands are recommended, as the moulding of the pulley can be sharp.

With the pulley and tapered cone removed refit the securing bolt to protect the threads and use a hide/plastic hammer to free the drum shaft from the bearings.

What you do next will depend on which type of bearing housing your machine has, either cast iron bearing housing, large metal back plate or moulded plastic outer tub.

When removing the bearing housing/drum, note the position and assembly of the sealing system both on the bearing face and the lower end of the drum shaft. Depending on the make and model a cupped/lipped seal or spring-loaded carbon seal system may be found. Ensure that the replacement kit is the same as the one already fitted to your machine. With cup seal systems check they are fitted the correct way up by making a note of the old seal before removing it. When removed, clean the shaft base thoroughly and use a little sealant to secure the new seal in position. DO NOT contaminate the front skirt of the rubber lip seal. The old bearings and seal can now be knocked out and the new set fitted (ball race types will be pre-greased – no extra required). Refit the front seal system/contact plate, again sealant can be used around the edge, but DO NOT allow contamination of the smooth metal/carbon surfaces. With the rubber cup seal system the contact between the smooth metal plate and the shaft seal skirt is all that creates the watertight seal, cleanliness is therefore essential.

It is a good idea to apply a little petroleum jelly (a slight smear only) to the new shaft seal skirt and its metal contact plate on the front of the bearings prior to assembly. Refitting is a simple reversal of the stripdown process, however you may find that the shaft of the drum does not protrude far enough through the new bearings to allow the fitting of the pulley. This is usually due to the new bearings being a little tight on the shaft. To overcome this problem, open the door of the machine, and with the flat palm of the hand, hit the rear of the inner drum to seat the shaft firmly into the new bearings. Do not use tools for this as they could dent the drum rear. Although the pulley can be fitted, failure to seat the drum shaft correctly will allow water to bypass the new seal.

Cast iron bearing housing

A Zanussi machine has been chosen to illustrate a typical cast iron bearing housing stripdown. Many manufacturers use similar systems and the information given can be adapted to those machines, where possible additional details are given. In this particular range of machines two types of bearings can be found – a conical bearing (one single outer case with two inner races) or two normal ball race types, the sizes of which will depend on the individual model.

Refitting is a simple reversal process, but remember to make sure that the captive washers on the centre bolts go behind the plate with slots in and NOT between the plate and the spider unit, otherwise leaking will occur. Another tip is to glue the washers to the bolt heads prior to refitting so that they cannot go out of position. When refitting the outer bolts, ensure that the two bottom bolts go in first. This allows all the compression of the new rubber seal to be done when lining up the top bolt. You may find that the shaft of the drum may not protrude far enough through the bearing to allow the fitting of the pulley. This is due to the new bearings being a little tight on the shaft. To overcome this problem, open the door of the machine and with the flat of the hand, hit the rear of the inner drum to seat the shaft firmly into the new bearings, DO NOT use tools for this as they may dent the rear of the drum.

Note: *Details of machines with 50/50 split shells can be found in the chapter: Useful tips and information.*

1 With the machine fully isolated remove the top and back panels

2 Remove the drive belt, locking tab, bolt and pulley

3 If it is stuck to the shaft, loosely refit the centre bolt and tap the bolt with a hide/plastic hammer to free it off

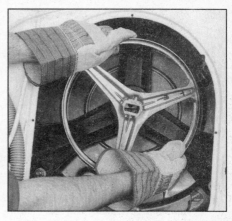
4 When loosened, waggle the pulley free without using too much force, (gloved hands are recommended, as the moulding of the pulley can be sharp)

5 Refit the securing bolt and use a plastic hammer/hide mallet to free the drum shaft from the bearings

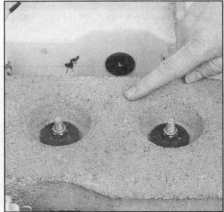
6 On some models you may need to remove the concrete top block to gain easy access to the top bolt of the bearing housing, however this is not required in this instance

7 With suitable protection carefully lay the machine on its face for the following sequences

8 Remove the end bolts securing the remaining legs. For models with additional centre bolts, loosen but do not fully remove the three centre nuts

Note: On Zanussi and similar models these are in captive slots and do not need complete removal. However, this may not be the case with other makes/models. A finger inserted behind the centre lip can usually detect if captive slots are used.

If you cannot get a spanner (13mm) behind to hold the bolt head, a good tip is to hold the exposed thread of the centre bolts with self-locking grips and undo the nut a few turns. As the nut need never be completely removed, thread damage is no problem

Note: This can only be done on machines with captive slot fixings.

When the outer bolts are out and the inner bolts loosened, the spider is free to be rotated clockwise 5–7mm (2–3in) allowing the captive bolts to be free of their slots

9 Next, pull the spider from the drum shaft and manoeuvre the housing out of the back of the machine

10 Ensure the shaft and the phosphor bronze bush on the drum shaft are clean and free from scale, etc.

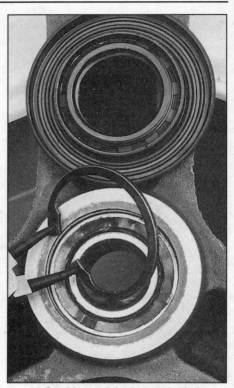

11 On this model a large circlip is located behind the shaft seal and you need to lever out the old seal to gain access to remove it with circlip pliers before trying to remove the bearing(s). Bearings without circlip fixings can be simply knocked out and the new set fitted. It is a good idea to apply a little petroleum jelly to the new seal and bush on the shaft to allow them to slip together when refitting

Chapter 31
Main drive belts

The drive belts used in automatic washing machines are of two distinctly different types. Both kinds come in a multitude of size variations, but each machine must be correctly fitted with the exact size and type and no other. The two types of belt are the Vee, so called because of its location on V-shaped pulleys, and Multi Vee belts which are much flatter and have a series of Vee formations on the drive face. The use of a Multi Vee formation gives a greater contact surface area in relation to the belt width. This is necessary as the belt is designed to be driven by a much smaller and therefore faster rotating drive pulley than the larger single Vee drive pulleys.

In general Vee belts are to be found on washing machines with induction motors and Multi Vee belts are found on washing machines with brush gear motors of all types. Three-phase induction motors also use multi vee belts.

What are drive belts made of?

Both types of belt consist of woven nylon cords upon which a synthetic rubber is moulded. The single Vee belt has sides of approximately 40 degrees and terminating in a flat base, see cross section D. The Multi Vee belt is a series of peaks and troughs, the number of which varies with the work load requirements of the belt, see cross sections A, B & C. Always ensure that a replacement belt is the correct size and width, most belts have sizes or size codes printed on the outer face. However, such marks are often illegible on old belts due to wear. Take a note of the make, model and serial number of your machine along with any legible belt code when obtaining a replacement belt.

Removal and renewal

The single Vee belt drive system requires both drive pulley (the one on the motor) and drum pulley (the larger one on the drum shaft), to have a recessed groove the same dimensions as the belt. Multi Vee systems can have two variations.

1 Both drive pulley and drum pulley are grooved to accept the Multi Vee configuration of the belt.

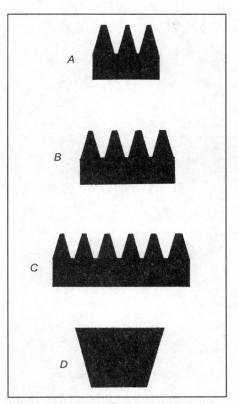

Shown are cross sections of the various types of belt to be found
A 3 point MultiVee
B 4 point MultiVee
C 6 point MultiVee
D A typical single Vee

2 Only the drive pulley is grooved (to aid grip on its much smaller surface area) and the drum pulley is smooth and slightly convex in shape. Grip is created on the drum pulley purely by it having a greater contact area to the belt when in use even though this is only on the peaks of the belt. The convex shape keeps the belt in place on the grooveless pulley and reduces wear if misalignment occurs.

Slacken off the motor bolt to reduce tension and pull the belt towards you midway between the pulleys whilst carefully rotating the drum pulley slowly clockwise. This will allow the belt to smoothly ride out of position. Reverse this process for refitting. **Note:** *It is advisable to use protective gloves as the pulleys on machines can have very sharp edges.*

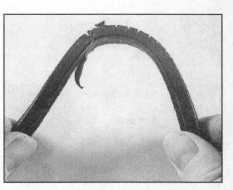

To inspect a belt turn it inside out and check the whole length thoroughly. The Vee belt shown has clear signs of cracking on its inner surface and shedding of the outer cover material. Renewal is the only answer to such problems

Belt care
Ensure pulleys are in good condition, i.e. not chipped or buckled, etc., and are aligned correctly. Misalignment will shorten the working life of both types of belt. Poorly aligned belts will shed the rubber compound coating from the nylon cords leaving tell-tale dust or flakes in the base and surrounding area of the machine. This may block the Vee section of Multi Vee belts and cause the belt to fly off usually on a spin cycle. Single Vee belts may twist within the Vee section when misaligned. Close inspection of belts is essential and turning the belt inside out and bending it is the best way to inspect them. Check the full length in this way. If any defects are found, renew the belt.

When removing a belt for inspection or during repair, care must be exercised to avoid damage to the belt itself. Do not use screwdrivers or similar to prise belts on or off as this can easily damage the belt cords and moulding of the soft aluminium pulleys used on washing machines.

Belt tension
It is natural for some degree of stretching and wear to occur during use which will result in the need for re-tensioning. Some machines may be self-tensioning, i.e., the weight of the motor keeps the belt under tension (this system was popular with some early washer driers). However, the majority of washing machines rely on motor adjustment, i.e., two fixed bolts and one slotted, to tension the belt.

Setting the correct tension is essential. Too

Adjust belt tension by moving the motor position up or down to attain correct belt displacement

Machines that have fixed motor positions use special elasticated drive belts. Ensure you obtain the correct type of belt

tight will quickly wear the belt and worse still, it will damage the drive pulley and cause premature motor bearing failure. Too slack and belt slip will occur resulting in poor wash, excessive vibration or heating of the belt which will result in belt damage or failure. On machines with aluminium pulleys, slipping can create ridges on the pulley grooves. If this does happen, the damaged pulley/pulleys will need renewing as any new belt fitted to such a pulley will soon become damaged by the uneven pulley surface.

Note: *Many modern machines including models in the Hoover and Zanussi range use belts with an elastic braid construction that do not require adjustment and do not have any provision for adjustment. The intention being the belt should last the lifetime of the machine. However, renewal is sometimes required and it is essential that the correct version of belt is obtained for these machines. Removal and renewal are by winding off and winding on as described earlier and there is no need to loosen the motor.*

The correct tension of a belt depends on its free distance between pulley contact points. As a rule a 12mm deflection per 30cm of free belt is required. Most washing machines have in the region of 30cm of free belt between pulleys and therefore a 12 to 13mm deflection is optimum. When fitted and tensioned correctly the belt will have a springy feel. Some stretching will occur to new belts, but modern good quality belts are much less

affected. However, the belt will need to be checked at a later date and re-adjusted if required. Do not over-tension a new belt in the misguided hope that this will overcome any initial stretching that may occur. Over tensioning can lead to belt damage and motor bearing wear.

Elasticated Multi Vee Belts

These belts are made with an internal elasticated braid and can be found on many modern front loading automatic washing machines, combined washerdriers and tumbledriers. Using this type of belt on tumbledriers eliminates the need for jockey pulleys. Due to this the drier is much quieter when in operation. No adjustment is required or available on most models with these belts and this may create fitting problems on some models and may require the slackening of the motor support bolts to aid fitting. Re-tightening the motor mounting bolts creates the correct tension.

The use of elasticated Multi Vee belts is now common on automatic washing machines and

several models in the Whirlpool, Hoover and Zanussi ranges (among others) use them. They are expected to last the service life of the machine and therefore no adjustment system is provided. Should it be necessary to renew the belt (for whatever reason) simply pull on the centre of the free section and slowly rotate the drum pulley, this will allow the belt to ride free from the pulley. Refit in a similar manner ensuring that the belt is positioned correctly on both the motor and drum pulley. There should be no need to slacken the motor mounting bolts when renewing or replacing this type of drive belt.

Points to note

It is not uncommon for belts to be warm after use even when correctly tensioned. This is due to the energy absorbed as the belt flexes and is proportional to the load. If the belt is hot or very warm after use, this would indicate incorrect tension or overloading causing belt slip and friction heating. Correct the problem but check the belt for any cracking caused by overheating. If in doubt, renew the belt.

Noise

This is usually a squealing type of noise most often heard on wash rotation and prior to spin (distribute) when the belt is under most load. This may simply be incorrect tension, or worn pulleys, i.e., ridges, misaligned or machine overloaded. Again, isolate and correct fault and inspect belt closely for damage. If in doubt, renew it. It may be possible to reposition the drive pulley on some motors. Use a long straight edge to check alignment.

Ensure Multi Vee belts align correctly if both drive and drum pulley are grooved, note position of original belt, i.e., first groove on drive pulley is used then first groove on drum pulley is used. Misalignment on Multi Vee belts is easily done, so ensure that they are correctly fitted to avoid premature belt wear or the belt flying off during spin or wash cycles.

Machines with centrifugal clutch systems, see *Motors* chapter, create quicker belt wear due to the constant squeezing and movement of the belt. Check the drive pulley closely for wear ridges and be prepared to change belts more frequently on this type of drive system to maintain peak performance.

Chapter 32
Electrical circuit testing

Throughout this book, references have been made to meters and their use in continuity testing of individual parts of appliances and their connecting wires. All such testing and checking for 'open' (i.e. not allowing for current flow), or 'closed' circuit (i.e. allowing current to flow), must be carried out using a battery powered multi-meter or test meter. Under no circumstances should testing be carried out on 'live' items, i.e. appliances connected to the mains supply. **Remember:** *completely isolate the appliances from the mains supply before starting any repair work or testing.*

Although some meters and testers have the facility to check mains voltages, I do not agree with their use in repairs to domestic appliances. Faults can be easily traced by simple low voltage (battery power) continuity testing, proving that the simplest of meters or even a home-made one like the one described are perfectly adequate for some faults. Remember that safety is paramount and under no circumstances should it be compromised. Always double check that the appliance is unplugged; a good tip is to keep the plug in view so that no-one else can inadvertently plug it in. The simple home-made continuity tester described later will help trace faults only in the wiring of the appliance. A multi-meter similar to the ones shown will be required for individual component testing.

If you decide to buy a test meter, you could find yourself faced with quite a variety to choose from. Do not be tempted to get an over-complicated one as it could end up confusing and misleading you when in use. Before using your new meter, read the manufacturer's instructions thoroughly and make sure that you fully understand them. The 'rapitest' meter is very simple to use when continuity testing and has a scale that reads 'open' circuit or 'closed' circuit. It was purchased from a local DIY store and was very reasonably priced. The meter will also help locate faults with car electrics, but as previously stated, using on live mains circuits should not be entertained.

Some multi-meters are able to show the resistance value of the item being tested as well as indicating continuity. This can be extremely useful if the correct value of the item being tested is known, i.e. correct resistance of motor winding, armature and element, etc., although this is by no means essential. Detailed use of the multi-meter for this function will be found in its accompanying instruction leaflet.

Testing this heater for continuity on the 0–200 Ohms range of the meter provided a reading of 22.7Ω which is within the range expected for a 2,500-watt element. Although the exact reading obtained is of interest, in reality you are checking for continuity (closed circuit – heater OK) or lack of continuity (open circuit – heater failure)

Checking this drain pump coil for continuity provided a reading of 160.7Ω, which again could be detected using the 0–200 Ohms range on the meter. Once again, although the exact reading obtained is of interest, in reality you are checking for continuity (closed circuit – coil OK) or lack of continuity (coil open circuit – failure)

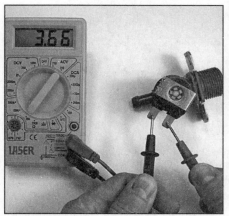

Checking this water valve coil for continuity required the meter to be set to read K Ohms (thousands of Ohms) as the coils of this type have high resistances and would appear open circuit if the wrong range was selected. The digital reading obtained is 3.66KΩ equating to 3,660 Ohms, which is within the expected range. Yet again, although the exact reading obtained is of interest, in reality you are checking for continuity (closed circuit – valve coil OK) or lack of continuity (open circuit – valve coil failure)

Checking this timer motor coil gave a reading of 9.75KΩ (9,750Ω) which is within the range expected. The exact reading obtained is of interest, but in reality you are checking for continuity (closed circuit – motor coil OK) or lack of continuity (open circuit – motor coil failure)

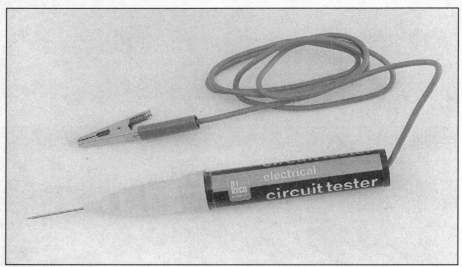

This simple continuity tester was purchased quite cheaply from a local automart. It is a manufactured version of the home-made type described

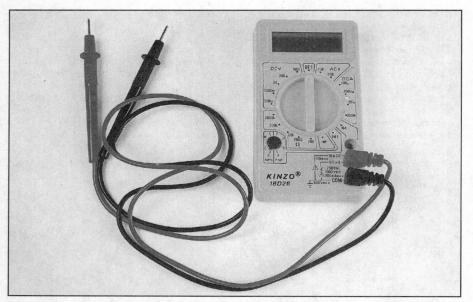

Small digital test meters such as this one are now widely available and readings easier to interpret. They are also available in auto-ranging versions, which automatically display the correct scale

Electrical fault finding

A simple continuity tester for wiring. This simple device can be used to trace wiring faults in most appliances and is very easy to make. It uses the lack of continuity to its full advantage. To make this tester, you will need a standard battery, bulb and three wires 1 x 13mm (5in) and 2 x 25mm (10in). Connect the short wire to the positive terminal of the battery and the other end of that wire to the centre terminal of a small torch bulb. Attach one of the longer wires to the negative terminal of the battery and leave the other end free. The other wire should be attached to the body of the bulb again, leave the end free.

The two loose ends now act as the test wires. Press the two ends of the wires together, and the bulb will light. If not, check that the battery and the bulb and all connections are OK. When 'open circuit', the light will stay off, and when 'closed circuit', the light will be on. **Note:** *Low voltage bulb type testers of 1.5 volts or 3 volts are unsuitable for testing the continuity of components within the machines. A test* meter like the ones shown will be required to test high resistance items such as pumps, timer coil, valves, etc. Ensure that the machine is isolated from the main supply before attempting to use a meter.

How to test for continuity using a test meter

To test for an open circuit, note and remove the original wiring to the component to be tested. (If this is not done, false readings may be given from other items that may be in circuit.) The ends of the two wires of the meter should be attached to the component that is suspected. For example, to test a heater for continuity, place the metal probes on the tags at the end of the heater and watch the meter. The needle should move.

If the heater is 'open circuit', i.e., no movement, the heater can then be suspected and tested further. If closed circuit, the heater continuity is OK.

To check for the correct resistance you will need to select the correct scale and reference to the instruction booklet for your particular meter will be required (unless you have an auto-ranging digital meter).

Often the most effective way to trace a fault is to use a very simple, but logical approach to them. One such approach is called the leap-frog method and can be used to find the failed/open circuit part or parts. In this instance, let us assume that the appliance does not work at all when functionally tested, therefore you cannot deduce where the problem lies purely from the symptoms. A quick check of the supply socket by plugging in another appliance known to be OK will verify (or not) that there is power up to that point. This confirms that the fault lies somewhere in the appliance, its supply cable or plug. We know that during normal conditions, power flows in through the live pin on the plug, through the appliance (when switched on) and returns via the neutral pin on the plug. The fact that the appliance will not work at all even when plugged in and switched on indicates that an open circuit exists somewhere along this normal live to neutral circuit.

Leap-frog testing – using a meter

First, test that the meter is working correctly, i.e. touch test probes together and the meter should indicate continuity. With the machine unplugged (isolated) connect one probe to the live pin of the appliance's plug and the other on the live conductor connecting point in the plug. Continuity should be found which confirms that the pin, fuse and their connections are OK, but faulty if open circuit occurs. If this check proves to be satisfactory, move the probe from the live conductor point in the plug to the live conductor connection in the terminal block within the appliance. Again, continuity should be found, if not, a fault between plug and terminal block is indicated. **Note:** *On cable continuity testing, it is best to move the cable along its length during the test to ascertain if an intermittent fault may exist.*

If this test is OK, move the probe to the next convenient point along the live conductor, in this instance, the supply side of the on/off switch, which may be part of the main programme switch on some machines (usually the front terminals).

Again, continuity is required. An open circuit indicates a fault between terminal block and switch connection. The next step is to move the probe to the opposite terminal of the switch. Operate the switch to verify correct action (i.e. 'on' continuity, 'off' open circuit). If OK proceed to the next point along the wire, in this instance the door interlock connection. Again continuity is required, if OK, move probe to the terminal on the return side of the heater within the interlock. See *Door switches (interlocks)* chapter. This again should indicate continuity through the heater of the interlock. At this point we will assume that an open circuit has been indicated, so go back to the last test point and verify continuity up to that point. If found to be alright, then a fault has been traced that lies within the interlock which requires renewal.

This simple, methodical approach is all that is required to find such problems. With more complex circuits it is best to break them down into individual sections, i.e. motor, heater, switch, etc., and test continuity of each section from live through the timer and the individual parts and back to neutral. This may involve moving the live probe that would normally remain on the plug live pin to a more convenient supply point within the appliance to avoid misleading continuity readings from other items within the appliance circuit. With practice, faults can be found even in complex wiring in this way.

Note: *The action of switching within the interlock of power back to the timer cannot be verified but continuity of the wiring can be checked in a similar leap-frog manner. In this instance, due to the heater being 'open circuit' the interlock would fail to operate and the action of power being returned (switched) to the timer for distribution to other parts could not take place. A fault with the main switching action of the interlock would have been indicated during the functional test. See* Functional testing, *i.e. when the machine was switched on, the door locked but nothing else would operate other than the door locking. This is due to most (but not all) machines having the interlock as the first item in circuit when switched on, therefore incorrect latching of the door or failure of the*

interlock (other than short circuit of the internal switch) will render the appliance inoperable.

DO NOT trace faults by looking for mains voltages. There is no need to consider or use such dangerous techniques. All testing can and should be carried out with the appliance completely isolated, i.e. switch off, plug out, using only a battery powered meter or tester to indicate continuity or open circuit.

The ohms reading will differ from item to item. Test for open or closed circuits only. Any reference to an ohm (Ω) reading is a guide only as resistances differ from machine to machine. The objective is to test for either continuity or the lack of continuity of the item being tested.

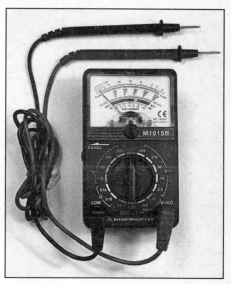

A typical multi-meter of the type available in most DIY stores. Try to obtain a meter with a good informative booklet. The meter shown proved to be useful for many other jobs around the house and car

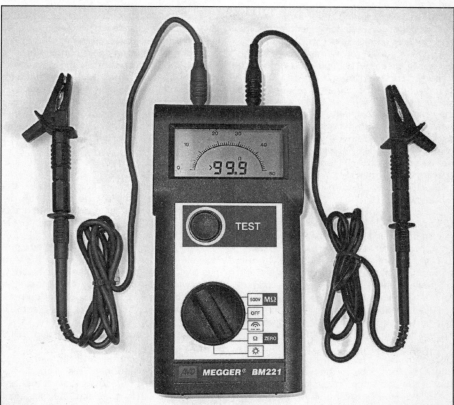

This commercial meter can be used for low Ohms readings as the scale can only provide readings up to 99.9Ω and would therefore be unable to test items with resistances above that level. Items such as the pump, valve coil and timer coil shown previously, would appear open circuit on this meter. Before using a meter ensure that it is capable of reading the expected resistance and that it is set to the correct scale. Although this meter has limitations for simple resistance checking of components it does have the ability to check insulation which the simpler (and cheaper) meters could not

Chapter 33
Wiring and harness faults

The term harness is used for all of the wires that connect the various components within the appliance. On large appliances they are usually bound or fastened together in bunches to keep the wiring in the appliance neat and safely anchored. Smaller appliances, however, may sacrifice neatness for safety and route the wiring to avoid contact with heat, sharp edges, etc.

At first sight, the harness may look like a jumble of wires thrown together. This is not the case. If you take the time to inspect the harness, you will find that each wire is colour coded or numbered (either on the wire itself, or on the connector at either end). This allows you to follow the wiring through the appliance easily. With practice, any wiring or coding can be followed.

As most of the wires in the machine either finish or start at the timer unit, it may be helpful to think of the timer as the base of a tree, with the main wiring harness as the trunk. As the trunk is followed, branches appear (wires to the valves, pressure switches, etc.). Continuing upwards, the trunk gets slowly thinner as branching takes place to the motor, pump, module, etc.

Each item is therefore separate but linked to the timer by a central bond of wire. This in turn can be likened to a central command post, communicating with field outposts.

The connecting wires to and/or from a component are vital to that component and possibly others that rely on the correct functioning of that item.

Luckily, wiring faults are not too common. but when they do occur they sometimes appear to result in big problems, when in reality it is only a small fault that has occurred, i.e. one poor connection can cause a motor not to function at all, and render the appliance unusable.

Do not fall into the trap of always suspecting the worst. Many people, including engineers, blindly fit parts such as a motor or a heater for a similar fault to that mentioned, only to find it did not cure the problem. Often the timer is blamed and subsequently changed. This does not cure the problem and is an expensive mistake. Stop, think and check all wires and connections that relate to your particular fault. Always inspect all connections and ensure that the wire and connector has a tight fit. Loose or poor connections can overheat and

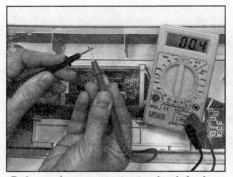

Before using your meter to check for low resistances – such as the continuity testing of a ribbon cable connection – touch the test leads firmly together and note the reading obtained, i.e. the reading of just the test leads (in this instance 0.4Ω). Deducting this reading from that obtained when checking for continuity will give the resistance of the item being tested

cause a lot of trouble, especially on items such as the heater.

Poor connections to items such as the main motor or pump will be aggravated by movement of the machine when in use and may not be so apparent when a static test is carried out.

One of the most easily missed faults is where the metal core (conductor) of the wire has broken and the outer insulation has not. This wire will appear perfect from the outside but will pass no electrical current. To test for this, see the chapter *Electrical circuit testing*.

It must be remembered that such faults may be intermittent. That is to say that one reading may be correct and the same test later may prove incorrect. This is due to the movement of the outer insulation of the wire first making, then breaking the electrical connection.

When testing for such intermittent faults, pull or stretch each wire tested. An unbroken wire will not stretch whereas a wire that is broken internally will stretch at the break point and rectification is a simple matter of renewing the connection with a suitable connector. Do not make the connection by twisting the wires together and covering them with insulation tape. Use only the correct rating of connector and ensure a secure and insulated joint is made. If a joint is required in a position of

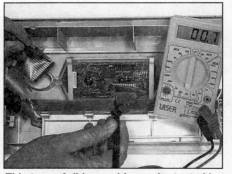

This type of ribbon cable can be tested by placing the test probes of the meter on the open connections immediately behind each connector block. In this instance a reading of 0.7Ω is shown but the original reading of the leads on their own (0.4Ω) must be deducted from this figure to obtain the true reading of the cable itself (0.3Ω in this instance). When testing the continuity of electrical connections such as this, as low a reading as possible is required, but the quality/accuracy of your test meter will have a bearing on this. An open circuit is an obvious problem, however, high resistances in cables and connections are also a problem, especially on low-voltage connections within electronically controlled machines

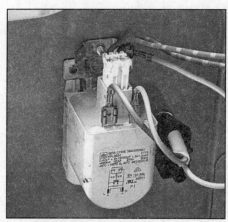

The terminal block is the first distribution point of the power into the machine. Ensure all connections are sound, as heat will be generated if not

Note: *This appliance combines the terminal block with the mains suppressor unit, i.e. the mains supply lead connects directly to the suppressor.*

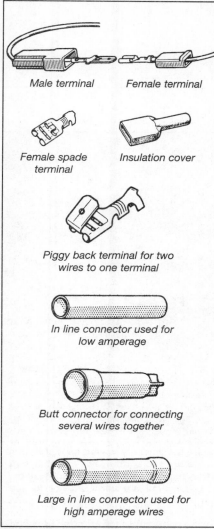

Male terminal   *Female terminal*

Female spade terminal   *Insulation cover*

Piggy back terminal for two wires to one terminal

In line connector used for low amperage

Butt connector for connecting several wires together

Large in line connector used for high amperage wires

All of the above are 'crimp' fitted to inner and outer of the wires. When used make sure that they fit securely and will not easily part

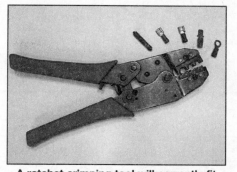

A ratchet crimping tool will correctly fit the connectors shown. The one seen in the photograph has changeable jaw ends (anvils) to suit the type of crimp required. This tool has the colour-coded jaws fitted that are used for correctly fitting the insulated terminals and connectors (those on the right-hand side in the above diagram)

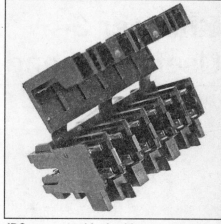

IDC connector block with cover open and ready for wiring to be inserted

An IDC connection block prior to closing the cover, showing that wiring is inserted without removing the outer insulation. It can be seen the outer insulation has been breached by the internal 'V'-shaped terminals

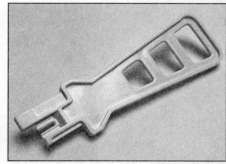

To ensure a sound connection within IDC connectors a dedicated IDC insertion tool should be used. The one shown is a low-cost alternative to the larger ratchet-type used commercially

cable movement, e.g. wiring from shell to outer tub unit components, it is advisable to renew the whole length of wiring or the joint made in a fixed section of cable. The use of rigid connections in movable wiring must be avoided. Take time to do a few simple checks. It saves time, patience and money.

Note: *Ensure that the harness is secured adequately to the shell of the machine, at the same time allowing for free movement of the motor, heater, etc.*

Take care that any metal fastening clips are fitted correctly and do not chafe the

plastic insulation around the wires. Also make sure that wires are not in contact with sharp metal edges such as self-tapping screws etc. **Warning:** *Before attempting to remove or repair the wiring harness or any other component in the appliance, isolate the appliance from the mains electrical supply by removing the plug from the wall socket.*

IDC connectors

As well as the more conventional connectors described previously, many manufacturers also use IDC connectors, this standing for Insulation Displacement Connection.

IDC fittings are often used in multi-wire connection blocks to components such as printed circuit boards, pressure switches, motors etc. Wires are simply cut to length and offered into the open fitting without the need to remove the outer insulation. A tool is then used to firmly press the wire into position. As the wire is pressed into position a 'V' shaped groove in the metal terminal cuts through the outer insulation and makes contact with the conductor within it. When all the wires are fitted the plastic outer cover of the terminal is clicked into position. Originally used for low-voltage fixed installations such as telephone systems, this type of fitting is becoming widely used in appliances. As the electrical connection is in effect a simple contact fit (not firmly crimped) poor connection, breakage and high-resistance problems can arise. On low-voltage connections increased resistance can lead to problems such as impulses/signals failing to be picked up by the electronic circuitry. On high-voltage/high-amperage circuits localised over-heating of the connection can occur like the one shown. Ensure all IDC connections are sound and correctly fitted by using the relevant insertion tool.

Chapter 34
Useful tips and information

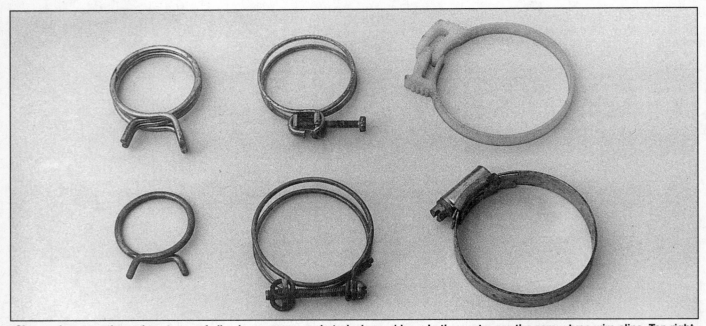

Shown above are the various types of clips in common use in today's machines. In the centre are the screw type wire clips. Top right is the new type toothed clip. This new clip is much easier and quicker to fit as grips or pliers are used to tighten jaws together. Left are two types of Corbin spring clips. Care should be taken in removing this type of clip, as they have a tendency to 'spring' under tension. For removal, Corbin pliers are best, however, with care, ordinary grips may be used. Lower right is a worm drive or Jubilee clip. This again is a simple but effective clip

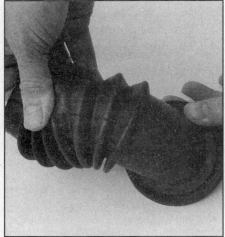

Check all hoses thoroughly for perishing and/or cracking. With corrugated hoses (as shown) stretch the hose to ensure a thorough check.
(It is wise to check any new hose before fitting)

On some machines the door interlock jams the door shut when it fails. As the fixing screws are behind the locked door, it may be difficult to open the door. It may be possible to move the door latch with a screwdriver, as shown. Be careful not to scratch the paintwork

A little washing-up liquid or fabric conditioner can be smeared on grommets or rubber mouldings to assist fitting

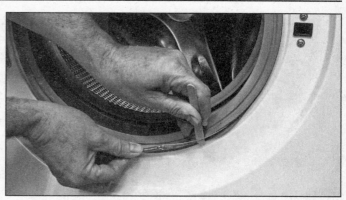

Some machines may have a wire surrounding the door seal. This retaining ring can be removed using a flat bladed screwdriver
Note: *When removing wire-only door seal securing bands (those without springs like the one shown), it is advisable to wear eye protection. This is also essential when drifting out old bearings. Wear sturdy gloves to protect your hands from the rough casting or other sharp edges when handling cast aluminium pulleys.*

If you experience problems refitting a spring clamp band with your fingers a tip to avoid damaging the front of the appliance with a metal tool, is to use a sturdy wooden lolly stick to help ease it into position. If you also feel the need to have a third hand to help hold the band in place as you fit it employ a small plastic clamp – refer to the door seal section to see one such item in use

Machines with slide-in worktops

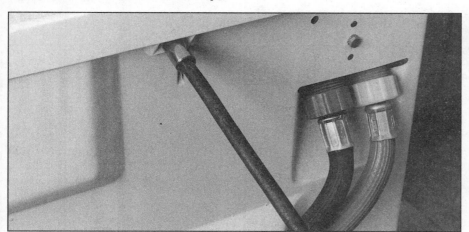

1 On some machines with fitted work tops, the top removal may not be straightforward. Firstly, remove the self-tapping bolts on the rear plastic panel section

3 The top is now ready to be moved from its position. Push or pull the top towards the back of the machine and remove. This may require some force, especially if the top has not been removed for some time

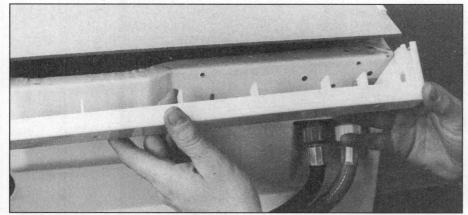

2 Remove the rear plastic surround completely. As always, ensure that the machine is isolated. This is because many machines will reveal open terminals behind the plastic moulding

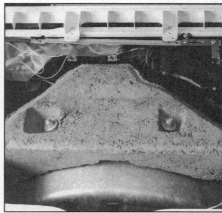

4 Access to the top half of the machine is now possible. To aid the refitting of the top, a little washing-up liquid may be smeared on the plastic slides of the machine

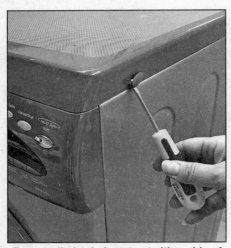

Two small plastic inserts at either side of this lid hide the lid securing screws. Use a small, flat-bladed screwdriver to carefully ease them out of position

Removing both screws allows the lid to be removed from the appliance

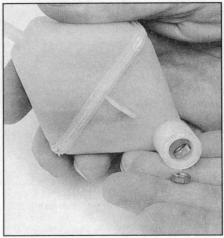

If you have difficulty trying to clean a sealed pressure vessel simply pop in a couple of small nuts, add a little water and shake. Rinse and repeat until the vessel is clean and the water runs clear

Access to machines with 50/50 split shells

Sealants like the one shown can be used for pressure system hoses and for aiding the fitting and sealing of new hoses, grommets, etc.

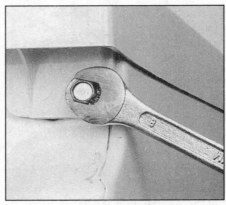

1 Remove the screws securing the work top and slide the top backwards to remove it

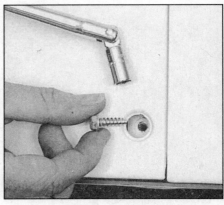

3 Remove the two screws exposed when the caps are removed

Damage or scratches on white appliances can be corrected by using these or similar products

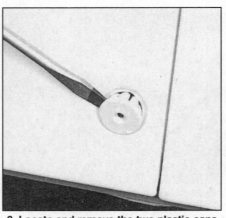

2 Locate and remove the two plastic caps on each side of the cabinet near the base

4 Remove the two securing screws at the bottom rear
Note: *On combined washerdriers a third screw will need to be removed.*

5 At either side of the top of the machine is a metal plate bridging the shell joint, remove only the rear fixing screws

7 Carefully ease the rear half of the shell away from the base

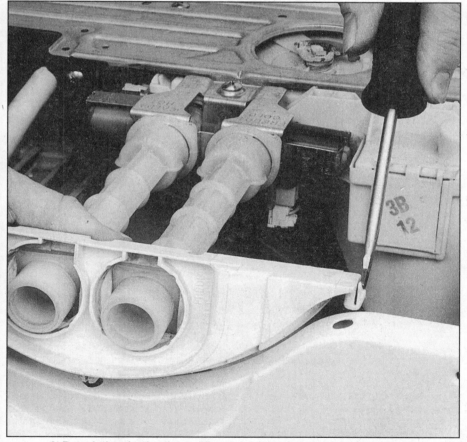

6 Detach the plastic clips holding the cable grip and inlet valve support
Note: *Some models may have screw fixings as well as plastic clips.*

Removing the front facia on 50/50 split shells

The front half of the shell can also be removed in a similar manner. The best way to do this is by first removing the rear panel as shown. This allows access to the various internal components that need to be disconnected to allow the front shell to be removed, such as the wiring loom supports and the two screws securing the front shell to the base. The control panel must now be removed from the front of the machine. Start by removing the selector knobs by inserting a small screwdriver in the hole and turning anti-clockwise (this can be a little tricky). Removing the knob front covers exposes the shaft fixings (usually simple nut or plastic locking tab) and carefully remove the control knob components. Now remove any screws/clips holding the front shell to metal cross member (this may include the timer screws/plastic cam clips) and remove the soap dispenser drawer. The plastic facia panel can now be removed by disengaging the plastic tabs/clips along the top (holding the facia to the cross member) and similar clips along the bottom edge of the facia.

Note: *The bottom tabs/clips are accessible through slots along the bottom edge of the facia and disengaged using a flat bladed screwdriver.*

Next refit the rear shell and its top fixings and carefully lay the machine on its back (with suitable support/protection). Remove the screws securing the top of the front panel and free the door seal from the shell lip after first removing the front clamp band. Next remove the screws securing the door interlock unit and ease the shell upwards and free from the

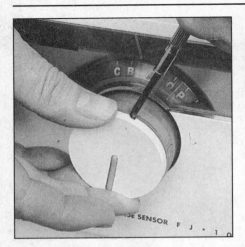

1 A small screwdriver and a twisting action are used to disengage the knob cover on this particular machine

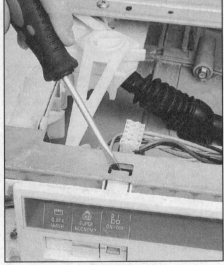

2 The top of this facia is held in place by plastic tabs/clips. Disengage each tab/clip by pressing them and easing the facia forward. Use only enough force to free the fixing, do not over-stress the plastic

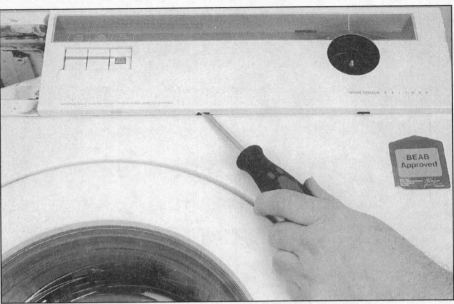

3 The lower facia tabs/clips are accessed through slots along the bottom edge

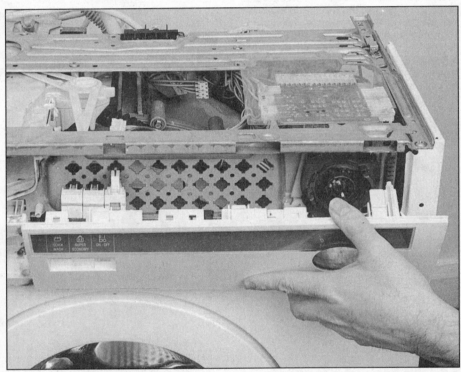

4 When all the fixings have been removed the front facia can be lifted free

base checking for any other fixing that may need removal/disengaging (due to changes in models, etc.).

One of the most awkward tasks you can come across when repairing your machine is that of removing the control knobs. There are no particular ways in which control knobs are secured and each manufacturer has their own and often individualistic methods. Due to the wide variety of fixing methods used it is not possible to show each and every variation. The range of fixing methods differs from the simplest push-fit versions to rather ingeniously disguised and complex hidden varieties. The following photographs and information is provided to illustrate several of the most common principles and methods of fixing. Use this information along with other instances that are shown throughout this

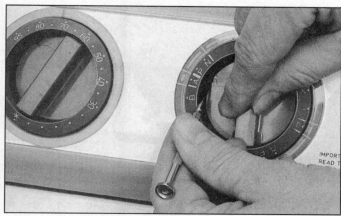

1 With this early Zanussi timer knob a small screwdriver is inserted into the hole on the outer edge of the knob inner

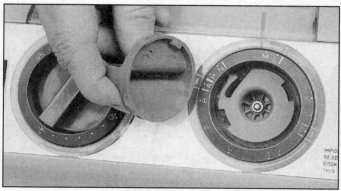

2 Press down on the small plastic catch and twist the knob anti-clockwise. Removing the knob/cover exposes the internal fixing securing the indicator barrel to the shaft. In this instance a nut is used but plastic tabs/clips will be found on thermostat and drier timers

The knob of this washing machine is used for both programme selection and turning the appliance on and off and therefore needs to be secured to the timer shaft, yet free to move. Closely inspecting the plastic moulding revealed that the knob has a cover which was latched to a second inner plastic moulding held in place by the small pip arrowed

A close-up of a knob inner with plastic latch

This appliance has an on/off button and the selector knob is a one-piece moulding which indicates that it is a simple push-fit on to the shaft

Note: *Prior to removal make a note of the position of the knob, or turn it to a known position as this will help refitting.*

By gripping the control knob firmly it could be eased from its position. If you need to use a tool for this purpose ensure you protect the plastic surface

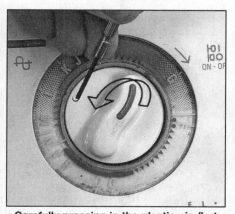

Carefully pressing in the plastic pip (but not too far) and turning the knob slightly anti-clockwise unlatches it. The knob cover can then be removed to expose the inner fixing which, in this case was, a recessed nut

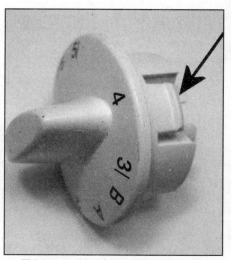

This type of knob is held in place by securing lugs which need to be depressed from behind the facia with the lid removed

Although the position of this knob was noted prior to removal the inner part of the knob and shaft are 'keyed' to ensure correct positioning

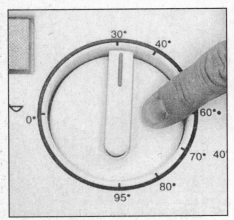

1 Some knobs are a simple push fit. If they cannot be pulled off by hand remove them using a pair of pliers/grip and a piece of cloth

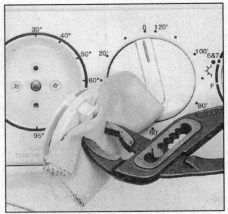

2 Place the cloth between the jaws of the grips and apply firm but not excessive pressure and ease the knob from the shaft

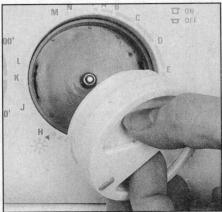

This Philips/Whirlpool model has similar looking control knobs. However, both are secured in different ways. The timer control knob is removed by turning the knob backwards. This unlatches the knob from the inner and it can then be removed. However, if you do the same to the thermostat knob you will break the knob or the shaft. These are only simple push fit knobs and must be removed as shown

Note: *This particular style of machine may also be seen under Servis and Electra brand names.*

book to access the type of fixing that your particular machine has and to adapt the methods shown for use on machines that vary from these particular types.

Smells originating from washing machines

Smells in washing machines are commonly caused by leaving the door of the machine closed and/or 'under-dosing' (using too little detergent over a period of time). The latter allows the build up of soiling in the warm, damp atmosphere of the machine, creating an ideal environment for common micro-organisms to multiply and cause a smell.

The micro-organisms responsible are widespread in nature. They can be found in water supplies, but are more likely to originate from the soiled laundry. Normally these organisms would be destroyed in the washing process – either by temperature, or chemically by the bleach components found in some detergents.

Nowadays, many washes are carried out at lower temperatures and many 'Colour' products and liquid detergents do not contain bleach. However, when these products are used according to the manufacturer's instructions, the results are excellent, there is no build up of soiling in the machine, and there is no likelihood of a smell developing.

If, however, higher temperature washes are never carried out, and a detergent containing a bleach is never used, 'under-dosing' will increase the chances of the washing machine developing a smell. This can be prevented by the use of an occasional high temperature wash, or by the occasional use of a detergent which contains a bleaching ingredient.

Where a smell has already developed, carrying out a 'maintenance' wash – high temperature, without a wash load and using a detergent containing a bleaching ingredient can cure this. Alternatively, again without a washload, a final rinse, preferably incorporating a rinse hold, can be carried

out, with a domestic hypochlorite bleach such as Domestos being added in place of fabric conditioner

To help prevent recurrence of the malodour, and also to help prevent door gaskets becoming sticky, ensure the door gasket of the machine is cleaned at the end of each wash programme and leave the door slightly ajar to allow air circulation to take place for a short while. **Warning:** *It is possible for small children to climb into washing machines and injure themselves; ensure measures are taken to avoid this.*

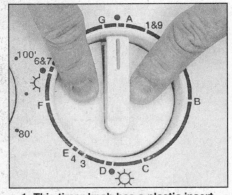

1 This timer knob has a plastic insert, which clips into the centre of the knob. When closely inspected the joint between the two pieces can be seen. Use a pair of grips to ease it out of position

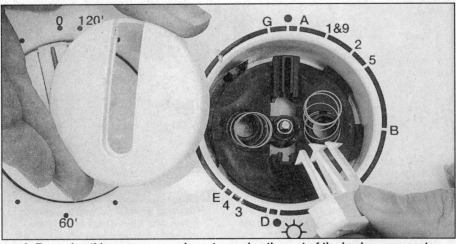

2 Removing this cover exposed a nut securing the rest of the knob components

Chapter 35
Buying spare parts

The aim of this manual has been to assist in the DIY repair of your automatic washing machine. I hope that now you will not only have a greater knowledge of how these machines work, but also the knowledge to prevent faults.

Above all, I hope that, armed with this information, you will feel confident enough to tackle most (if not all) of the faults that may arise with your machine from time to time.

However, all this knowledge and new-found confidence could be wasted if you are unable to locate the spare parts needed to carry out the repair. In the past this would have been a problem, but in recent years the availability of spares have increased for several reasons:

1 The reluctance of people to pay high call out and labour charges for jobs that they feel they can do themselves.
2 The general interest in household DIY coupled with the saving from call out and labour charges, gives a feeling of satisfaction when the job is successfully completed.
3 The growth in size and number of DIY stores in recent years.
4 The improvement in the availability of pre-packed spares.

Many independent domestic appliance companies have been reluctant to supply parts for the DIY market in the past, but the current trend is to expand the amount of pre-packed spares. This has been confirmed by the three biggest independent spares suppliers of genuine and non-genuine (patterned) spares. The range of 'off the shelf' spare parts in both retail outlets and mail order companies is most welcome, and many machine manufacturers who do not have local dealerships will supply parts by post if requested.

One way of obtaining the parts you require is to find a local 'spares and repairs' dealer through the *Yellow Pages* or local press. This is best done before your machine develops a fault, as you will then not waste time when a fault arises. In many instances you may possess more knowledge of your machine than the assistant in the shop, so it is essential to take the make, model and serial number of your machine with you to help them locate or order the correct spare part for your requirements.

You may also find it quite helpful to take the faulty part(s) with you if possible, to confirm visually that it is the correct replacement. For instance, most pumps will look the same from memory, although quite substantial differences may be seen if the faulty item is compared with the newly offered item. The casing or mounting plate, etc., may be different. It is most annoying to get home only to find that two extra bolts are required.

Patterned parts

Certain parts that are widely available are marked 'suitable for' or 'to fit'. These are generally called patterned or patent parts. Such terms refer to items or parts that are not supplied by the manufacturer of your machine, but are designed to fit it.

Some are copies of genuine parts and others are supplied by the original parts manufacturer to an independent distributor, which are then supplied to the retailer and sold to the customer. This avoids the original manufacturer's mark-up as it is not an official or genuine spare part. This saving is then passed onto the customer.

Many of the appliance manufacturers disliked this procedure in the past, as the parts were of an inferior quality, but this is not the case today as the supply of parts is very big business and quality has improved dramatically. Although great savings can be made, care must be taken not to save money by buying inferior spare parts. Check the quality of the item first wherever possible. A reputable dealer should supply only good quality patterned or genuine parts.

Many of the original machine manufacturers are now discounting their genuine authorised spares to combat the growth in patterned spares. This is very good as it can only benefit you, the customer.

Genuine parts

Parts supplied by the manufacturer of your machine or by their authorised local agent, are classed as 'genuine' and will in many cases, carry the companies trade mark or colours, etc., on the packaging. Many of the parts in today's machines are in fact not produced by the manufacturer of the finished machine, but a sub-contractor who may also supply a distributor of patterned spares with identical items.

Patterned spares producers will only take on items that have volume sales and leave the slow moving items to the original manufacturer of the machine. Generally it is a long procedure to obtain spares 'direct' from the manufacturer as many are unwilling to supply small orders direct to the public. Another system used to deter small orders is to use a 'pro-forma' invoicing sheet that will delay the receipt of parts until your cheque has cleared.

With the increase in DIY, manufacturers are slowly changing their view regarding spares supply. This is simply to fend off the patterned spares, by making the original parts more available and competitively priced. Again this will in turn benefit the consumer.

Parts by post

Through the company below you can readily access almost every domestic appliance spare part available in the UK, the range of spares covering all major manufacturers and brands. Simply write or e-mail your requirements to:

UK Whitegoods
19–21 Nursery Street
Kilmarnock
KA1 1RQ
Tel: 0845 226 1273
Fax: 0845 226 2508
E-mail: spares@ukwhitegoods.co.uk

Parts orders and inquiries can be sent by post, fax, telephone or e-mail. All are supplied at competitive prices and payment can be made by cheque, credit or debit card, Paypal and NOCHEX.

Ensure you quote the make, model and serial number of the relevant machine(s).

A range of both DIY* and more technical training material (manuals and videos etc.) is also available.

*An interactive DVD which complements the information relating to washing machines given in this publication is being produced for launch in late 2007. For further details please see websites www.dixontraining.co.uk or www.ukwhitegoods.co.uk.

Exchange reconditioned timers and modules

The following companies offer a range of reconditioned timers and speed control units for a wide range of makes and models. For details of the service provided and a catalogue contact:

E.M.W. Electronics
Units 11 & 12 Oaktree Business Park
Mansfield
Nottinghamshire
NG18 3HQ
England
Tel: 01623-647537 Fax: 01623-634200
Website: emwelec.co.uk
E-Mail: tech@emwelec.co.uk

QER Ltd
Quality House
Reedlands Road
Workington
Cumbria
CA14 3YF
Tel: 01900 67913
Freephone order (UK only): 0800 2798912
Website: www.qer.biz

In conclusion

Finally, the decision between genuine and patterned spares is yours, cost and speed of availability may have to be taken into consideration, but do not forsake quality for a small financial saving.

As a guide we have compiled a list of manufacturers' names and telephone numbers where parts may be obtained. It may also be helpful to check your local *Yellow Pages*.

Further information

Note: *This information was correct at the time of publication, but may change with the course of time.*

Make	Telephone No.
AEG	01753 872 325
Ariston	01895 858277 *(or see Yellow Pages under Merloni Domestic Appliances)*
Asko (was Asea)	0181 568 4666
Bauknecht	01345 898 989
Bendix	*Yellow Pages*
Bosch	0990 678 910
Candy	0990 990 011
Colston	*see Ariston* (above)
Creda	*Yellow Pages*
Electra	*see Electricity Board*
Electrolux	01325 300 660
Fagor	01245 329 483
Frigidaire	01977 665 590
Hotpoint	*Local Directory*
Hoover	*Yellow Pages*
Indesit	01895 858 277 *(or see Yellow Pages under Merloni Domestic Appliances)*
Kelvinator	0151 334 2781
Miele	*Yellow Pages*
Merloni	01895 858 277
Philco	0181 902 9626
Philips (now Whirlpool)	01345 898 989
Servis	0121 526 3199
Whirlpool (was Philips)	01345 898 989
Zanussi	*Yellow Pages/Local Directory*
Zerowatt	0151 334 2781

Chapter 36
Know your machine

Most of us, you'll agree, would be completely lost without the range of gadgets we've become accustomed to using every day. Learning to take advantage of these time and energy-saving appliances, particularly your automatic washing machine, will give you the freedom to look after yourself and your family in more important ways.

With your special needs in mind, washing machine manufacturers have carefully developed automatic washing machines which will make the task quick and effortless however often you wash. There are several types of washing machines available.

Used properly, a fully automatic washing machine provides a most efficient and thorough method of washing. The special wash action of front and top loaders with a horizontal rotating drum mechanism creates sufficient agitation to effectively remove all dirt particles and even stubborn stains. However, it is important to use the correct type of washing powder in these machines.

Overloading your machine will greatly reduce cleaning efficiency, as free movement of the clothes is restricted. Your machine has a maximum load capacity which should not be exceeded.

On the next page is a handy table to help you check your dry weight loads compiled with the help of Lever Brothers.

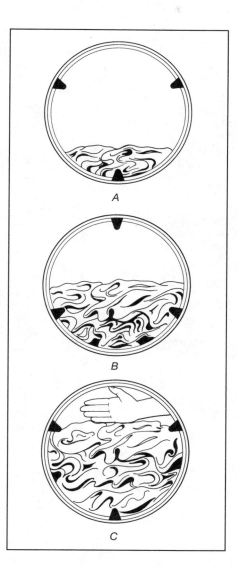

A

B

C

Rule of thumb
To help in assessing the correct wash load, the drawing illustrates the maximum dry load size per selected programme.

A Woollen and other fine fabrics requiring gentle washing – only a quarter of the drum should be occupied.
B Synthetic and man-made fibres requiring delicate washing – only half the drum space should be occupied.
C Cottons and robust fabrics requiring higher temperatures and normal wash action – can occupy a greater proportion of the drum, leaving approximately a hand's width space at the top.

This information is for guidance only and the spaces represent the space left when the clothes are loaded normally. Do not compress the load to achieve the recommended amount of vacant space.

Clothes

Blouse	cotton other		150g 100g	(5oz) (3½oz)
Dress	cotton other		500g 350g	(1lb 2oz) (12oz)
Dressing Gown			700g	(1lb 8oz)
Jeans			700g	(1lb 8oz)
10 Nappies			1000g	(2lb 3oz)
Nightdress			150g	(5oz)
Pyjamas	cotton		350g	(12oz)
Shirt	cotton other		300g 200g	(10oz) (7oz)
Skirt			200g	(7oz)
Suit, bulked polyester			1500g	(3lb 5oz)
Sweater	wool other heavy lightweight		400g 350g 200g	(14oz) (12oz) (7oz)
Tracksuit			1000g	(2lb 3oz)
Teeshirt			125g	(4½oz)
Vest			125g	(4½oz)

Household items

Bedspread	candlewick	(D) (S)	3000g 2000g	(6lb 10oz) (4lb 6oz)
Blanket	wool acrylic	(D) (S) (D) (S)	2000g 1500g 1500g 1000g	(4lb 6oz) (3lb 5oz) (3lb 5oz) (2lb 3oz)
Cot Sheet			200g	(7oz)
Duvet Cover	cotton other	(D) (D)	1500g 1000g	(3lb 5oz) (2lb 3oz)
Pillow			900g	(2lb)
Pillowslip			125g	(4½oz)
Tablecloth	large small		700g 250g	(1lb 8oz) (9oz)
Tea Towels			100g	(3½ oz)
Towel	bath hand		700g 250g	(1lb 8oz) (9oz)
Sheet	cotton other	(D) (S) (D) (S)	1000g 750g 500g 350g	(2lb 3oz) (1lb 10oz) (1lb 2oz) (12oz)

D = Double   S = Single

Chapter 37
Understanding the wash process

In order to ensure good wash results, the four factors of washing must be borne in mind – Time, Temperature, Agitation, Detergent. If one is to be reduced then another may need to be increased to compensate. Important points to remember are:

1 Temperature and agitation should never be increased beyond that recommended on the garment's wash code label.
2 Time can be increased by soaking before or during the wash.

Note: *some fabrics should not be soaked. Check the label of the garment.*

Detergency is constantly being 'increased' as technological developments make it possible to include new and more effective ingredients in the formulation, ensuring cleaning products really do give best results for today's wash.

The composition of the wash load is constantly changing. Today there are more multi-coloured articles than ever before. Man-made fibres are often mixed with natural fibres, e.g. Polyester cotton. This means that wash temperatures have had to be reduced to prevent any damage to colour or fibres. Currently over 70% of washing is done at 50° or below.

The wash process is also affected by what goes into the machine – Water, Washload and Detergent.

Water
Too high a temperature may cause damage, e.g., colour transfer and creasing. Hard water means that extra detergent is required. Low water pressure can lead to problems when the detergent is dispensed through the dispenser drawer of the machine. In some areas water contamination in the form of peat, iron or other naturally occurring minerals can cause discoloration to the wash load, or even to parts of the machine, such as the door gasket.

Wash load
The wash load has to be considered carefully to ensure that the correct fabric types are being put together, e.g., cottons and linens; synthetics; machine washable woollens. The colour and size of the load, together with the nature of the soiling, all have to be taken into account. Help is at hand when sorting the wash load if all the wash codes, found on the garment labels, are followed. These advise maximum temperatures and agitation recommended for that particular type of fabric. If the fabrics

require different wash conditions then it is advisable to split the load and perhaps use the half load facility on the machine if available. This will ensure better wash results.

Detergent
Detergent is available in either a powder, tablet or liquid form. These detergents are then split into high suds, e.g., Persil and Stergene – or low suds, e.g. Persil Automatic and Radion. High suds detergent are for use in twin tub, tub type top loaders and hand washing. Low suds detergents may be used in any type of washing machine as well as for hand washing. The lather level in low suds detergent is controlled so that the vigorous wash action of a front loader does not cause too much foam to be created. Most low lather, or automatic detergents, are now available in concentrated powder or liquid forms.

A detergent, either powder or liquid, is a complex mixture of ingredients, designed to help wet the fabric, remove soiling and suspend the soiling in solution until the machine pumps out. Ingredients are included to cope with every type of soiling found on the average wash load. Also built into the formulation are ingredients designed to soften the water, protect the machine, prolong it's life and efficiency.

Dosage of detergent is therefore crucial. It is important that the dosage information on the individual packets and bottles is followed in order to achieve perfect wash results. The amount of detergent required can only be reduced if the water is soft, smaller loads are being washed or if the items are only lightly soiled.

During the final rinse a fabric conditioner, such as Comfort, should be added to the wash load. A fabric conditioner eliminates static cling – essential if the wash load is composed of man-made fibres – as well as giving a soft feel to the wash. Freshness, less creasing, easier ironing and improved spin efficiency are other benefits of using a fabric conditioner.

In order to obtain the best possible wash results from a machine, it is important to follow the machine manufacturer's instructions, the care labels on the items being washed, and the information on the detergent packs. These guidelines will help to ensure successful washing, time and time again.

Choosing the correct detergent

Over the last few years there has been a significant increase in the number of different

detergents on the market. People have realised that one product cannot necessarily deal with all their laundry needs. The garments making up today's wash load have become more varied in terms of fabric type, and colour. Also, types of stain and soiling differ.

More and more people are choosing to buy two or three different types of detergent to meet their different washing requirements. For example a typical mix may be:
1 A biological powder for whites and heavily stained articles e.g., Persil Performance or Radion with Sunfresh Automatic.
2 A colour liquid for dark coloured clothing, or matching household linen e.g. Persil Colour Care Liquid.
3 A light-duty product for delicate garments made of wool or silk, e.g. Persil Finesse.

There are a number of decisions to be made before picking one or more detergents to suit the required criteria:
1 Is an automatic product needed?
2 Is biological or non-biological detergent preferred?
3 Would powder or liquid be the best choice?
4 What benefits would a concentrated product give?
5 When should a colour product be considered?

Automatic or 'low foaming' detergent
Traditionally, detergents such as Lux Flakes, Persil and Surf for twin tubs produced high foam levels, and the foam level was used as an indicator that sufficient detergent was present in the wash solution.

As front loading and top loading type machines now dominate the washing machine market, the majority of detergents now on sale are, 'Automatic' or low foaming. A drum-type machine cannot cope with too much foam, and automatic detergents contain ingredients to prevent excessive foam being produced in the wash. Automatic detergents can be used in any type of clothes washing situation – machine or hand wash. If automatic detergents are used in a twin tub or Hotpoint top loading machine, the dosage given on the pack should be approximately doubled as the water capacity and size of wash load is much greater with this type of machine. All concentrated detergents are low foaming.

Biological or non-biological?
Biological detergents contain enzymes, non-biological detergents do not.

What are enzymes?

Enzymes are natural substances, which help to break down different types of soil into smaller particles, making the task of removing stains easier for the detergent.

There can be up to three different types of enzyme in a biological detergent, each working on a different type of stain:

1 Lipase – helps break down fatty stains such as butter or margarine.

2 Protease – helps break down protein based stains such as blood or gravy.

3 Amylase – helps break down starch based stains such as chocolate.

Biological detergents are more effective than non-biological at removing the above types of stain. In addition they are especially effective at lower temperature washing, i.e. 40–60°C which means both energy and money can be saved by their use on a regular basis. Garments made from delicate fibres, however, such as wool and silk, should not be washed in a biological detergent. Persil Finesse has been especially developed for fabrics of this type. It is fair to say that it is not possible to formulate a detergent which will be suitable for everyone under all conditions, some people with sensitive skin often prefer to use a non-biological detergent.

Liquids or powders?

Liquids are easy to pour out and dissolve quickly. They also have the added benefit of being able to be used neat to pre-treat difficult stains (though colour fastness should be checked first on a piece of the fabric that does not show). Most powders (except 'colour-care' products) include a bleach ingredient for tackling stains like fruit juice, tea, coffee and wine. Liquid detergents do not contain bleaching agents, so are not as efficient as powders at removing this type of stain, particularly on higher temperature washes. Both powders and liquids are now available in 'refill' bags or cartons helping to reduce the waste of packaging materials.

Concentrated or conventional?

A recent development has been to introduce concentrated variants of familiar brands which are now available in powder form, biological, non-biological and colour.

Concentration is all about using fewer resources, fewer chemicals per wash, reducing the impact of manufacturing and transporting the goods, and having to produce, carry, store and dispose of less packaging. They are therefore more acceptable in terms of the environment.

Concentrated powder detergents, will normally give the best results when dispensed using an 'in-the-machine' dosing device, usually a plastic ball net. This ensures that all of the detergent is used in the wash and none is wasted, either by remaining in the dispensing drawer, or being washed directly into the sump at the base of the machine.

Special colour detergents

The most recent types of detergent to be launched are those for Colour Care.

'Colour' detergents are biological, and come as powders or liquids. The other products previously mentioned are formulated to give maximum cleaning under the toughest wash conditions. Some contain bleach, which can fade certain dark colours, and some contain optical brightening agents which can cause shade changes in some pastel coloured garments. Colour detergents are formulated without bleach or optical brightening agents.

Whilst these products are designed to take care of coloured articles in the washload, they should not be confused with 'light duty' wash products, such as Stergene, Lux Flakes or Persil Finesse, which are suitable for delicate fabrics like wool or silk.

Detergent tablets

The biggest revolution in the use of laundry detergents for more than a decade has been the advent of detergent tablets. They have been developed in direct response to customer wishes for a more convenient washing product. The new tablets make doing the washing less of a chore – they are simpler, less messy and less wasteful than existing products because there is no need to measure out detergent. They also offer great value for money, especially for people who currently use too much powder. They offer brilliant cleaning, dissolve evenly and thoroughly, and yet, are strong enough to stay in one piece during the journey from factory to supermarket to kitchen. Tried and tested ingredients have been put together in a unique way to ensure that the tablets give superb cleaning performance.

A net is provided in which the tablets are placed before being placed on top of the washload inside the machine. Using a net is the best way to make a washing tablet disperse evenly and thoroughly all around the wash. Two tablets normally provide the correct dosage for most wash conditions. A wrapper keeps the tablets dry, and keeps the ingredients and perfume fresh. The net is made from soft polyester material of the kind used for washing bags for delicate items.

Chapter 38
Identifying poor washing problems

Effectively diagnosing the root cause of poor wash problems will help plan the correct course of action needed to alleviate or rectify the problem. Remember, not all problems are a direct result of mechanical failure or malfunction of the appliance. There are a whole range of external criteria that can affect the washing process and lead to poor wash results. Without a thorough understanding of the washing process it is only too easy to embark upon a random stripdown of a correctly functioning machine only to find sometime later that it was an external problem. Worse still you may decide it is time to change your old machine for a new one only to find that the poor wash problem remains!

The following help and advise is a direct result of experience they will be of help in three ways:
1 To help identify the cause of existing problems.
2 To help prolong the life of the appliance.
3 To give advice on how to achieve the best wash results.

It is essential to understand that any washing machine, new or old, cannot produce the best possible wash results without the correct use of the detergent. In addition to poor wash results, premature failure of components may also result from the incorrect use of detergent or the bad habits of the user!

To help in developing the fault finding process the following information has been split into four sections:
1 How to get the best possible wash results.
2 Help when things go wrong.
3 Causes of staining during washing.
4 How to prolong the life of your machine.

How to get the best results

Always ensure that the appliance is correctly installed, set correctly and is being used in accordance with the manufacturer's instructions.

Ensure the correct type of detergent is being used
For front loading washing machines, the detergent, whether powder, liquid or tablet must be specially formulated for use in automatic washing machines. This means it produces a controlled amount of lather. Non-automatic detergents will give too much lather, reducing the agitation of the washload and leading to poor cleaning.

Ensure the correct amount of detergent is being used
The use of insufficient detergent will lead to poor wash results, and over a period of time will cause damage to the machine itself. Dosage is determined by the size of the wash-load, the degree of soiling and water hardness. Details of the recommended dosage can be found on the packs. Refer to this for guidance. Underdosing will cause garments to dull in colour as soil removed during the washing process is redeposited onto the load. Too little detergent can also mean that stains may not be fully removed. Heavily soiled items should be given a pre-wash to remove most of the soiling prior to the main wash. Good quality detergents contain many ingredients which are not only important for cleaning but also protect components within the machine.

TO MAINTAIN OPTIMUM CLEANING IT IS VITAL THAT DOSAGE IS NOT REDUCED TOO MUCH

Ensure the detergent is being measured correctly
The instructions on the pack will have details of the correct dosage for the varying levels of soiling. Some concentrated powders and concentrated liquid detergents must be poured into a dosing 'bubble' and placed in the drum of the machine on top of the washload. Tablet detergents are placed inside a mesh bag.

Ensure the machine is not overloaded
The clothes should be placed one at a time into the drum leaving a section of the back of the drum visible, or there is a danger of the machine being overloaded. Man-made fibres are lighter in weight than cottons therefore the weight of a 'man-made' washload must be reduced or the volume of these fibres can lead to reduced agitation and therefore poor wash results.

Ensure the correct wash programmmes are being used
It is important that clothes are washed at the temperature and level of agitation recommended on the garments' labels especially for synthetic fabrics and machine washable wool. Remember 'Quick Wash' programmes are only for lightly soiled garments. The best wash results are achieved by using the programme recommended on the garment label.

Ensure correct rinsing takes place
Soiling and detergent residues are removed by rinsing the clothes. Several rinses are necessary to do this effectively. Water taken into the machine mixes thoroughly with the clothes diluting the concentration of the soiling and detergent present. Each rinse further dilutes the soiling and detergent until the garments have been thoroughly rinsed. It is important that you allow the machine to carry out ALL rinses, and that you do not advance the programme during the rinsing stage. Paradoxically, reducing detergent dosage does not generally lead to improved rinsing because, at low dosage, more soil (and detergent residues) are redeposited onto the load (see *Ensure the correct amount of detergent is being used* above). If you are particularly concerned about efficient rinsing (for example because of allergic sensitivity), then the best solution is to give extra rinses and reduce load size.

Fabric conditioner is added during the final rinse to eliminate static, soften the wash and leave a fresh perfume on the clothes.

Overfilling the fabric conditioner compartment can cause premature dispensing of fabric conditioner due to syphoning. This may cause mild blue or peach coloured staining. Conditioner stains should be treated by gentle rubbing with a bar of soap, followed by rewashing in the usual way.

Cloudiness of the rinse water can often be mistaken for poor rinsing. In reality the opposite is often the case as turbidity (cloudiness) during the rinse agitation cycle relates to the efficiency of the machine in removing the soil residues from the washload and is perfectly normal.

Help for when things have gone wrong

Removing redeposition
Regular underdosing or overloading machines can lead to a build-up of soiling on the inner surfaces of the machine. Reintroducing the correct wash procedures can release this build-up which may then be redeposited onto or stain the washload. In other words the clothes may come out of the wash worse than when they went in. To avoid this potential problem after identifying an underdosing or overloading problem,

carry out a 'maintenance wash' to clean the inside of the machine prior to using the machine with a wash load. A maintenance wash consists of selecting the highest temperature programme, using the recommended detergent dose but no washload in the drum. In situations where redeposition has already occurred, the clothes will need to be re-washed using the recommended wash programme and detergent dosage. However, if the soiling is particularly heavy, it may take several washes before any significant improvement is noticed.

Note: *When efforts to do the correct washing procedures are made, do not expect instant results. The conditions that caused the problem may have been present for some considerable length of time and in such instances visible improvements may also take a little time. Improvement may be gradual and take several washes. This may lead you to think that nothing is happening and revert back to the old system. Avoid this problem by holding back one of the original items (it helps if it can be one of two similar items), place it in a drawer and do not wash or use it. After five or six normal washes you can compare your 'control' item with those that have been washed correctly. The comparison can often be quite remarkable.*

Washing at lower temperatures

It is now common practice to mix items in the washload, this can be done safely as long as the wash codes are followed. Most fabrics that require maximum agitation can be mixed together but must be washed at the lower temperature, i.e. wash a mixture of 90°C, 60°C and 40°C labels at 40°C. Fabrics needing medium agitation can be mixed in the same way 50°C and 40°C, wash at 40°C. However, if fabrics are never washed at their maximum recommended temperature, then stain removal can be a problem. The occasional wash at the full-recommended temperature should ensure perfect results. Care should be taken if white fabric is included in the washload when mixing loads.

Causes of staining during washing

Occasionally, marks may appear on garments during the washing process. In such instances it is all too easy to blame the machine for causing the marks as they were not visible on the garments when they were put into the machine. The following list of common causes of staining is provided to assist you in the correct diagnosis of staining and if used correctly it will help avoid unnecessary repairs to your machine.

Stain	See Cause
Black/Grey marks	DJ
Blue	AI
Brown	AB
Green	AF
Grey	ACDFI
Lighter patches	CG
Pink	ABCD
Rust	E
White/Grey specks	I

A Dye transfer

The most frequent cause of coloured staining is from dye that has leaked in the wash solution. This dye can then be transferred onto other articles in the wash. Nylon and elasticated items tend to pick up loose dye easily. Loose dye may also remain in the sump of a machine and contaminate the next load. Tiny coloured fibres can also attach themselves to other articles being washed, e.g. wool from a blanket onto a sheet, fibres from a sweater onto a shirt.

TREATMENT. Dye solvent e.g. Dylon or one of the products from the Stain Devils range may be required.

PREVENTION. Test new items for colourfastness and never mix white and coloured items. Carry out an occasional 'maintenance wash' especially before washing valued items. **Note:** *Nylon is particularly 'good' at picking up loose dye.*

B Metallic compounds in wash water

Iron in the water can cause brown, pink or orange marks. Copper causes grey/green stains. The 'spots' often occur in the same pattern as the holes in the drum of the machine.

TREATMENT. Rewash when conditions causing contamination have been corrected, i.e. road works, heavy rainfall. **Note:** *Periods of drought can make contamination occur. If possible reduce the spin speed and dosage of fabric conditioner as metallic particles may adhere to the conditioner on the garments.*

PREVENTION. As above under treatment.

Footnote: *Discoloration of the washload (or even parts of the machine) due to water contamination can be difficult to verify because by the time problem is identified, the water supply may be back to normal.*

C Chemicals in wash water

Some chemicals which may already be on the garment can be colourless but react with alkalinity of the wash solution and show up as staining e.g. pink staining on baby clothes can be caused by phenolphthalein in teething powder. Lighter patches occurring on pillows and sheets can be caused by skin preparations, acne treatments or hair treatments with the alkalinity of the wash solution. Grey/brown staining can be caused by a high level of grease on garments, e.g. clear petroleum jelly on babies nappies may be contaminated by soiling from the rest of the wash. If this type of redeposition occurs, the grey/brown stains may be in the form of grease balls which collect in the corners of articles such as pillowcases, shirt collars etc. This type of fault can give a very greasy feel to the stain. **Note:** *Grease balls can also be affected (spread out) by the heat from ironing. In addition to marks on garments burnt residues may build up on the sole plate of the iron.*

TREATMENT. Grease balling can be removed by re-washing with sufficient detergent. Where a lightening effect has occurred, the damage is usually permanent, Stain Devils may help to remove some of the stains.

PREVENTION. Pre-treat heavily soiled areas prior to washing or add a pre-wash to the normal washing programme. Try to prevent skin preparations such as acne and hair treatments from coming into contact with fabrics.

D Mildew

Mildew is a mould growth which develops usually on unwashed articles which have been left damp for a length of time. It may also show as pink or red spots, as well as the more usual grey.

TREATMENT. For white cottons use a very dilute hypochlorite bleach solution – add 1 eggcup full of household bleach (such as Domestos) to 1 gallon of water in a bucket or bowl and mix thoroughly before adding the affected article. For coloureds rub the affected area with hard soap and allow it to dry naturally before carrying out a prewash.

PREVENTION. Wash damp clothes as soon as possible to prevent mildew growth. Do not store clothes in the damp atmosphere of the washing machine. Ensure washed articles are dried thoroughly before they are stored.

E Rust marks or iron mould

The most common causes of rust stains are direct contact with rusted metals (screws, nails, etc., left in pockets or lodged within the appliance), rusted flakes from water pipe, blood stains (from the iron content), some red wines, medicines, tonics and certain inks.

TREATMENT. Mild stains can be removed with lemon juice applied to the stain and ironed through a damp cloth. For heavier stains use a proprietary rust remover such as those found in the Stain Devils range is recommended.

PREVENTION. Pretreat blood, wine, medicine and ink stains prior to washing.

F Copper staining

Grey/green staining is often the result of a high level of copper in the wash solution from new plumbing or filings on work overalls.

TREATMENT. Needs specialist treatment. Dry cleaners may be able to help.

PREVENTION. Loose copper particles that may be within the pipe work after repairs have been carried out should be completely flushed out of the system prior to use. Overalls (especially those of plumbers) should be shaken to remove copper particles prior to washing.

Note: *A high copper content in the wash may also have a damaging effect on the door gasket.*

G Uneven fluorescers take up

This problem often makes areas of the fabric appear 'extra white' making the original whiteness look 'yellow' by comparison. This cannot occur during the normal washing process.

Note: *Most leading washing products contain fluorescers.*

TREATMENT. Constant re-washing may remove fluorescer, however in some cases the staining may be permanent.

PREVENTION. This problem can arise if neat liquid detergent is allowed to dry on damp washing. When using liquid detergent for pre-treatment, the item must be washed immediately. Do not use undissolved detergent powder directly on wet washing.

H Hard water deposits

In very hard water areas, calcium in the water supply can show up on dark items as small white/grey specks. These are often mistaken for undissolved detergent powder.

TREATMENT. Re-wash using sufficient detergent. May be necessary to carry out a 'maintenance wash' with detergent but no washload. This will help remove the build-up of hard water deposits from inside the machine.

PREVENTION. Use recommended dose of detergent for hard water area.

Note: *Hard water deposits can shorten the life of the heating element.*

I Undiluted fabric conditioner

Blue staining may occur if undiluted fabric conditioner has come into contact with the washing. This may happen if the conditioner is prematurely dispersed. These stains are not expected to be permanent.

TREATMENT. Rub the affected area gently with a bar of soap and re-wash in the usual way.

PREVENTION. Always ensure the conditioner is diluted before use. This is done automatically in most front loading automatics. Ensure that the fabric conditioner compartment is not overfilled as this may cause the conditioner to be dispensed prematurely.

J Door seal marks

Marks caused by the door seal normally have a 'rubbery' feel and are the same colour as the seal. The most likely cause is serious overloading or by an article being trapped between the rotating drum and the stationary seal.

TREATMENT. Very difficult to remove. Dry cleaner may be able to advise.

PREVENTION. Don't overload the machine. Reduce load for man-made fibres. Ensure the washload is placed well into the drum before door is closed and ensure nothing is trapped, i.e. buttons, shirt cuffs, collars, etc. Also ensure that the machine is level to prevent clothes in the drum from riding forward.

Fair wear and tear

Occasionally physical damage to washed garments is blamed on the machine when in fact it is due to fair wear and tear. Marks that occur during the wash may follow a pattern and may be limited to parts of the garment such as the collar and cuffs of a mans shirt. However, if water contamination or dye transfer had caused the problem, then the marks would be across the whole garment. Therefore in this instance the indications are that the cause of the problem was most likely on the garment prior to washing.

Pulled threads on knitted or loosely woven garments are often caused by jewellery or buckles and zips on other garments in the same washload. Fabric damage to the backs of shirts/sweaters is mostly the result of rough surfaces on chairs. Inspect as many items as possible to see if a pattern of damage is present.

Many synthetic fabrics will 'pill' (go bobbly) due to friction caused when the garment is being worn. A good example of this is the 'baby grow' all-in-one suit. As the child crawls the fabric is rubbed against the carpet or the underside of the sleeve of a jumper. The same type of damage can be caused in the washing machine if the wrong wash agitation programme is selected, for instance, if synthetic items are washed as cotton items.

Note: *Synthetic fibres are weak when wet and are therefore more susceptible to damage. Care must be taken when washing and then handling wet synthetic fabrics. When physical damage has occurred to garments, careful assessment of the problem must be made.*

How to prolong the life of the machine

How long a particular machine will last depends on a number of factors, the most important being that the machine is being used for the purpose for which it was designed. Many small businesses (hairdressers, care homes, etc.) purchase domestic clothes washing machines and tumble dryers when in reality they should use their commercial and more robust counter parts. Factors which most often lead to a reduction in the life of the machine generally, relate directly to the way in which it is used and the level of attention given to correct use and maintenance.

Excessive lather

Excessive lather in the wash can lead to poor wash results, due to the reduction in agitation given to the washing, as the foam provides a cushioning effect. It can also result in over-foaming and malfunction of the drain pump, should it become 'locked' with lather. Modern machines with narrow drum-to-outer tub gaps can also be affected by foam locking due to excessive lather caused by over-dosing of detergent. Excessive foam between the drum and outer tub can create a braking effect which in severe cases can cause the wash motor to overheat and trip its internal T.O.C. Blocking of the pressure vessel resulting in nuisance tripping of the pressure switch may also occur. A wide range of problems may ensue, depending on the make and model of machine, and computer controlled machines may terminate the wash programme altogether. To avoid the problem ensure the correct amount of high quality automatic detergent is used as they contain ingredients to suppress lather.

Pre-treating heavy stains with dishwash liquid, or chemicals within the soiling can also lead to excessive lather. The use of water softening additives can also lead to excessive lather as they can lead the user in to believing that it is possible to reduce the amount of detergent required. Where a domestic water softener is installed in the house it should be recommended that the washing machine is connected to the mains supply, and not to the artificially softened water, or excessive foaming, even when using an automatic detergent, may occur. In extreme circumstances, in very soft water areas, excessive foaming may occur when a vigorous wash action has been selected and serious under-dosing of detergent has taken place.

Door seal deterioration

Rubber is naturally an unstable substance. For this reason, rubber items that are intended to give long service have special stabilisers added to them prior to moulding. Washing machine door seals fall into this category. In normal use, the stabilisers remain in the rubber for between 4-6 years, protecting it from decomposition. However, the rate of decomposition of the door seal fitted to a machine is influenced by the original quality of the gasket, by the frequency of machine use, and to some extent by the number of higher temperature wash cycles used (higher temperatures tend to increase the rate of decomposition). Most high temperature or 'boil' washes are for babies' nappies, where hygiene is as important as good wash results. Modern biological detergents can now achieve 'Boil wash' hygiene at temperatures as low as 50°C. In addition to time and temperature there are certain substances that can have adverse affects on the composition of the door seal and greatly reduce its working life. These substances fall into three main categories.

A Oils, fats, grease, solvents such as polish, baby ointments, Vaseline, solvents on working clothes, etc. Many of these substances are absorbed into the rubber causing it to swell and deform whilst other cause the stabilisers to migrate from the rubber, leaving it sticky to the touch.

B Metals in the wash (copper and iron). Copper is a known 'catalyst' of many chemical reactions. In other words high concentrations of metals like copper and iron can speed up the decomposition processes. In addition to increasing decomposition copper and iron in the wash can also cause discoloration of the door seal.

C Pre-treatment products. The use of certain pre-treatment products containing high levels of non-ionic detergent or hypochlorite based bleaching agents can also accelerate door gasket decomposition.

This most often occurs when articles treated with these types of products are placed directly into the machine without first rinsing to remove the pre-treatment product, e.g. nappy sterilising solutions. Another common cause can be the use of clothes previously used with bleach solutions being used to mop and wipe the door seal after use. This simple action can greatly reduce the life of a door seal.

To prolong the life of the door gasket:
1 Always use recommended dosage of detergent, taking the size of load, degree of soiling and water hardness into account.
2 For heavily soiled articles use the pre-wash facility.
3 Always dry the door gasket after use with a clean bleach free cloth and if possible leave the door of the machine slightly open to allow circulation of air. **Note:** *Take care to avoid creating a hazard and to prevent children from gaining access to the drum of the machine.*

Constant overloading
Overloading of the machine can result in poor washing, rinsing and spin efficiency and can also lead to machine damage. Remember when washing man-made fibres the load must be reduced. In extreme cases of overloading, the pressure of the fabric against the door of the machine can lead to marks being left on the wash load from the door gasket.

Enamel and aluminium alloys
Heavy duty washing products create an alkaline wash solution which can slowly dissolve enamel and aluminium components. High quality detergents contain an ingredient which chemically prevents this happening, thereby ensuring that components such as vitreous enamel

outer tubs, aluminium alloy back plates or drum spiders, etc., do not fail prematurely. **Note:** *Protection will only occur when sufficient detergent is used. As mentioned previously it is inadvisable to reduce the dosage of detergent products especially where alkaline water softeners (some wash additives), which contain no corrosion inhibitor, are included in the wash.*

Heating elements
The formation of scale on a heating element can reduce its efficiency and lead to premature failure. Hard water requires the full dosage of detergent to prevent heater scale. Reducing the amount of detergent will reduce the life of the heating element.

Summary

Automatic washing machines and automatic detergents are designed to work together to provide the best wash results. In dealing with faults with your machine you may find that the problem is not due directly to a fault of the machine, or that a component has failed prematurely due to an external factor. It is necessary to think beyond the mechanics of the machine and try and establish what factors may have contributed to the problem in hand.

Many problems arise from not fully appreciating or understanding how your machine or the wash process works and this in turn can lead to either poor wash results or premature component failure. I advise you to read and ensure you fully understand your machine's instruction book and the information given on the detergent pack that you use.

Chapter 39
Common causes of poor washing results

Poor washing is mainly due to the incorrect operation of the machine by the user, rather than a mechanical or electrical fault of the machine. The most common user faults are listed below.

1 Have you read the manufacturer's manual?

Improvements on poor colours and whites will not happen magically, the process is very gradual. Good results can only be achieved if the correct programme and dosing is followed.

2 Incorrect Programme Control

a) To achieve good consistent results, you must have a good understanding of your machine and its controls. Always remember – you tell the machine what to do. If in doubt, read the manufacturer's manual.

(b) Does the selected programme have the right water temperature, agitation and length of wash for the fabrics being washed?

3 Incorrect dosage

a) The amount of detergent that should be used is usually displayed on the powder pack. Please remember that this is only a guide, and the amounts have to be adjusted to load size, type and degree of soiling, and the 'hardness' of the water supply.

b) Is the container used for measuring the detergent accurate? With the recent advent of 'compact' powders, use the scoop provided.

c) Have you made allowances for special types of soiling? Ointments, thick creams, heavy perspiration and the like, use up the suds activity very quickly.

Note: *Poor soil and stain removal, the greying of whites or the appearance of 'greasy balls' on washed clothes is a clear indication of under-dosing. It is never due to over-dosing.*

4 Detergency

Detergents are formulated to do several tasks.

a) Overcome water hardness.

b) Wet-out the fabrics.

c) Remove the soiling from the clothes.

d) Hold the soiling in suspension, away from the clothes so that it can be pumped out with the water.

The harder the water, the harder the detergent has to work. More detergent should be added in the case of hard water, less in the case of soft water – simply follow the dosage information given on the detergent pack. The local area water authority should be able to inform you of the hardness of water in your area.

5 Incorrect loading

a) Overloading the machine will result in the clothes not being able to move freely inside the drum, resulting in poor soil removal.

b) Some programmes require reduced loads. If one of these programmes is used, reduce the load. If you are not sure, check the manufacturer's manual.

6 Other factors

a) How old is the machine? Like any mechanical/electrical item, a washing machine has a limited life span. In the case of an automatic washer, the average life span is approximately eight years.

b) When was the machine last serviced?

c) Poor whiteness is a result of constant under-dosing (See 4). With the soiling not being removed, there is a gradual build up of deposits in the clothes. This can only be corrected by always washing with the correct loads.

d) Domestic changes can reflect the quality of the wash, i.e., have you moved area? (See 3). Is there a new addition to the family? (See 2c).

e) Are the poor results evident on all programmes or only on specific programmes? (See 4).

Most of the manufacturers recommend a maintenance wash with detergent but no load 2 to 3 times a year to keep the machine clean and free from deposits.

Six golden rules for best results

1 Wash clothes frequently.

2 Use the right amount of detergent. Refer to the detergent pack for the correct dosage. Remember under-dosing leads to poor soil and stain removal, and the greying of whites.

3 Choose the recommended programme for the fabric. To safeguard colour and finish, preserve shape and minimise creasing, never wash hotter, wash longer or spin longer than indicated by the correct wash code for the fabric.

4 Rinse thoroughly. Thorough rinsing is essential – always allow the machine to complete its full programme.

5 Treat stains quickly. Never allow stains to dry in. Blot out as much as possible and keep wet until the item can be washed thoroughly. Never rub a stain as this may push it further into the fabric.

6 Dry fabrics correctly. Check the instructions on the garment label for line dry, dry flat, tumble dry etc.

7 Do not forget to check pockets for coins and tissues, etc., and fasten all zippers.

Marks which appear on the wash

If, during use, certain chemicals come into contact with fabrics, irreparable damage may occur. This is often not apparent until after the item is washed.

These chemicals may be present in relatively innocent personal products – skin preparations, hair mousse, perfumes, etc., as well as household products such as cleaning agents, polishes, etc.

The position of the marks and the type of item on which they appear can help to identify the cause. In most situations the marks appear ONLY on certain items in the wash – very often towels, or perhaps only tops or trousers. The fabric is almost always cotton, linen, viscose or poly-cotton, all of which are absorbent, and will hold the chemical within the fibre.

The marks can be split into two different types:

Light marks – where colour loss has occurred.

Greyish darker marks – where dye transfer is the most likely cause.

Lighter marks

The most common cause of this type of marking is skin creams and ointments containing benzoyl peroxide. This colourless ingredient reacts to the temperature of the wash water to release peroxide bleach removing the dye from the item with which it has come into contact. Skin creams usually have an oil base, which helps them adhere to the skin, but this does mean that they can rub off onto towels from the hands after washing, onto bed linen, and onto the necks of T-shirts, etc. The marks are usually only present on the garments or items used by the person using the preparation. No problem will be apparent until the item is washed and the wash temperature activates the bleach. Most, although not all, of these products will state on the label, contact with fabrics should be avoided, and the presence of benzoyl peroxide may also be listed under the ingredients. Unfortunately, as these marks are colour loss, due to the bleaching action, they are permanent and the colour cannot be restored.

Darker marks

The most common cause of this type of marking is from a chemical which has come into contact with the fabric during use, and which acts as a scavenger during the wash, attracting soiling or dye from the wash solution on to it.

Hair mousse, hair treatments and skin preparations may contain chemicals which can act as scavengers during the wash.

The majority of problems in this area involve hand towels, which have been used in the bathroom and have inadvertently come into contact with a preparation, which has then attracted loose dye from the wash solution.

It is also possible for dye from a previous wash to remain in the sump of the washing machine or around the inside of the machine's outer tub and subsequently transfer on to articles in the following wash.

Soiling removed from other items in the same washload and suspended in the wash water can also be attracted to the affected area of the article.

As previously mentioned, the marks only normally appear on items, which have been used by the person using the preparation, and once again, in most instances, these marks are permanent and cannot be removed.

Chapter 40
Successful stain removal

Stains on washable fabrics fall into two groups:

Group one –
stains that will wash out in soap or detergent suds

Type of stain
Beetroot, Blood, Blackcurrant and other fruit juices, Chocolate, Cream, Cocoa, Coffee, Egg, Gravy, Ice lollies, Jam, Meat juice, Mud, Milk, Nappy stains, Pickles, Soft drinks, Sauces, Soup, Stews, Syrup, Tea, Tomato Ketchup, Wines and Spirits and Washable Ink.

Method
Fresh stains – Soak in cold suds to keep the stain from becoming set in the fabric. Then wash in the normal way according to the fabric. Old dried-in stains – Lubricate with glycerine. Apply a mixture of one part glycerine to two parts water to the stain and leave for 10 minutes. Then treat as fresh stains. Residual marks – White fabrics only. Bleach out with Hydrogen Peroxide solution (One part 20 volume hydrogen peroxide to nine parts water). Leave soaking in this solution for 1 hour. Then wash in the normal way. Blood stains may leave residual iron mould marks, which should be treated as for iron mould.
Special note: *For 'built' stains such as egg (cooked), chocolate and mud, scrape off surplus staining matter first before putting to soak. Blood and meat juice stains whether fresh or old should be soaked in cold water first.*

Group two –
'treat-and-wash' stains

What you will need:
Glycerine (for lubrication)
Methylated Spirit (handle carefully: Inflammable, Poisonous).
Turpentine (Inflammable).
Armyl Acetate (handle carefully highly inflammable).
Hydrogen peroxide.
Proprietary grease solvent – 'Thawpit', 'Beaucare', 'Dab-it-off', etc., (Do not breathe the vapour: Use in a well ventilated room).
Photographic Hypo.
White vinegar (acetic acid).
Household ammonia (keep away from eyes).
Cotton wool, paper tissues, etc.

Handy hints
1   Act quickly to remove a stain and prevent it 'setting'. The faster you act, the milder the remedy needed.
2   Never rub a stain, as this pushes it further into the fabric. 'Pinch out' as much as you can, using a clean cloth or a paper tissue.
3   Never neglect a stain. The more drastic remedies for 'set' stains may harm delicate fabrics. If some stains are left on man-made and drip-dry fabrics in particular, they can be absorbed permanently into the fabric itself. Stains such as iron mould (rust) can weaken cellulosic fabrics and may eventually cause holes.
4   When applying solvents, always work from outside the stain towards the centre to avoid making a ring.
5   Always try a solvent on a hidden part first (e.g. under hem or seam allowance) to make sure it does not harm colours or fabric.
6   Stains on garments to be 'dry-cleaned' should be indicated on the garment (e.g. with a coloured tacking thread). Tell the cleaners what has caused the stain. This facilitates the task of removal and lessens the risk of the stain becoming permanently set by incorrect treatment.

Absorbent pad method
Using two absorbent pads of cotton wool, one soaked with the solvent and other held against the stain. Dab the underside of the stain with solvent and the staining matter will be transferred from the material to the top pad. Change this pad around to a clean part and continue working in this way until no more staining matter comes through. To remove last traces of the stain, wash in usual way.

Type of stain	Solvent	Method
Ballpoint ink	Methylated spirit. (INF) (Benzine for acetate and 'Tricel')	Absorbent pad method.
Bicycle oil	Proprietary grease solvent	Absorbent pad method or follow manufacturer's instructions
Black lead	Proprietary grease solvent	Absorbent pad method or follow manufacturer's instructions
Chalks and Crayons (Washable)		Brush off as much as possible while dry. Then brush stained area with suds (one dessertspoonful to a pint of water). Wash in the usual way
Chalks and Crayons (Indelible)	Methylated spirit (INF) (Benzine for acetate and 'Tricel') (INF)	Absorbent pad method
Chewing gum	Methylated spirit (INF) (Benzine for acetate and 'Tricel') (INF)	Absorbent pad method. Alternatively rub the gum with an ice cube to harden it. It may then be picked off by hand. Wash as usual to remove final traces

Type of stain	Solvent	Method
Cod Liver Oil, Cooking Fat, Heavy grease stains	Proprietary grease solvent	Absorbent pad method or manufacturer's instructions
Contact adhesives (e.g. Balsa cement, 'Evostick')	Amyl Acetate (INF)	Absorbent pad method
Felt pen inks	Methylated spirit (INF) (Benzine for acetate and 'Tricel') (INF)	First, lubricate the stain by rubbing with hard soap, and then wash in the usual way. For obstinate stains, use Methylated Spirit and absorbent pad method. Wash again to remove final traces
Grass	Methylated spirit (INF) (Benzine for acetate and 'Tricel') (INF)	Absorbent pad method
Greasepaint	Proprietary grease solvent	Absorbent pad method or follow manufacturer's instructions
Hair lacquer	Amyl Acetate (INF)	Absorbent pad method
Iodine	Photographic Hypo	Dissolve one tablespoon hypo crystals in one pint warm water. Soak the stain for about 5 minutes, watching closely. As soon as the stain disappears, rinse thoroughly, then wash in the usual way
Iron mould (rust marks)	a) Lemon juice (for wool, man-made fibres and all fine fabrics)	Apply lemon juice to the stain and leave it for 10–15 minutes. Place a damp cloth over the stain and iron. Repeat several times, as necessary. Rinse and wash as usual.
	b) Oxalic acid solution (for white cotton and linen only) use with care	Dissolve ½ teaspoonful oxalic acid crystals in ½ pint hot water. Tie a piece of cotton tightly round the stained area (to prevent the solution spreading) and immerse the stained part only. Leave for 2 or 3 minutes. Rinse thoroughly and wash in rich suds
Lipstick and Rouge a) light stains b) heavy stains	Proprietary grease solvent	Soak, then wash in usual way. Absorbent pad method or follow manufacturer's instructions
Marking ink	Marking ink eradicator (from stationers)	Follow instructions on the bottle label carefully
Metal polish	Proprietary grease solvent	Absorbent pad method or follow manufacturer's instructions
Mildew (mould on articles stored damp) a) coloured articles		The only treatment is regular soaking, followed by washing in rich suds – this will gradually reduce the marks
b) white cottons and linens without special finishes	Household bleach and vinegar	Soak in one part bleach to 100 parts water with one tablespoonful vinegar. Rinse thoroughly, then wash
c) white, drip-dry fabrics	Hydrogen peroxide solution	Soak in one part hydrogen peroxide (20 volume) and nine parts water until staining has cleared. Rinse thoroughly then wash in the usual way

Type of stain	Solvent	Method
Nail varnish	Amyl Acetate for all fabrics (INF)	Absorbent pad method
Nicotine (Tobacco juice)	Amyl Acetate for all fabrics (INF) (Benzine for acetate or 'Tricel') (INF)	Absorbent pad method
Non-washable ink	Oxalic acid solution (For white cottons and linens only)	See method (b) under iron mould
Paint		
a) Emulsion	Water	Emulsion paint splashes sponged immediately with cold water will quickly be removed. Dried stains are permanent
b) Oil	Turpentine or Amyl Acetate (INF)	Absorbent pad method
Perspiration		
a) Fresh stains	**Ammonia. Do not inhale the fumes**	Damp with water, then hold over an open bottle of household ammonia
b) Old stains	White vinegar	Sponge with white vinegar, rinse thoroughly, then wash in usual way
'Plasticine' Modelling clay	Proprietary grease solvent or lighter fuel (INF)	Scrape or brush off as much as possible. Apply solvent with absorbent pad method – wash to remove final traces
Scorch a) Light marks		Light stains will sometimes respond to treatment as for Group 1 – washable stains
	Glycerine	If persistent, moisten with water and rub glycerine into the stained area. Wash through. Residual marks may respond to soaking in hydrogen peroxide solution
b) Heavy marks	Heavy scorch marks that have damaged the fibres cannot be removed	
Shoe polish	Glycerine and proprietary grease solvent	Lubricate stain with glycerine, then use solvent with absorbent pad method or follow manufacturer's instructions. Wash to remove final traces
Sun tan oil	Proprietary grease solvent	Absorbent pad method or follow manufacturer's instructions
Verdigris (green stains from copper pipes, etc.)		Treat as iron mould

INF: *Inflammable*

Special Note: *Cotton garments with flame-resistant finishes must not be treated with household (chlorine) bleach or hydrogen peroxide in stain removal treatment, since this may impair the finish*

Keep solvents securely closed, labelled and out of children's reach

Chapter 41
Textile care labelling

For generations, washing advice was passed down from parent to child. Washing was done by hand and the items washed were usually cotton or wool. The arrival of the washing machine, modern detergents and more importantly the introduction of man-made materials meant that more detailed help was needed to ensure fabrics were washed according to their needs.

The Home Laundry Consultative Council (the UK National Textile Care Labelling Authority) introduced a system of wash codes and symbols. The codes and symbols are designed to indicate whether the fabric can be washed, or needs to be dry-cleaned; the maximum temperature the fabric can be washed at, the most suitable means of drying and the temperature the fabric should be ironed at. The original codes were updated in 1987 and this 'new' care labelling scheme is now in line with that used in Europe.

Washing –
What the symbols mean

 The wash tub indicates the most appropriate programme for that particular fabric.

 The maximum temperature is shown in °C. These will be 95, 60, 50, 40 or 30°C.

In addition to the temperature a bar may be present below the wash tub symbol.

 Where there is no bar below the wash tub maximum agitation is recommended. This symbol appears on robust fabrics such as cotton and linen.

 Where a single bar is shown beneath the wash tub, the washing action (agitation) should be reduced. This symbol is found on more delicate fabrics such as polycotton, acrylics and viscose.

 A broken or double bar beneath the wash tub symbol shows that only the most gentle wash action is required, as the fabric is likely to contain washable wool or silk.

In addition to indicating the agitation required the 'no bar', 'single bar' and 'broken bar' programmes have different water fill levels on most machines and also different spin speeds which relate to the absorbency of the fabric. For instance 'no bar' will require a long fast spin to remove as much water as possible from the absorbent fabric such as cotton. 'Single bar' fabrics such as poly-cotton and acrylic are less absorbent and may be severely creased if spun too fast or for too long.

 The wash tub symbol with a cross through it means that the fabric is not suitable for washing.

 Where a hand is shown in the wash tub, the garment may be hand washed but should not be machine washed.

Bleaching –
What the symbols mean

In the UK, the use of household hypochlorite bleach, such as Domestos, does not form part of the normal washing process. However, in some European countries, it is used on certain fabrics. Most dyes are sensitive to chlorine bleach and a triangular symbol is used to indicate if the fabric is suitable for bleach treatment. The household hypochlorite bleach should not be confused with the oxygen based bleaching agents which are present in many of the formulations of washing detergents

 Chlorine bleach may be used.

 Do not use chlorine bleach.

Dry-cleaning –
What the symbols mean

The symbol used to indicate that a fabric can be dry-cleaned is a circle.

 The letter within the circle advises the dry cleaner which type of solvent can be used.

 A circle with a cross means that the garment is unsuitable for dry-cleaning.

Ironing –
What the symbols mean

Most irons now carry the same symbols as the garments care label. The 'dot' system takes the guessing out of just how hot the iron should be for different fabrics. The iron shaped symbol carries one, two or three dots, each indicating that the temperature is suitable for fabrics which have care labels with the same number of dots.

 One dot = Cool

 Two dots = Warm

 Three dots = Hot

 Cross = Do not iron

Drying

The vast majority of textile articles can be safely tumbledried. Care labels may be used to indicate either that tumbledrying is the optimum drying method for a particular article, or that tumbledrying should not be used if the article is likely to be harmed by this treatment.

In cases where the tumbledrying prohibition symbol is used, any special positive instructions, such as 'dry flat' for heavier weight knitwear, should be given in words.

Drying – what the symbols mean

 The information shown in the square gives the recommended drying method for that particular fabric.

 Today many fabrics can be tumble-dried and this is indicated by a circle within the square. The most suitable heat setting for for the garment is indicated by the addition of 'dots' within the circle.

 One dot indicates low or half heat is required – normally synthetic fabrics.

 Two dots indicates high or full heat is required – normally cotton fabrics.

 A cross within the circle, or across the square indicates that the garment should not be tumbledried.

Other less used drying symbols.

 Drip drying is recommended.

Hang = line-dry.

Dry flat.

Mixed fabric group loads

Ideally fabric groups should not be mixed to make up a washload. Unless care is taken it does increase the risk of shrinkage, or dye contamination and discoloration of white things (particularly nylon) from articles which prove non-colourfast under the wash conditions. However, if for convenience or for the sake of economy, there is no alternative, always select the mildest wash conditions.

Special note on velvet

Velvet is a construction term, not a fibre. It may be silk, cotton or an acetate/nylon blend, e.g., 'Tricelan' For best results look for the wash-care label and follow the instructions faithfully. If in doubt, dry-clean.

Soft furnishings in velvet weave, e.g., Dralon – it is helpful to remove surface dust with a vacuum cleaner or soft brush. 'Dralon' velvet is not washable. It can be cleaned with a dry-foam shampoo. Avoid saturating cotton backing, vacuum or brush foam off when dry. When dry-cleaning, state fibre content.

Flame-retardant fabrics and finishes

Apart from nylon and wool, which are regarded as being of low flammability, there are two ways of giving fabrics flame-retardant properties:

a) by the application to cotton fabrics of a special finish such as 'Protean', 'Pyrovatex', 'Timonox'. Also in certain cases to wool, though this as yet is not being widely used for apparel purposes.

b) by the modification of the fibre itself, e.g., fibres like acrylic but with modified properties. The generic term for these is modacrylic, e.g., 'Teklan' or Monsanto's modacrylic. They are inherently flame retardant.

The appropriate washing codes for the above are:

1 Cotton
2 Wool
3 Modacrylics

Important: *Flame-retardant fabrics, e.g., modacrylics or fabrics with a flame-retardant finish must not be bleached, or soaked in any washing product.*

Fabrics with a flame-retardant finish must

not be washed in soap or non-automatic powder as soap can mask the properties of the finish. Other types of washing product, including automatic powder may be used with safety. Rinse very thoroughly.

Hand care

To get the best results in the hand wash make sure the powder is thoroughly dissolved before washing and the clothes thoroughly rinsed afterwards.

After each wash by hand, rinse your hands and dry them thoroughly. People with sensitive or damaged skin should pay particular attention to the instructions for use and avoid prolonged contact with the washing water.

'Special finish' labels

E.g. 'machine washable wool'. Sometimes the finish given to a fabric changes its washability.

No label provided

If in doubt wash under the mildest conditions, i.e., use warm 40°C suds only; do not soak; wash through quickly and gently; rinse thoroughly; blot off surplus moisture with a towel and dry carefully. If washing by machine, choose the gentlest programme. If ironing seems appropriate, use a cool iron.

Labels with unfamiliar symbols

These will be found detailed.

Wash for the fabric, never mind the shape!

Remember always that it is the fabric and its construction rather than the type of article that decides the washing treatment. A polyester shirt will be grouped with a textured polyester suit, a small boy's polyester trousers and his sister's polyester blouse. They are all different shapes and sizes but all will be washed as polyester requires, in hand-hot suds with cold rinsing and a short spin.

Different fabrics require different washing temperatures and agitation times. So ignore the shape of the article and concern yourself only with what it is made of and then wash it according to the appropriate Care Labelling Code.

Blends and mixtures

A blend fabric is one which has been woven or knitted from yarn made by the blending of two of more fibres, prior to the yarn being spun. A mixture fabric is one where two or more different yarns are used during weaving or knitting (e.g., a nylon warp woven into a viscose or cotton weft). In both cases the fibre which needs the milder treatment influences the wash conditions suitable for the fabric. For example a polyester/wool blend should only be washed in warm suds, because of the wool content; polyester/cotton and acrylic/cotton are both washed at temperatures lower than the maximum for cotton. If in doubt, wash as for the fibre requiring the milder treatment.

Colour fastness

Test for colour fastness by damping a piece of the hem or seam allowance and iron a piece of dry white fabric on to it. If any colour blots off, wash the article separately in very cool suds, and rinse at once in cold water. Put to dry immediately. If the colour is very loose, dry cleaning may be advisable (check the label).

Soaking

There are occasions when heavily soiled or stained articles benefit from a soak before washing, particularly those included in fabric Group 1. Before soaking any coloured article it is important to make sure that: the dye is fast to soaking – if in doubt, do not soak; the washing powder is completely dissolved before putting in the articles; the water temperature is not too high for the fabric or the dye; the article is not bunched up, it should be left as free as possible; white and coloured articles are not soaked together – this is especially necessary where white nylon is concerned as nylon stockings and tights, for example, are seldom fast to soaking for long periods; the articles do not have metal buttons or metal fasteners – soaking can encourage iron mould (brown stains). Articles made from wool or silk or from fabric with a flame-retardant finish, whether white or coloured, should *never be soaked in washing products of any type.*

Chapter 42
Jargon

Amp – Short for ampere. Used to measure the flow of electricity through a circuit or appliance.
Armature – Wire wound centre of brush motor.
Bi-metal – Two different metals which have been joined together. When heated the strip bends in a known direction.
Boss – Protection around entry point.
Burn-out – Overheated part of item.
Bus bar – An electrical conductor.
Cable – Conductors covered with a protective semi-rigid insulating sheath, used to connect the individual components within a wiring system.
Carbon face (seal) – Watertight flat surface seal.
Centrifugal – Force that increases with rotation causing movement away from its centre.
Circuit – Any complete path for an electric current allowing it to pass along a 'live' conductor to where it is needed and then to return to its source along a 'neutral' conductor.
Clamp band – Large adjustable clip used for holding door boot.
Closed circuit – A normal circuit that allows power to pass through.
Collet – Tapered sleeve of two or more parts designed to grip a shaft passed through its centre.
Commutator – Copper segment on motor armature.
Component – Individual parts of the machine, i.e., pump, valves, motors, are all components.
Conductor – The metallic current carrying 'cores' within cable or flex.
Consumer Unit – Unit governing the supply of electricity to all circuits and containing a main on-off switch and fuses or circuit breakers protecting the circuits emanating from it.
Contact – Point at which switch makes contact.
Continuity – Electrical path with no break.
Corbin – Type of spring hose clip.
Damped – To have reduced movement of suspension, i.e., reduce oscillation of tub unit during distribute and spin cycles.
Dispenser – Compartment that holds detergent ready for use.
Dispenser hose – Hose that supplies the tub with detergent and water from the dispenser compartment.
Distribute – To balance load by centrifugal force, i.e., a set speed calculated to even out wash load prior to faster spin.
Door boot – Flexible seal between door and tub.

Door gasket – Flexible seal between door and tub.
Door seal – Flexible seal between door and tub.
Drift – Soft metal rod used for bearing removal.
E.L.C.B. – Earth leakage circuit breaker- see R.C.C.B.
E.M.F. – Electromotive force. Source of energy that can cause a current to flow in a circuit or device.
Early – Machine not currently on the market.
Energize (Energise) – To supply power to.
Energized (Energised) – Having power supplied to.
Flowchart – Method of following complicated steps in a logical fashion.
Functional test – To test machine on a set programme.
Garter ring – Large elastic band or spring used to secure door boot.
Grommet fitting – Method of fitting hoses, etc., requiring no clips.
Harness – Electrical wiring within a machine.
Hertz (Hz) – Periodic cycle of one second, i.e., cycles per second.
'Hunting' – Oscillating.
Impeller – The blades of the water pump.
Insulation – Material used to insulate a device or a region.
Isolate – To disconnect from the electrical and water supply, etc.
Laminations – Joined metal parts of stator.
Late – Current machine on market.
Lint – Fluff from clothing that may cause a small blockage.
Live – Supply current carrying conductor.
Make -1. Manufacturer's name.
2. When a switch makes contact it is said to make.
Microprocessor – Miniature integrated circuit containing programme information.
Miniature Circuit Breaker (MCB) – a device used instead of fuses to isolate a circuit if fault/overload occurs.
Neutral – Return current carrying conductor.
O.O.B. – Out of balance detection system.
Open-circuit – Circuit that is broken, i.e., will not let any power through.
Outer casing – Cabinet, 'shell' of the machine.
P.S.I. – Measurement of water pressure, pounds per square inch, e.g. 38 p.s.i.
Pawl – Pivoted lever designed to engage ratchet gearing.
P.M.E. – Protective multiple earthing.
Porous – Item that allows water to pass through.

Potentiometer – Variable resistance device.
Processor – Main central processing component of computer control circuitry.
Programmer – See Timer.
R.C.C.B. – Residual current circuit breaker (also known as R.C.D.)
R.C.D. – Residual current device. See also – E.L.C.B. and R.C.C.B.
Reciprocating – Mechanical action of backwards and forwards movement.
Reverse polarity – A situation where live and neutral feeds have reversed, e.g., connected incorrectly at supply, socket or plug.
Ribbon cable – Flat cable used for low voltage P.C.B. connections.
Rotor – Central part of an induction motor.
Schematic diagram – Theoretical diagram.
Seal – Piece of pre-shaped rubber that usually fits into a purpose built groove or between two surfaces, therefore creating a watertight seal when subjected to pressure.
Sealant – Rubber substance used for ensuring watertight joints.
Shell – Outer of machine.
Spades – Connections on wires or components – remove gently.
Stat – Abbreviation of thermostat.
Stator – Electrical winding on motor.
Terminal block – A method of connecting wires together safely.
T.O.C. – Thermal overload cutout. At a pre-set temperature, the T.O.C. will break electrical circuit to whatever it is in circuit with, i.e., prevents motors, etc., overheating.
Thermistor – A semi-conductor device, the resistance of which is affected by temperatures.
Thermostat – Device used to monitor temperature.
Thyristor – Electronic switching device.
Timer – Programme switch.
Triac – Electronic switching device.
Volt – Unit of electrical pressure (potential) difference. In most British homes the mains voltage is 230V.
Volatile (when relating to computer control applications) – Unable to store information when power is turned off.
Non-Volatile (when relating to computer control applications) – Retains information for a set period even with power turned off.
Watt – Unit of power consumed by an appliance or circuit, the product of the mains voltage and the current drawn (in amps). 1000W = 1 kilowatt (kW).